Wood

Wood

The Best Of **Fine WoodWorking**

The Taunton Press

Cover photo by Alec Waters

Taunton
BOOKS & VIDEOS
for fellow enthusiasts

©1995 by The Taunton Press, Inc.
All rights reserved.

First printing: 1995
Printed in the United States of America

A FINE WOODWORKING Book

FINE WOODWORKING® is a trademark of The Taunton Press, Inc.,
registered in the U.S. Patent and Trademark Office.

The Taunton Press, Inc.
63 South Main Street
P.O. Box 5506
Newtown, Connecticut 06470-5506

Library of Congress Cataloging-in-Publication Data

Wood.
        p.   cm. — (The best of fine woodworking)
     "A Fine Woodworking book" — T.p. verso.
     Includes index.
     ISBN 1-56158-099-6
     1. Woodwork.   2. Wood   I. Fine woodworking   II. Series.
TT180.W593   1995
674—dc20   95-15
                                                                       CIP

Contents

Introduction

Ask a dozen woodworkers why they took up the craft, and you'll likely hear a dozen different answers. But the one common element that brings woodworkers together is a love for the wood itself.

In the hands and eyes of a woodworker, wood becomes a sensuous mix of texture, color, figure and grain, but with the romance come some practical considerations, too. Whether you're turning a bowl from a burl or making a dining-room table from some choice cherry lumber, transforming wood into an object of craft means coming to terms with its physical properties: how it dries and changes with the seasons, how it reacts to tools and finishes. Woodworkers learn fast that few successes come from overpowering the wood. Rather, they must apply their skill to bring out the best in the material.

This book contains 32 articles originally published in *Fine Woodworking* magazine that look at wood from the craftsman's perspective. There are pieces on all the common North American cabinet woods, as well as a few exotics, and there's solid information on buying, drying and storing wood. The articles tackle both the romance and beauty of the material and the practical knowledge necessary to work it. If you love wood and love making beautiful things from it, you'll surely learn something in these pages, but more important, you may rediscover the magic of wood that caused you to become a woodworker in the first place.

—The Editors

The "Best of *Fine Woodworking*" series spans ten years of *Fine Woodworking* magazine. There is no duplication between these books and the popular *"Fine Woodworking on..."* series. A footnote with each article gives the date of first publication; product availability, suppliers' addresses and prices may have changed since then.

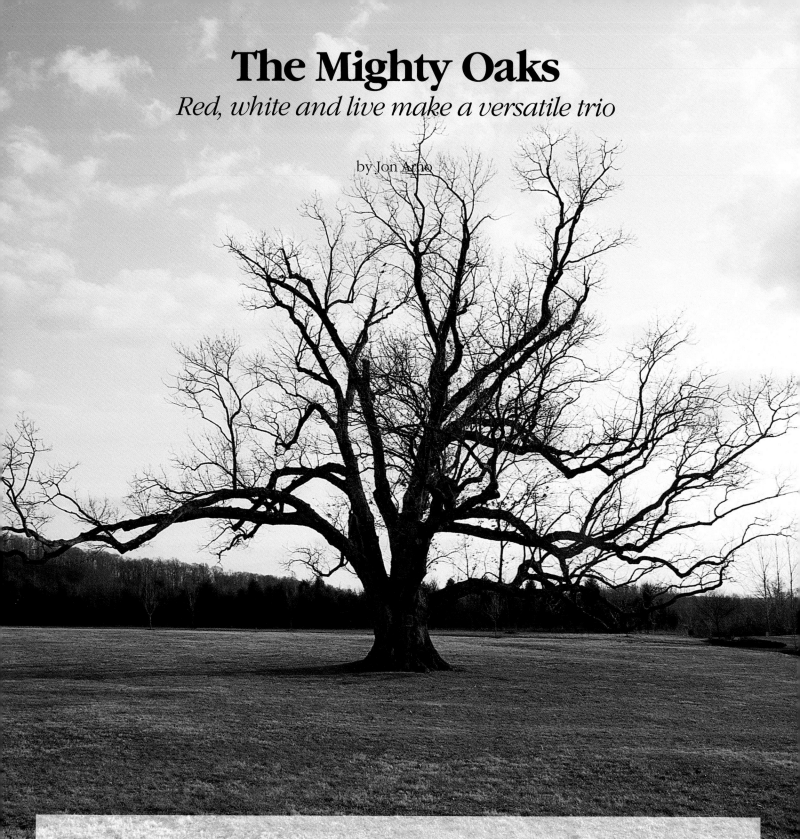

The Mighty Oaks

Red, white and live make a versatile trio

by Jon Arno

O ur senses tell us it is nothing more than a coarse-textured wood with showy rays and a harsh acidic scent. Yet there's something about oak that causes most of us to think of it in human terms: bold, strong and dependable. There can be little doubt why.

These trees, their fruit and their timber, are an inseparable part of the story of humanity. Acorns predated grain in the diet of our Stone-Age European ancestors. The pagan Germans worshipped oak, and in England, dense groves of the European white oak, *Quercus robur*, served as holy places for Druid rites well before written history began. From ancient times until just before our grandfathers were born, oak served as a strategic military and economic commodity, being the primary naval timber for ships of the line and tall Yankee clippers.

Oak's role in the modern world may be somewhat less romantic, but it has not diminished. Oak remains our most-used hardwood for interior trim, cabinets, flooring, furniture and for many heavy construction applications. The two primary factors that have made oak so enduringly popular are its abundance and its utility. Before exploring these topics, though, let's examine the great diversity of the timbers we lump together botanically as oak.

Oak's family tree

Oaks belong to the beech family, Fagaceae. That this family should be referred to as the beech family is one of the more irrational snubs in taxonomy. Of the 600 or so species in the family, including the beeches, chestnuts and chinquapins, well over 500 of its most important members belong to the oak genus, *Quercus*.

The oaks are also the most abundant and widespread genus of hardwoods in the Northern Hemisphere. In the United States alone we have a growing stock of 100 billion cu. ft. of oak—more than twice our reserves of any other hardwood genus. The natural abundance of the oaks is due to their genetic vigor and their resulting adaptability. Oaks hybridize with very little difficulty. Over millions of years, this natural, genetic experimentation has resulted in a host of species ideally suited to almost any viable environment.

In the course of evolution, the genus divided into two botanically distinct groups: white oaks and red oaks, which are sometimes called black oaks. (There's also a third group—the live oaks, which are climatic variants of the white and the red. I'll discuss live oaks later.) The most significant botanical difference between the two is that white oaks mature their acorns within a single season while the red oaks require two seasons. To tell them apart, all you really need to know is that most white oaks have round-lobed leaves, and the lobes on red-oak leaves come to a point.

Other differences in the cellular anatomy of the woods are of particular interest to the woodworker. Woods in the white oak group tend to have larger rays and smaller, but more abundant, thin-walled pores. The red oaks have fewer, but larger, thick-walled pores, and the rays tend to be smaller and darker in color (see the photos on p. 10). Also, the pores in white oak are almost always clogged with foam-like structures known as tyloses, but the pores in red oak are normally unobstructed (see the photos on p. 11). Because these features are responsible for many of the functional properties of these woods, the lumber industry has adopted essentially the same groupings as the botanists, marketing oak lumber as either white or red. Beyond this, little or no effort is made to differentiate the species. For most construction applications, this broad-brush approach is adequate, but for furniture and finer craft work, it leaves much to be desired.

Within the oak genus there's an extremely broad range of cabinetwoods. The softest of our domestic oaks, with a specific gravity of 0.52 (see the box at right for a definition of specific gravity and a comparison of some of the more common North American species), is the Southern red species *Quercus falcata*. This species is only about as dense as black walnut (0.51). Some of the live oaks have specific gravities approaching 0.90, making them even denser than rosewood. No other genus of domestic hardwood spans such a broad range. In the United States alone, there are 58 formally classified domestic species and perhaps a third again as many recognized hybrid varieties and naturalized foreign species.

Genetics alone, however, do not account for all of the variation in the oaks sold as cabinetwood. Climate, soil and even the way the lumber is processed can produce lumber of the same species with strikingly dissimilar characters, both in appearance and working properties.

The most significant factor besides genetic makeup that determines an oak's character is climate. Red oaks and white oaks that grow in our temperate North-American forests are ring-porous woods. At the beginning of each growing season, these trees pro-

The oaks
Some common North American oaks arranged by group

Common and botanical names	Specific gravity	Volumetric shrinkage
White		
Eastern white, *Q. alba*	0.60	16.3
Bur, *Q. macrocarpa*	0.58	12.7
Overcup, *Q. lyrata*	0.57	16.0
Post, *Q. stellata*	0.60	16.2
Chestnut, *Q. prinus*	0.57	16.4
Swamp chestnut, *Q. michauxii*	0.60	16.4
Red		
Northern red, *Q. rubra*	0.56	13.7
Southern red, *Q. falcata*	0.52	16.1
Cherrybark, *Q. falcata, v. pagodifolia*	0.61	—
Scarlet, *Q. coccinea*	0.60	14.7
Willow, *Q. phellos*	0.56	18.9
Water, *Q. nigra*	0.56	16.1
Black, *Q. velutina*	0.56	15.1
Laurel, *Q. laurifolia*	0.56	19.0
Pin, *Q. palustris*	0.58	14.5
Live		
Live, *Q. virginiana*	0.80	14.7

Specific gravity is the ratio of the weight of a given piece of wood to the weight of water occupying the same volume. It reflects the relative density of the wood in question. The figures above are based on the wood's green volume and oven-dry weight.

Volumetric shrinkage is expressed as a percentage decrease from original green volume to oven-dry volume. Shrinkage indicates a wood's relative in-use stability.

duce a band of large earlywood pores, which accent the annual rings and give the wood a showy, open-grained character. Some live oaks are botanically related to the white oaks and some to the reds, but because live oaks do not experience seasonal interruptions in growth, they do not produce the usual bands of large earlywood pores. Instead, they tend to be less figured and much harder woods. As seen on the end grain, the pores in live oak form long radial chains, like the strings of bubbles in a glass of champagne, extending outward from the pith to the bark.

From the woodworker's perspective, categorizing the oaks into these three basic groups (red, white and live) provides a logical and useful framework, though this is only a starting point. The woods in each group share similar functional properties, but there can be considerable variation from one species to another even within each group. The live oaks make up the hardest and heaviest group; the white oaks are next in terms of weight, strength and durability; and the red oaks are the softest and lightest. Most species of white oak have slower growth rates, producing smaller-diameter pores and a more compact cellular structure. This gives the wood great strength and a high resistance to splitting. White oak's rays tend to be larger, tying the vascular (vertically oriented) cells together and giving the wood greater resistance to compression.

All oaks contain high concentrations of tannin (see the box

This majestic white oak (left), over 500 years old, serves as an eloquent explanation of why humans have imbued the oak with human characteristics, such as strength and dependability, and why ancient peoples worshipped such trees.

Photo facing page: Vincent Laurence
From *Fine Woodworking* (July 1993) 101:54-57

Size and distribution of rays and pores are the best way to identify the oaks. White oaks (left) have smaller but more abundant pores than the red oaks (center) and larger rays. Live oaks (right), because they're largely tropical in origin, have the most even distribution of pores of any of the oaks, as well as the greatest density and the least figure.

below), which provide at least a modest amount of protection in inhibiting decay. But white oak is substantially more durable than red oak when exposed to the elements because the pores of white oak are clogged with tyloses, which retard the absorption of moisture and help to prevent decay organisms from being established.

Which oak to use?

White—Given white oak's many favorable attributes, it is not surprising that many of the cabinetmaking and wood technology texts published in the 19th and early 20th centuries cite white oak as the preferred, or at least most useful, of our oak timbers. White oak's durability and strength made it superior for uses such as bridge beams and railroad ties, and its low permeability to moisture made (and still makes) it ideal for wine barrels and other cooperage applications. In contrast, a red-oak barrel, regardless of how well the staves were fitted, would leak because its contents would simply flow out through the wood's large, unobstructed pores.

For cabinetmaking, white oak also possesses the virtue of being much more flamboyantly figured than red oak, especially when quartersawn. This radially cut white oak is sometimes called silvered oak and was the height of fashion a century ago. Although red oak also can be quartersawn, its rays' darker color and relatively smaller size don't provide the same degree of splashy contrast as does the white.

Today, silvered oak is no longer the rage, and many of the construction and container duties that were once the exclusive domain of white oak are now being performed by metals and synthetics. White oak's clear-cut advantage over red oak has faded.

Eastern white oak is also not as plentiful today as it once was. In the American market a century ago, the term *white oak* was all but synonymous with Eastern white oak (*Quercus alba*). This plentiful species (along with a few virtually indistinguishable hybrids) provided almost all of the commercially processed, higher-grade cabinetwood in the white oak group. Although *Q. alba* still accounts for a large portion of the annual harvest, other species, most notably bur oak (*Q. macrocarpa*), are quite commonly sold as white oak today. Bur oak is a much coarser textured wood with a grayish color and exceedingly large rays. It doesn't turn as well or finish as smoothly as Eastern white oak, but it is not without its virtues. With an average volumetric shrinkage of 12.7%, green to oven dry, it is more stable than Eastern white oak (at 16.3%) and makes excellent hardwood flooring. However, the two woods are not totally interchangeable and should not be used together where their differing shrinkage properties could cause problems, such as in edge-glued tabletops or wide panels. Because of the lumber industry's propensity to commingle these species, buying white oak these days can be tricky. If at all possible, you should inspect any white oak before buying, or at least buy from a supplier who can guarantee that all the lumber you purchase for a project will be of one species.

Red—There's plenty of variety among the red oaks as well, with their average specific gravities (see the box on p. 9) spanning an

Tannin, pro and con

Chemically speaking, one of the most distinctive features of oak is its high tannin content. Indeed, the scent of most species is so powerful that it will linger in the air for hours after the wood has been milled. Although I very much enjoy the fragrance of many woods and view their aromas as one of the more pleasant aspects of working with wood, I find oak to be downright offensive. And for those of us who are sensitive to oak, exposure to the dust can cause watery eyes, skin

rashes and even heartburn.

Even so, the offending agent—tannin—magnifies oak's utility in many ways. Tannin has antiseptic properties, and the highest concentrations are in the bark; therefore, oak bark has long been used for preserving or tanning leather. Tannin also reacts with iron to produce black pigment, and oak-leaf galls were once a major ingredient in the making of ink.

For woodworkers, the interaction between tannin and iron is a mixed blessing.

On the one hand, care must be taken in using steel nails or screws in oak because over time the surrounding wood will develop an ever enlarging black blotch. Yet when oak logs are submerged in a swamp, this same chemical reaction creates bog oak, a unique and beautifully highlighted, silver-black cabinetwood that is much prized in the British Isles.

Tannin, because it's highly acidic, also reacts with ammonia to produce rich brown pigments. Although

modern oil-based wood stains are a lot easier to work with, ammonia-fumed oak was once a very popular finish. In this process, trays of highly concentrated (industrial strength) ammonia are placed in an airtight area along with whatever unfinished oak items are to be fumed. In a matter of hours (or days, depending on how dark a hue is desired), the raw oak becomes indelibly and deeply pigmented. For more on fuming, see "Craftsman-Style Comfort in a Morris Chair," *FWW* #101, pp. 38-42. *—J.A.*

Photos this page: Susan Kahn

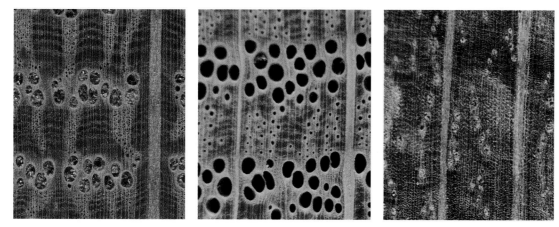

End-grain sections show one of the biggest differences between the oaks. White oak (left), which has been used for barrels for centuries, holds liquids because its pores are largely clogged by tyloses. But red oak's pores (center) are mostly unobstructed and allow liquids to pass through. The pores of most live oak (right) are also open, like those of red oak, but much smaller.

even greater range than the whites. Southern swamp (or cherry-bark) red oak (*Q. falcata var. pagodifolia*) is actually slightly heavier than Eastern white oak. Species like cherrybark, which are native to the extreme South where the climate is moist and the growing season is long, grow rapidly and produce proportionately more dense latewood within each annual ring than do Northern-grown oaks. Oaks from the temperate North tend to produce softer and more flamboyantly figured woods.

In recent years, Southern red oak has developed a somewhat tarnished reputation in the interior trim and cabinetmaking fields for being too streaky and often curly grained. Personally, I prefer this streaked, curly, Southern-Appalachian oak for the special character it lends some furniture projects, especially in tabletops and book-matched panels. But then again, I prefer red oak over white in most applications for rather pragmatic reasons.

Red oak is stocked by more of the high-volume lumberyards where construction contractors buy, so it's generally a little less expensive than white. Red oak is also softer than white, so it's easier to work. This is most noticeable with hand tools and when thickness planing because white oak's rays have a greater tendency to tear out. Neither red nor white oak are particularly well-suited for turning, but typically, gouges stay sharp a lot longer with red oak.

The rays in red oak are less pronounced than in white, so it is not as difficult to match boards. The thing to look for when selecting boards is whether a board is flatsawn or quartersawn. While both grain patterns are attractive, they tend to clash when used together in the same project, so I regard them almost as two different woods.

Finally, because the ray flecks are darker than the background wood in red oak, relatively dark stains can be used without any danger of overemphasizing the rays. With white oak, using a dark stain is not a good idea unless you really want to accentuate the rays. They'll inevitably stand out as contrasting yellow bands against the surrounding, more porous (therefore darker) wood tissue. If you're going to stain white oak, use a blond stain.

Live—Live oak has never been a commercially important furniture wood. One reason is that live oak is absolutely punishing to work with. Historically, live oak has only been used in very specialized applications. Our most plentiful domestic live oak, *Q. virginiana*, was much prized during the 18th and 19th centuries for building warships because of its superior ability to withstand a broadside attack. But given the hand tools of the time, it was never the oak of choice for finer work, and it never became associated with a popular period-style of furniture. This may change, though, in the years ahead. Modern power tools can handle it at least as well as rosewood, bubinga or purpleheart.

Moreover, prospects are high that the live oaks will remain in

good supply. In Mexico alone there are well over 100 species of oaks, and the vast majority of them belong to the live oak group. Though they contain fewer species, the forests of Central and extreme northern South America also contain large quantities of live oak, some of which have strikingly unusual ray patterns and vivid color. In fact, they're so different from our domestic species that often the only clues to their kinship with oak are the wood's tannic scent or the use of Spanish trade names containing the words *roble* or *encino*.

By whatever name, these tropical oaks are a world apart from our ring-porous domestic oaks in either the red or white oak groups. With few exceptions, they're brutally hard, but they polish extremely well. Although generally considered diffuse-porous woods (because the pores do not congregate in the earlywood), the live oaks are still relatively coarse textured and open grained compared to the familiar domestic species we think of as typical, diffuse-porous woods, such as maple and birch.

The live oaks have as much potential as cabinetwoods, but there has not yet been much research or technical data gathered on their working properties. Though our domestic live oak (*Q. virginiana*) is relatively stable, some imported species with high volumetric shrinkage have caused disappointment when brought into our somewhat dryer and more temperate climate...so be forewarned.

Forever in fashion

In construction, cabinetry and furnituremaking, as well as in a host of other fields, oak has been in style almost since Western history began. As many a surviving royal throne, treasure chest or ancient armoire will attest, it was the preferred wood throughout the Middle Ages and in the Jacobean period. Even in the 18th and 19th centuries, when mahogany alone would do for elegant pieces, oak was the primary wood for common, utilitarian items such as dry sinks, cupboards, tables and chairs.

In the New World, the Spanish conquest of the Southwest left us the legacy of mission oak. At the turn of the century, massive pedestal tables and rolltop desks in golden oak were popular. At mid-century, our soldiers returned home from World War II to raise their families in houses furnished with limed-oak coffee tables and dining-room sets. Oak still dominates the furniture and cabinetmaking scene, although nowadays, much of that coarse-grained look is actually veneer or synthetic laminate. And for kitchen cabinets, flooring and interior trim, the use of oak still far exceeds any other hardwood—and probably all other domestic hardwoods combined. Given their history, enduring popularity and the existing stock of oaks, they're likely to remain stalwart favorites for a long time. □

Jon Arno is a wood technologist and consultant in Troy, Mich.

Cherry
A rose among woods

by Jon Arno

To the American cabinetmaker, there's something special about our domestic black cherry, *Prunus serotina*. It's the second most popular hardwood (after oak) used by furniture manufacturers in this country. And if price is to be taken as a measure of popularity, only black walnut is consistently more expensive than cherry among our major native-grown timbers.

The mystique behind cherry's popularity (and I can't deny it influences me more than it should) is tradition. Cherry was a much-prized wood among Colonial cabinetmakers and also among the magnificently skilled Shaker craftsmen of the 19th century. Certainly, its great working characteristics were important considerations to these old masters at a time when hand tools were the *only* tools. But, I suspect, there was yet another, ulterior motive for its use, at least among the Shakers: Members of that religious sect disdained frills, and the natural beauty of cherry allows a woodworker to create a piece that's exceptionally appealing to the eye—without compromising the functional design with fancy moldings or bric-a-brac.

Cherry is a member of the rose family, *Rosaceae*. This family, with its more than 3,000 species, is one of the most important in the plant kingdom. Were the rose family to vanish tomorrow, it would take with it not only the beauty and fragrance of the rose, cherry wood and cherry pie, but also a host of other flowers and edibles—plums, peaches, apples, raspberries, almonds and many, many more. The so-called "rosewoods" of commerce, by the way, come from tropical species of the genus *Dalbergia*, which is a member of the pea family, *Leguminosae*. None of these

rosewoods is close kin to the true rose. The rose family is well-endowed with woody perennials, shrubs and even trees, some of which—like apple and plum—have been used in cabinetmaking for small items and woodenware since ancient times.

Like apple trees, orchard cherry trees don't produce a lot of usable wood because much of the tree's energy goes into fruit production, rather than toward making timber. Only our wild black cherry is plentiful enough—and energetic enough—to fight for its place in the forest canopy and produce logs of usable dimensions. Black cherry can attain diameters of 4 ft. to 5 ft. and heights of about 100 ft., but seldom in the same tree. A 3-ft.-dia., 80-ft.-tall cherry tree is a mighty respectable specimen. While black cherry is the giant of its family, it's a mere also-ran among the maples, yellow-poplars, oaks and walnuts it competes with in the wild.

Cherry has an average specific gravity of 0.47 (green volume to oven-dry weight), making it hard enough for most furniture and woodworking purposes. On the average, it's 8% to 10% lighter in weight than American black walnut, more than 15% lighter in weight than sugar maple and downright soft in comparison to most of the oaks.

For a wood that's so beautifully figured, cherry is exceptionally easy to cut with reasonably sharp tools. This is a great blessing on those tedious but necessary little jobs, such as mortising for hinges, hand-joining and surface-planing.

Cherry is excellent on the lathe. It's in a class with walnut and, according to USDA Forest Products Laboratory tests, even superior to maple, which is a primary wood for spindles, rollers and other turned articles. In many respects, cherry and maple have comparable working characteristics and are well-suited for similar applications. What cherry gives up to maple in terms of strength and wear properties, it more than makes up for in its ease of working and in the beauty of its color and figure (with the exception of some of maple's special grain patterns, such as fiddleback and bird's-eye, but these are not typical). In fact, one of the great virtues of cherry is its remarkably attractive figure. Across the spectrum of cabinetwoods, generally only the open-grained or ring-porous woods will rival cherry for figure. This is a key point in truly understanding cherry's unique place among the great woods of North America, because cherry is one of the very few woods that combine a diffuse-porous cellular structure with nearly ideal density and a truly beautiful figure. Although fine woods in many applications, other diffuse-porous woods—basswood, yellow-poplar, birch and maple, for example—are either too soft for furniture that will experience hard use, or too bland to produce a finish with real character.

Why cherry captures the important benefits of a diffuse-porous wood while offering a fabulous figure is perhaps best explained by contrasting its cellular arrangement to that of a more typical diffuse-porous wood, maple. The modest, flatsawn figure of typical maple results from thin bands of fibrous tissue along the annual rings that are produced by the tree at the end of each growing season. The pores are of small, uniform diameter and are very evenly dispersed throughout the wood. In cherry, however, the pores—formed early in the growing season—are slightly larger and form a band along the annual ring. This anatomical distinction is quite subtle, but it's significant enough to give cherry's figure far more character than maple and other typical diffuse-porous woods. In effect, cherry is a semi-diffuse-porous wood (see photo, below right), and owes much of its beauty to this feature.

America's other great (and, some would say, finest) timber, black walnut, approaches the other side of the spectrum in that it is semi-ring-porous. This distinction may seem academic—of little interest, except to botanists—but it's important. The size and arrangement of pores—or, more accurately, vessel cells—give cherry a clear advantage over walnut in at least one important furniture application: tabletops. Cherry's grain is so tight that it virtually never needs to be filled in order to achieve a glass-smooth finish. Just an extra coat of a reasonably high-bodied varnish followed by a good rubdown will do the trick. To use this same technique on walnut is possible but, at best, it's a labor of immense love because walnut will drink up the first two or three coats of varnish like an overworked camel.

It's my opinion that, among common domestic hardwoods, only sugar maple is functionally superior to cherry for tabletops. That's due to maple's finer, less-porous texture and greater dent-resisting hardness. Even this conclusion, however, is suspect when the issue of relative stability is brought into consideration. On this feature, maple is adequate, but cherry is outstanding.

Cherry is extremely stable in terms of expansion and contraction when exposed to changes in humidity. This feature made it a favorite species in the printing industry when poured-lead type was the state-of-the-art. A printer could set a page on a cherry-wood block and store it for months without fear of having the block distort the next time it was put on press. But while stability is indeed a great virtue of cherry, I must confess that when I was a much younger man, my blind faith in wood technology books—which universally extol the stability of cherry—led to one of my most embarrassing woodworking blunders.

I already had plenty of shop experience with cherry, but my first opportunity to get a real "steal" on the stuff came about when some trees had to be cut down to clear a lot in my neighborhood and make way for a new house. After years of paying $3 a board foot for store-bought stock, I was absolutely ecstatic when the builder told me these cherry trees were mine for the taking—*free!* With abject faith in the renowned stability of the species, I was totally certain that air-drying the wood was going to be a piece of cake. So, to hasten the process, I brought it home green from the mill and stacked it up with stickers in our very hot attic. There, it spent the months of July, August and September, completely undisturbed.

By summer's end, the wood was indeed dry, but as I lifted the attic door and turned on the flashlight, the sight that greeted me had the general dimensional configuration of a curly head of windblown hair, split ends and all. To this day—with the exception of what I fed to my fireplace—the only usable thing I've gotten out of what should have been well over 200 board feet of prime cherry is one Shaker cabinet doorknob. Aside from its potential in providing an occasional 6-in. lathe billet, the cherry that's left is totally worthless. To draw a moral from this story (and perhaps spare others the same experience), cherry is exceedingly stable *once* it's dry, but not necessarily *while* it's drying.

Over the years, I got to know the black cherry species well from many other perspectives. As a firewood, it is superb. When a stick or two of slightly green cherry is laid on the hot coals of a fire, the aroma is unforgettably delightful. The fruit is small, almost black in color and, in my opinion, it'll never replace the commercial Bing for flavor in the raw state. It's bitter to the point of unpalatability when eaten off the tree, but it makes a good wine with a deep purple-red color. In Colonial times, the fruit was packed into jars of rum to produce a potent favorite of the era called "cherry bounce." That, too, I've experimented with, and it is indeed tasty, but really not substantially different from a modern fruit brandy.

American black cherry is not a reliable producer of fruit—at

Photo: R. Bruce Hoadley

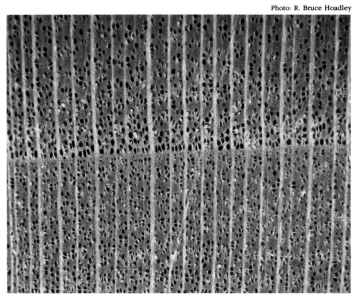

This ten-power macrophotograph of cherry endgrain shows the slightly larger pores at each annual ring. These give the wood a desirable grain pattern without making the grain hard to fill.

These three veneer samples show the range of cherry's character, from the very high grade on the left, to gummy (center), to the figured heartwood at right.

least, not in the harsh climate of northwestern Wisconsin where I cohabited with it. Some years it will hardly set fruit at all; in other, good years, the crop will be plentiful to the point of becoming a nuisance. The cherries litter the lawn, and their dark juice stains clothing. Swarms of birds devour, process and deposit them on cars, sidewalks, roofs and windows. The botanists would call this bird-to-cherry relationship "symbiotic" because it helps to propagate the species—not only to nearby fencerows and under telephone lines, but across considerable distances. As a result, black cherry has a sporadic and yet very extensive range. It's most plentiful in the hardwood forests of the eastern and midwestern United States and southern Canada, but its range extends down through the mountains of Mexico into Central America.

Like most other hardwoods, black cherry grows wild, not in planted stands. As long as there's a supply of seeds from local trees and sufficient sunlight, the trees do well. In fact, experiments over the last 20 years have proven that cherry does best if left alone: Efforts to produce knot-free wood by pruning low branches from selected trees seem to generate more branches.

The heart of cherry's U.S. range, and where it produces timber with maximum vigor, is in the central and Appalachian states. However, latitude, altitude and other macro-geographic and climatic factors are only part of what is important to the tree with respect to habitat. Cherry isn't very shade-tolerant. This, combined with its less than formidable maximum growth potential, makes good cherry lumber dependent on opportunistic natural events. The tree will grow vigorously in full sunlight along a fencerow, but it will branch out low, form a broad crown and, over time, pick up a fence staple or two when it happens to be growing right where a post ought to be. All of this, of course, degrades the quality of the wood.

The best source for cherry right now is in the mountainous region running up through Pennsylvania and into New York. That part of the country was almost completely clear-cut about 100 years ago, and cherry—being something of a pioneer species—got off to a good start. Seeds spread by birds were abundant, the saplings were mostly unshaded by older trees and competition between the trees made them reach up for light, promoting tall stems. Foresters in the early 1970s were delighted to discover the maturing resource, just at the time when the trees were reaching their peak. (If left unharvested over the next 100 years, these cherry trees would eventually succumb to the beech and maple growing in the forest's understory.) At the time, the demand for cherry was quite low, because there wasn't enough quality wood available from other parts of the country to promote and maintain much interest. As recently as the 1950s, cherry was one of the *least* used of our native timbers, having sunk to 28th place in the number of trees harvested. It was so scarce, in fact, that it ranked in price with rosewood and ebony. When the steady supply of Pennsylvania cherry began coming into the marketplace, however, popular demand grew as more and more people began to see the quality of the wood. Today, as mentioned earlier, the demand for cherry is second only to oak.

Cherry has a tendency to be a rather gummy wood, especially trees that have grown under less-than-ideal conditions. This gumminess can be a negative, especially when sanding the endgrain. The surface may quickly burn or darken when belt-sanded, requiring a great deal of tedious hand-sanding to soften the color. The safe approach is to give the endgrain a whisk or two with a sharp scraper, followed by gentle hand-sanding with a fine-grit sandpaper. Personally, I like "gummy" cherry. A certain amount of gum streaks well-dispersed in a slowly grown, wavy-grained piece of heartwood can be very attractive.

In furnituremaking, one of cherry's great attributes is the color it will eventually attain as time and chemistry work together to produce its unmistakable patina. The translucent, warm, amber-orange hue that only old cherry furniture exudes has eluded stain manufacturers to this day, and very likely always will. For starters, I have yet to find a convincing technical explanation of the chemistry of cherry's patina—I doubt if scientists really understand it yet.

Exposure to light definitely affects cherry and might accelerate the patina-building process, but I know from my own otherwise bitter experience in that absolutely pitch-dark attic, one of the few things my stack of cherry did right was to darken. (I think maybe I roasted it.)

The chemistry of cherry is certainly complex and not entirely friendly. Like peaches, almonds and some of its other close relatives in the rose family, cherry produces cyanic acid which, in high enough quantities, is lethal. Although the wood itself is non-toxic, wilted cherry leaves have poisoned livestock. There are traces of the poison in both the bark and the fruit pit. In fact, peach pits are high enough in cyanic acid to have once been an economically viable source for the deadly poison, cyanide.

I have no reservations about working with cherry wood and would do so far more often if it weren't for its price. Cherry is quite plentiful here in Wisconsin, but even here the best price I've found for FAS, kiln-dried stock is $2.80 per board foot, unsurfaced. I've chased down a few sources of freshly cut green material at well under $1 per board foot, but I'm understandably a little apprehensive about that alternative. Actually, I *have* successfully air-dried a few pieces of cherry since that disaster years ago (taking the normal care necessary with any wood), and my self-confidence has healed to the point that I would gladly take on the challenge again, but that's not the problem. I simply can't find good, wide pieces of cherry heartwood at the local mills. Demand for this "rose among woods" is intense, and doubtless the best of Wisconsin's production is shipped off to furniture factories and to woodworkers with fatter wallets than mine. What the mills here attempt to pawn off on us locals are narrow widths, slab cuts and sapwood. The art of avoiding that kind of "deal" is a skill the backwoods scavenger soon learns.

You know, come to think of it, it's only about a ten-hour drive from here to the cherry belt in Pennsylvania. □

Jon Arno is a woodworker and amateur wood technologist who recently moved from Brookfield, Wisc., to Schaumburg, Ill.

Walnut drops its leaves early in the fall, silhouetting its stark, open crown. It is a messy lawn tree, producing catkins in spring and large leaves—along with bushels of nuts—in autumn. In contrast to this open-field tree, a woods-grown walnut reaches for sunlight, resulting in a long, clear trunk, but the most recent 10 to 20 years of growth will be light-colored sapwood.

Walnut
The cabinetwood par-excellence

by Jon Arno

In lists of the various properties of cabinetwoods, American black walnut, *Juglans nigra,* stands near the middle in every category. There are dozens, if not hundreds, of woods that are stronger and denser. There are a few woods with better figure and richer color. Some hardwoods are substantially easier to work than walnut. And many fine cabinetwoods are a good deal less expensive.

Yet walnut is so flexibly appropriate for a broad range of uses that, overall, it rivals any other wood in the world. It might, in fact, be the very best cabinetwood of all. What does walnut bring to the party that causes it to stand out? To answer this question, we must consider not only its physical properties, but a number of subtle things that appeal to other senses and to our emotions.

Take gunstocks, for example. Of the four woods commonly used, only walnut is rated "excellent" in the physical attributes a gunstock requires. It has been the favored gunstock wood since colonial times, long before laboratory testing could comfirm our pioneers' instincts. The substitutes, hard maple, yellow birch, and sycamore may surpass walnut in one or two respects, yet, in the final balance, walnut becomes the standard, the perfect gunstock wood. In weight it is heavy enough to absorb some recoil, yet not so heavy as to be arm-wearying. For its weight, it is outstanding in strength, hardness and shock resistance. It is stable enough not to endanger the precise alignment between metal and wood. It machines beautifully. Walnut's dark color, aesthetics aside, is a particular asset—the runners-up all require staining lest they be conspicuous in the field, and are, therefore, more difficult to touch up if dented or scratched.

Notice how many of these attributes are also desirable for furniture. In the gamut of cabinetwoods, there are only a handful of woods as well endowed. In addition, walnut is neither ring-porous like oak or diffuse-porous like maple. It is what most experts call "semi-ring-porous," with a gradual transition between earlywood and latewood. This helps to make for little, if any, chatter in its resistance to the cutting edge, allowing shavings to peel off with a wax-like roll. Walnut has adequate ring-porosity to show a beautiful grain pattern, but is diffuse-porous enough to make the use of fillers optional in most furniture applications—if unfilled the pores will show but not be objectionable.

In walnut, we have a wood that is not too hard, not too soft, not too open-textured, not too plain...not too anything (except maybe too expensive). Like Baby Bear's porridge, it's just right.

I suspect that walnut has been so long entwined with human history that we have developed a genuine emotional attachment to it, one that runs deep. Walnut of the English or European variety, *J. regia,* has been with us both in our cabinetmaking and in our diet since ancient times, when our ancestors imported the tree from the Middle East and reestablished it in western Europe, where it had been extinct since the last ice age. In the 1600s,

European walnut supplanted oak as the premier furniture wood, until it, in turn, was supplanted by Honduras mahogany. During the American colonial period, when mahogany furniture imported from England was in style, walnut was sometimes stained red by domestic cabinetmakers in an effort to emulate the imports. It could be argued that, in Europe, mahogany is still the standard by which other cabinetwoods are measured. Yet in America this has not been the case for a long time. Today, we take Philippine "mahogany" (lauan and other species of *Shorea*) and stain it dark brown to imitate the walnut that is closer to our hearts.

Strictly speaking, current style is an intangible. Walnut has other intangible features as well. Particularly high on such a list is the pleasant aroma of a piece of walnut as it passes through the planer or the tablesaw. I am abnormally fastidious about keeping my shop clean because I know a clean shop is a safer shop. In fact, I will sometimes stop in the middle of a project to sweep the floor, but I have been known to let walnut shavings lie for days. To me, the scent of walnut ranks with fresh-ground coffee as one of life's great treats. Under certain conditions, however, particularly when a carving block of unseasoned walnut has been set aside to dry slowly, thriving micro-organisms can imbue the wood with a lasting, sourish odor best described as a stink. Even so, it helps clear the sinuses.

I should defer to the medical profession on this topic, but the reason the aroma of walnut evokes such pleasant emotions and a

About the other walnuts

My vote for the royal family of cabinetwoods must be *Juglandaceae.* This botanical family includes *Carya,* the hickories (including pecan), and the true bluebloods of the line, the *Juglans,* which are the walnuts and butternut. There are broad differences among the *Juglans* species, but most walnuts overlap so much in color and density that you may have to examine cell structure to tell them apart for certain.

The walnuts and the hickories comprise some 50 or so species worldwide. The hickories are limited to eastern North America and southern China, while the walnuts have a broader range in North America, Central America and northern South America, as well as in Eurasia.

The wood of the old-world tree, *J. regia,* is slightly softer and lighter in color than our black walnut, *J. nigra.* European walnut also shows subtle differences resulting from the climate and soil where it has grown, and for marketing reasons may be called French, Balkan, Italian, etc., but it is all the same species. Very little solid stock escapes Europe, although the veneer called circassian burl is sometimes seen on the market here.

Black walnut is not our only domestic species—there are *J. major,* or Arizona walnut, and *J. microcarpa,* which is called little walnut, Texas walnut or nogal. Occasionally, wood from the several species of walnuts from South and Central America shows up, called either tropical walnut or nogal. These are beautiful woods, a little softer, a little coarser textured and somewhat darker than our black walnut, judging from the few samples I have seen. These species are true walnuts, unlike African walnut (mansonia) and Queensland walnut, which have borrowed the name but not the pedigree.

The several Oriental species of true walnuts, native from northern India to Japan, produce woods that are almost never seen in our market. I haven't worked with Japanese walnut, *J. cordiformis,* but it is reputed to have a warmer, yellowish hue than our native wood.

Butternut, *J. cinerea,* is our other major domestic species of *Juglans,* and one of my personal favorites. While butternut is somewhat coarser in texture, its figure is virtually the same as black walnut. If you have ever wished there was a wood that worked as easily as pine or basswood yet looked like walnut, butternut is as close as you will ever get. With an average specific gravity of only 0.36, it is actually less dense than Ponderosa pine at 0.38 and substantially less dense than black walnut at 0.51. At the extreme ends of the scale,

though, the hardest, darkest-colored butternut and the softest walnut can be difficult to tell apart. Yet even then, butternut tends toward gray-tan and gingery tones, while walnut shows more purple.

Butternut has prevalent tension wood and tends to fuzz up a little in sanding. Being soft, it will generally drink an extra coat of varnish before it fills to a polishable surface, and it will not endure as well in daily use—this may be important if you are making a table, but it's almost irrelevant for a mantel clock or a picture frame.

Finally, claro walnut is a term used freely by lumber dealers on the West Coast, usually to describe highly figured walnut harvested from overmature trees in nut plantations. Some of this wood is probably English walnut that was grafted to a native rootstock, a practice that can promote a flame figure low in the stem. Other possibilities are two species native to California, *J. hindsii* and *J. californica,* found respectively in the northern and southern parts of the range. All of these claro walnuts are true *Juglans,* but the name is no guarantee of which species the walnut is, nor that it is particularly showy. I suspect at this point that I'm just splitting hairs. Let me affirm that in the walnut family tree there are some beautiful dark woods but no black sheep. I, for one, will welcome walnut under any name in my shop—none of it is what you could call bad.   —*J.A.*

sense of well being may be more than psychological. According to a USDA Forest Products Laboratory publication, walnut contains ellagic acid, a sedative and tranquilizer. They report an incident in which a dog chewed on a black walnut statue and fell into a deep sleep for two days. There are also reports that various tribes of American Indians used to throw crushed walnuts or butternuts into ponds to stupefy fish.

Walnut's chemical potency should come as no surprise to gardeners. One of our native black walnut's most active constituents is a substance called juglone, which is apparently part of the tree's biological defense system. Juglone is toxic to other plants, such as apple trees, and especially to members of the tomato family. It would appear to pose no problem to cabinetmakers, however. It polymerizes into dark pigments in the wood tissue, which, I presume, makes it inert.

One of the walnut tree's few shortcomings is that it produces logs with a relatively large amount of almost pure white sapwood. Slicing it all off would be an appalling waste. Fortunately, by injecting hot steam into the kiln during the drying process, the sapwood can be darkened somewhat. This procedure is certainly beneficial in view of our limited supply of walnut, but it seems to dull the richness of the wood's overall color. To my way of thinking, there is something special about a piece of carefully air-dried walnut with its subtle, almost translucent blue-purple highlights. Unfortunately, like flowers, youth, and so many of this world's beautiful things, the magic of a freshly planed piece of air-dried walnut is a fleeting pleasure. Age and exposure to light will bleach its vivid tones, and over the years the strikingly blue-purple highlights mellow out toward the gold or amber side of the spectrum.

As far as price goes, I wish I could offer some novel schemes for scavenging a deal on this stuff, but there aren't any. Even the small backwoods sawmills know what walnut is and what it is worth. Black walnut generally runs between $3 and $5 per board foot, depending upon the grade, and butternut (see box, facing page) usually costs about $1 less per board foot. The problem is, there is no such thing as an inferior species of walnut and everybody knows it. There is no compelling reason for walnut to be in scarce supply other than the universal demand for it. As it is, the demand makes the wood of this relatively plentiful tree seem scarce.

Walnut is a pretty tree with its deep brown, almost black bark and its bright light green compound leaves, but it is a beauty that belongs in the forest where competition for sunlight forces it to produce a tall, unmarred trunk. In this setting it is a capable competitor and will develop diameters in excess of 5 ft. and heights of 100 ft. or more. In the open, like most hardwoods it has a propensity to branch out, forming a dome-like crown which much reduces its value as a timber source.

Although its crop of tasty nuts is an important asset, the tree is not that popular for landscaping. Because walnut leafs late in the spring and loses its leaves early in the fall, its appearance is stark and dead looking for much of the year. There is no particular beauty to its flowering, it is a catkin producer, and a messy tree on a well-manicured lawn. Its nuts attract squirrels that are generally more skillful in collecting the crop than all but the most watchful homeowner, and add injury to insult by planting a few of them in gardens where they are chemically hostile to other plants.

While we woodworkers might unanimously agree that walnut plantings should be sharply increased, the economics of growing hardwood timber on valuable eastern land is, pardon the pun, a

Making walnut-husk stain

The pigments in all parts of the walnut tree are plentiful and, for better or worse, downright indelible. Anyone who has tried to husk walnuts by hand knows all about the durability of this stain. Even crushing the fresh leaves with bare hands will leave you with a dirty, two-pack-a-day, yellow stain on your fingers that defies a scrub brush. The pigments in the husk of the nuts and the root bark make excellent dye for cloth and, of course, they give the wood its much prized color. In the case of American black walnut, this is the well-known and often strikingly purple-streaked chocolate brown.

Those cabinetmakers with a flair for experimentation can get at this pigment and produce a stain that will transfer some of walnut's beauty to other less-endowed woods. To begin, collect a few pounds of the nuts, preferably those that have fallen to the ground and are beginning to darken and decompose. Husk them and loosely pack a quart jar full of the husks (sans the nuts—eat those). Fill the jar brim-full with non-detergent ammonia, the ordinary sort, not the sudsy kind.

Cap the jar and allow it to stand for a few weeks. The ammonia will leach out the pigment, and this mess can be strained through cheesecloth to produce a jet black liquid that, admittedly, is something of a trial to work with. Wear rubber gloves and apply the stain with a rag in a well-ventilated work space, preferably outdoors. The stain is water based, and two coats are generally necessary because the first coat raises the grain and must be rubbed down with fine sandpaper or steel wool.

It's a foul-smelling, messy process, but it works, and I promise that the results are definitely worth the trouble. —J.A.

Walnut-extract stain, best made from decomposing husks, is excellent for darkening mahogany, and produces a patina on pine that continues to darken with age. Woods shown, from front to rear, are poplar, pine, mahogany, cherry and maple.

tough nut to crack. But contrary to popular opinion, on good sites walnut is not a slow grower. It spurts up rapidly for the first decade or so and then begins to slow down as it enters into nut production. The tree seems to oblige us woodworkers with the reasonably quick accumulation of woody tissue, but then it taunts us in taking its own sweet time mellowing it into the rich brown heartwood we seek. □

Jon Arno is an amateur wood technologist in Milwaukee, Wisc. He is currently seeking information from other woodworkers about the properties and working qualities of unusual native woods.

Bird's-Eye Maple
Nature flaunts her 'Midas touch'

by Bill Keenan

Collecting and stockpiling interesting woods for pet projects is characteristic of woodworkers, and I'm no exception. I have a particular soft spot for bird's-eye maple. Once a lumber dealer steers me to the yard's maple stash, I quickly find myself out of control and reaching for my checkbook. But what is the mystique about bird's-eye maple that turns woodworkers into wood worshippers? It may be its golden-grain beauty and rarity, or it may be that nobody can explain how the eyes form. Like a jewel scattering light, this unique wood provides few clues to the mysterious process that forged it.

The distinctive figure, named for the way each tiny swirl resembles the eye of a bird, is usually found in the sugar or hard maple (*Acer saccharum*), one of North America's most distinctive trees, known for its shade, cream-color lumber and sticky harvest of sap. The bird's-eye figure can be found wherever maples grow, but it's most common in the harsh growing conditions of the north country. Occasionally it's found in other wood species, including soft maple, yellow birch, ash and ponderosa pine. Whatever the cause of the figure, it's a result that woodworkers prize. When a bird's-eye log is split along a plane tangent to the growth rings, the wood separates, exposing a bulging cone that extends inward on the bark-facing side of the wood and a matching pit on the log's other side. When a log is sliced lengthwise or rotary-cut for veneer, the result is the familiar bird's-eye pattern.

Individual eyes can be as tiny as pinpricks or the size of a quarter. Once bird's-eyes begin to appear, they propagate, becoming larger through succeeding outer layers of growth. Often the bird's-eyes continue to form throughout the life of the tree. Or, they may end abruptly several inches beneath the surface of the log—happy surprises that lie in wait for woodworkers.

Bird's-eye and other maples have figured prominently in American woodworking and furniture history. I'll tell you a little about it before discussing what we know about bird's-eye formation and the practical aspects of how to work with it.

Bird's-eye history—American furnituremakers have used bird's-eye veneer for more than two centuries. Although little has been recorded about its use, early furnituremakers often used maple in intricate inlays. In the late 1700s, for example, bird's-eye flourishes were common on furniture of the Federal period.

By the late 19th century, detailed handwork combined with lavish bird's-eye touches had found its way into art-nouveau furniture and the resurgent Louis XV movement. In the late 1920s, a time of transition marked by the merging of a new linear functionalism with ornate traditionalism, the bird's-eye pattern found its niche as a stylistic ornamentation playing counterpoint to the crisp geometry associated with design trends such as Art Deco.

Virginia Boyd, a University of Wisconsin-Madison historian who specializes in American interiors, says bird's-eye maple was also used at this time for reproduction work—Chippendale and other colonial-revival pieces. Though seldom used in the originals, bird's-eye, to the 20th-century mind, became associated with the nostalgic. "It was a hearkening back to an older time and style, even though it wasn't an accurate look back," Boyd said.

Today, bird's-eye maple has found favor as a highly prized specialty wood in the repertoire of many woodworkers. While Europeans, especially Germans and Italians, seem to favor bird's-eye veneer, American woodworkers employ both veneer and solid wood. It's not unusual in the United States to find furniture made entirely of solid bird's-eye maple.

Origins—As long as bird's-eye maple has been around, so have questions about its origin. Why does bird's-eye occur almost exclusively in maple? Why does it appear in such varied patterns throughout a given tree? Like random splotches from a frenzied painter's brush, bird's-eyes may appear over the entire length of a tree, be confined to one side or scattered in irregular patches. Why, no one knows.

Theories about what causes the swirling figure have been as varied as the patterns of the figure itself. Early investigators thought it was caused by a parasitic fungus that attacked the cambium, the thin layer between bark and wood that produces new wood cells. Others suggested it was caused by boring insects, or that wounds inflicted by birds during the tree's early growth resulted in pits or grooves, which over time were filled in with fresh layers of wood growth. But these explanations don't make sense, because wounds

From *Fine Woodworking* (January 1989) 74:78-80

Long prized by woodworkers for its distinctive figured pattern, bird's-eye maple requires sharp tools and a deft touch to shape and smooth successfully.

in live parts of a tree normally heal over and disappear as new layers of growth are added. In bird's-eye maple, the eyes grow radially, like spokes on a wheel, and they usually increase in size. Another theory attributed the eyes to undeveloped buds that remain dormant in the inner bark. If this explanation were valid, you would expect the bird's-eyes to have dark cores and project in an outward direction. But the cores are clear and the eyes grow as conical indentations pointing inward, toward the tree's pith, as shown in the drawing at right.

In the wake of this speculation, wood scientists began to systematically sort out clues to the bird's-eye mystery. First, they noted that bird's-eye logs characteristically had dark stains or rotten heartwood. They also observed that figured trees were usually found in a dense portion of even-aged stands; they were often unhealthy and deformed. Researchers determined that maples with the bird's-eye pattern took an average of 60 years longer to reach an 18-in. dia. than the normal, unfigured trees growing in open stands. Regardless of how vigorous the trees' later growth, old bird's-eye maples had narrow early-growth rings, typical of young trees in a crowded stand that must fight for available light. Whatever the direct cause of bird's-eyes, suppression of the tree is probably linked to their development.

In the most recent effort to unravel the bird's-eye mystery, a researcher at the U.S. Forest Service's Northeastern Forest Experiment Station observed that a viral agent fit the known facts of bird's-eye formation better than any hypothesis so far. However, to date, the experimental work has been inconclusive: Nature continues to guard her secret well.

Finding bird's-eye maple — The value and popularity of bird's-eye maple, especially during the 1930s, prompted researchers to attempt to mass produce it using graftings of tissue from highly figured trees — without success. So bird's-eye aficionados cling to the few available clues to guide them in their search. Bird's-eye has been found in trees as small as 2 in. in diameter, and tiny depressions found on 1-in. maple saplings may be a sign of its beginning. As the tree adds layers of growth, these small depressions grow in size, sometimes extending through the bark. When present, and

Bird's-eye configuration

Bird's-eyes cause local distortion in annual rings, appearing like spokes in a wheel.

Quartersawn face

Bird's-eyes generally grow larger from point of origin; distorted annual rings create cone-like structures.

Indentations in cambium may or may not extend through and be revealed in bark.

Photo: Michele Russell Slavinsky; drawing: Lee Hov

often they're not, these depressions are advertisements for a buried treasure.

If you're in the woods looking for bird's-eye maples, check along hollows and gullies or on the northwest slopes of hills. These are areas where young trees have to tough it out, and consequently, are ideal environments for bird's-eye formation. It also helps to know if bird's-eye maples are apt to grow in your region. In southern Wisconsin, which is not prime bird's-eye maple country, foresters say you might find one tree out of 10,000 with good bird's-eye figure. But loggers say that 300 miles north, in Michigan's upper peninsula—bird's-eye maple heaven—you'll find approximately one maple in 400 with the figure.

Characteristics—Structurally, bird's-eye maple isn't much different from normal hard maple. Because figured maples grow slower, you might expect the wood to be a bit denser. Air-dried bird's-eye maple weighs 47 lbs. per cubic foot and has a specific gravity of .68, a bit higher than the .63 for normal air-dried maple.

Bird's-eye maple is a hard, tough wood. It has a uniform texture, glues well and takes a good finish. Its creamy white wood is often streaked amber to brown, usually the result of defects or disease in the tree. Technologists at the Forest Products Laboratory say grain deviation in mildly figured bird's-eye maple won't affect strength, but they caution that highly figured wood won't be as strong as straight-grained wood for spindle support members, such as chair legs.

Bird's-eye maple seasons slowly, and because of its wild grain, has a higher shrinkage factor than ordinary hard maple. This can cause buckling as it dries. In fact, careful drying of the wood is critical. Air-drying or the use of a solar kiln with a slow drying schedule are best. Rapidly kiln-dried bird's-eye maple can result in twisted lumber with eyes eager to chip out. Hairline cracks around the eyes are a sure sign the wood has been dried improperly. Because of the way the eyes grow, most bird's-eye lumber is plainsawn to reveal the full figure; if quartersawn, the figure will be masked.

Prices for bird's-eye lumber vary widely depending on the amount of figure. Strangely enough, through a quirk in the National Hardwood Association's rules, bird's-eyes, like so many knots, are counted as defects. Consequently, bird's-eye maple that's not sorted for specialty markets at the sawmill may be graded low. This, no doubt, accounts for a lot of 2-in.-wide bird's-eye maple strips I've seen ignominiously gracing gymnasium floors. Fortunately, loggers are a pretty shrewd bunch: Before maple logs are run through the sawmill, the obvious bird's-eye logs are sorted out. Good bird's-eye can bring a sharp-eyed logger an extra $100 per 1,000 bd. ft.

European veneer buyers also have a warm spot for bird's-eye logs. According to one veneer exporter, the Europeans have their own grading system for bird's-eye veneer logs. He says they look for white wood, large eyes and a lot of curl. They examine a log by scooping out small portions of wood with a knife and by checking for the spoke-like pattern of bird's-eye on the ends of a log. Most woodworkers, however, aren't so particular: Some prefer bird's-eye maple that has rich streaks of brown in it, feeling that it gives the wood more character.

Working with bird's-eye—Despite my affection for bird's-eye maple, I use it sparingly. Because it's so "busy" visually, I think it requires a well-developed design eye to make it work effectively. But with some thought, this extravagantly figured wood can transform nice work into special work. The deviating grain around the eyes gives the wood a chatoyant quality: It gathers light in ripples, providing a luster as changeable as that of a fire opal.

The very qualities that make this wood so appealing to the eye

also make it a nightmare to work. The swirling grain is notorious for chipping out, so planing it can be an exasperating experience. The dense wood will burn on a belt sander if you aren't careful, so make sure your belts are reasonably new, and keep the work moving to avoid burn marks.

I've had good luck using a hand scraper for finishing touches. Hone the scraper and then put a light burr on it by running a burnisher over the edge once or twice. Use a shallow angle, and pull the scraper lightly across the wood's surface.

To find out how others approach the surly stuff, I talked to some woodworkers who use bird's-eye maple regularly. Some of them, especially the ones that require precise dimensions for joinery, don't like to mess with thicknessing it themselves. They prefer to buy it to thickness or glue it up and take it to someone who has a heavy-duty thicknessing sander. The dollars spent, they claim, are well worth the time saved and the avoided aggravation.

Those who do plane it themselves use varying techniques seasoned with a lot of common sense. Planing only the side of the board closest to the pith is a logical approach to bringing it to the desired thickness (the other side is just thickness-sanded). Because bird's-eye grows as a series of cones pointing toward the tree's pith, the planer blades, in theory, slice off the protruding cones, leaving a smooth surface. Another woodworker takes a similar approach with an added twist: He sharpens his planer blades and then gives them a 10° back bevel. In effect, the blades act as scrapers, so he can't remove much—sometimes as little as ¹⁄₆₄ in. on a pass, depending on the wood's figure. But, he ends up with a satin-smooth surface on bird's-eye maple and other troublesome woods, like quartersawn cherry.

Machining bird's-eye wood on a jointer is straightforward, but common sense should prevail. Examine the grain to determine which way to run the plank through. A reliable method is to run your thumb along the edge to feel the stubble of the opposing grain so you can tell which direction is the path of least resistance and thereby minimize tearout. Make sure your blades are razor sharp, then run the wood through slowly, taking off ¹⁄₃₂ in. or less on each pass.

The cross forces exerted by the wild grain in bird's-eye wood probably help to stabilize it. Once flat, bird's-eye lumber will generally stay that way. However, like other woods, bird's-eye lumber can cup if it dries unevenly. If you have the time, it's a good idea to let it adjust to conditions in your shop after preliminary machining. After a couple of weeks, you can true it up.

Bird's-eye maple turns nicely, and I haven't run into any problems with chipping: I keep my gouges and scrapers sharp and use a light touch. The orientation of the bowl blank on the lathe is a matter of preference, not utility.

Working with bird's-eye maple veneer isn't much different than working with other veneers, but according to furniture designer Dick Wickman of Verona, Wisc., bird's-eye veneer tends to crack along parallel lines that can break through the finish.

Bird's-eye maple can be finished like most other woods, but here's how professional woodfinisher Rob Ray of Madison, Wisc., finishes bird's-eye solid wood and veneer: First, he applies one coat of lacquer, diluted 3:1 with lacquer thinner, and allows it to dry. This fills the pinholes and makes loose fibers stand up. Then, he scuffs the surface lightly with 320-grit sandpaper, being careful not to sand through the lacquer surface. Now he applies a color-matched paste wood filler, thinned with naptha. He let's this just barely dry, then wipes the surface with burlap and rags. He applies the surface finish of his choice, and completes the job by hand-rubbing. □

Bill Keenan, formerly a forester, is now a writer, editor and woodworker. He lives in Madison, Wisc.

Maple: A Versatile Timber
Sometimes fancy, sometimes plain, but never dull

by Jon Arno

Maple has something to offer every woodworker, from general contractors to turners. Even though maple's inconspicuous figure lacks the striking contrast that gives ring-porous woods, such as oak and ash, their bold character, this diffuse-porous wood is subtly beautiful. Unlike colorful walnut or cherry, light-colored maple has warm brown accents and a translucent, opalescent quality in the way light plays off its surface. And most maple is easy to work and readily takes a finish, and can be used in anything from the finest furniture to packing crates, floors, bowling alleys and pins, cabinets, chairs and eating utensils.

Best of all, maple is exceptionally plentiful and often inexpensive. The latest USDA Forest Service statistics estimate that approximately 42 billion cu. ft. of maple stock (including both hard and soft maple species) is growing on timber lands in the Eastern United States. Most of it is relatively young second growth, but enough of it is of adequate size to produce sawtimber yielding more than 90 billion bd. ft. And this doesn't include stands of bigleaf maple in the Pacific Northwest, maple in unharvestable reserves, or both soft and hard maple available for logging in Canada. Of the commercially important hardwood cabinetmaking timbers native to North America, only the oaks are more plentiful than maple. Sugar maple, *Acer saccharum*, (the tree shown here), which is harder than most oaks, is the most common maple cabinetmaking wood; however, softer maples, such as red maple *(A. rubrum)*, are also abundant and can be cost-effective substitutes.

There are about 125 species of maple distributed primarily in the Northern Hemisphere. About two-thirds of all these maples are native to China and the bulk of the remainder is spread out from England to Japan. North America claims only 13 native species and just 6 of these represent important commercial sources of timber. Despite the limited number of species, though, the United States and Canada provide the vast majority of the world's total production of maple lumber. Commercially, the lumber is divided into two groups: hard maple and soft maple, as given in the chart on p. 23.

Differences between hard maple and soft maple – Hard maple is stronger than soft maple and is better suited to woodwork that takes abuse, such as floors and countertops. Hard maple is cut from two closely related species: sugar maple and the less plentiful black maple, *A. nigrum*. The woods of these two trees, which grow in the Northeastern and Central United States and Southeastern Canada, are virtually indistinguishable in appearance. While black maple tends to be slightly lighter in weight, sugar maple has an average specific gravity of 0.56 (oven dry weight/green volume). Both hard maples are about as heavy as northern red oak and heavier than black walnut and black cherry. (For more on specific gravity, see Bruce Hoadley's book, *Understanding Wood*, The Taunton Press, 1980.)

This sugar maple growing on a hillside field in Connecticut is more than 4½ ft. in diameter at chest height and stands over 100 ft. tall. Wood from these trees is known commercially as hard maple.

Even though all of the soft maples are substantially lighter in weight than hard maple (and therefore inferior for applications such as flooring), red maple really isn't all that soft. Its average specific gravity is 0.49, which falls midway between that of black cherry (0.47) and that of black walnut (0.51). When it comes to first-rate domestic cabinetwoods, that's pretty good company to be keeping. And red maple is more plentiful and usually much less expensive.

With a little careful selection, cost-conscious woodworkers can come up with some excellent wood among the soft maples. The key is choosing the right species for any given job, and soft maples are diverse enough to span a great many applications. Most of the

From *Fine Woodworking* (November 1990) 85:73-75

grain patterns found in hard maple also occur in soft maple, but some of the soft maple species actually possess more interesting color. For example, the heartwood of red maple, which grows throughout most of the Eastern United States, is usually darker than that of sugar maple. It has interesting gray highlights and sometimes dark, chocolate-brown markings.

The softest and lightest soft maple is box elder *(A. negundo)*, which is found throughout most of the United States. It's also the finest textured of the maples, making it very pleasant to work with and a favorite among turners. Bigleaf maple, a Western species, and silver maple *(A. saccharinum)*, which is plentiful throughout the East, are the remaining two major U.S. timber-producing soft maples. Both of these species are relatively soft and easy to work, and they have the additional advantage of being much more stable than hard maple. In fact, bigleaf has an average volumetric shrinkage of only 11.6%, which is quite comparable to black cherry.

Maple's many faces—In most woods, figure is produced by variation in texture between the springwood and summerwood. In maple, however, the figure is produced by bands of warm-brown- or amber-colored fibrous tissue demarcating the annual rings from the wood's overall creamy yellow hue. Like the annual rings, the medullary rays in maple are much darker than the background tissue, and they pepper the tangential surface with short, thin lines, which are similar to the ray flecks in beech. But maple's rays are softer and more subdued, like the weave of shear fabric. Even plain-figured maple, shown in the top, left sample on the facing page, seldom produces absolutely straight grain and the figure on its tangential surface usually curls and contorts like the veins in fine marble.

In some instances, ordinary maple trees may produce extraordinary figures, which are commonly referred to as fiddleback, quilted and bird's-eye maple. Bird's-eye figure (shown in the top, right sample on the facing page) ranks among the world's finest and most sought after cabinetwoods. (For more on this, see "Bird's-Eye Maple," pp. 18-20.) Curly figure (shown in the bottom, left sample on the facing page) is sometimes called fiddleback or tiger-stripe maple and is often used for the back of stringed instruments, like violins. Quilted figure (shown in the bottom, right sample on the facing page), which occurs most often in the Western bigleaf maple, *A. macrophyllum*, is prized for tabletops and inlay. Only a small percentage of maple woods brought to market have these

Which maple is which?

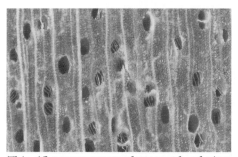

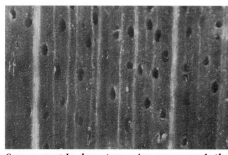

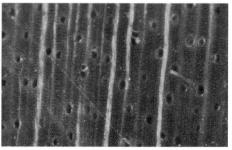

This 15-power macrophotograph of river birch endgrain reveals characteristics that are not visible to the unaided eye. The rays of river birch are narrower than the diameter of its largest pores.

Sugar maple has two size rays and the widest are as wide or wider than its largest pores. Sugar maple is the most common maple cabinetmaking wood. This species is also related closely to black maple.

Soft maples, such as the silver maple shown here, generally display more uniform ray width than hard maples. Distinguishing between species of maple, however, is difficult without chemical analysis.

Maple is so common that you usually know when you are looking at it. But of all the wood you could confuse maple with, birch is the most similar. Birch and maple have a long history of being used in the commercial manufacture of cabinets, and so they're often encountered—sometimes together in the same project. Both are fine-textured, light-colored woods and have similar working characteristics. Even when you look closely, you can see that both have relatively small, uniform-size pores that are evenly distributed.

With a little practice, distinguishing maple from birch is not difficult. Some cabinetmakers can differentiate the two by smell. When fresh, maple and birch have distinctly different scents, and you can train your nose to recognize the difference.

You can also see physical differences between maple and birch. Birch generally has a somewhat chalky, less-lustrous surface than maple, and birch has an ash-gray cast, while maple is often yellowish beige. If you look closely at maple's cleanly crosscut endgrain, you can see its medullary rays, which diverge from the center of the tree. On the tangential surface of maple, the rays appear as a profusion of evenly dispersed, very fine, dark brown lines that run parallel to the grain. Each ray is only about $\frac{1}{64}$ in. to $\frac{1}{32}$ in. long, but they're in such abundance that they lend a warm color to the wood. On the radial surface, the rays appear as distinct, narrow, amber-orange bands that run across the grain, occasionally $\frac{3}{4}$ in. to 1 in. long if you're lucky enough to have cut directly through the ray. The rays in birch, however, are so fine and so similar in color to the background tissue that they are virtually invisible on either the tangential or radial surfaces without magnification.

To differentiate between maple and birch with certainty, you should examine their endgrain using a 15-power hand lens. Cleanly slice the endgrain of both samples with a razor blade and compare what you see through the lens with the three photos above of river birch, sugar maple and silver maple. In birch, the diameter of the largest pores is greater than the width of the widest rays.

It is extremely difficult, however, to distinguish between various species of maples (as you can see from the photos above, center and right). Some technical references report that soft maples have rays that are relatively uniform in width, while hard maples have both wide and narrow rays. Also it is possible to distinguish red maple from sugar maple by chemical analysis. When a water solution of ferrous sulfate is applied to the surface of these woods, red maple turns bluish-black, while sugar maple turns green. —*J.A.*

Photos this page: John P. Limbach, Ripon Microslides

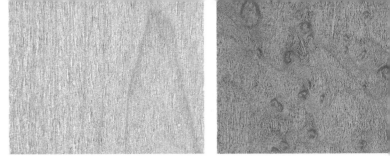

special figures, which are the result of abnormal growth. In some instances, the tree's living, wood-producing layer (the cambium layer, located just inside the bark) develops spots that fail to produce wood tissue at a normal rate. While this process may not affect the entire tree, it generally persists for years, as the spots enlarge and build up layer upon layer of convoluted grain. Depending upon the degree of malformation and how you cut the log, a number of distinct figures may be obtained from a single piece.

Machining and finishing maple — Plain-figured maple machines exceptionally well and will hold very sharp details. In fact, the latin name for the maple genus, *Acer,* means sharp because lances and skewers made from it held a sharp point. Plain maple's even grain allows it to be sawed, chiseled, handplaned or machine planed, or drilled without much chipping or tearout. When it is routed, it has a tendency to develop burn marks that are difficult to sand out, and so you must use a sharp, clean bit and keep your feed speed high. Because of hard maple's density, working it with hand tools requires some muscle, but the results are gratifying. Figured maple, on the other hand, can be very difficult to handplane or scrape cleanly, and it requires using a plane with a surgically sharp blade. Hard maple turns so predictably and yields such defect-free products that it has long been favored for commercial production of round items: kitchen utensils, bowling pins, furniture parts, dowels, spindles, spools and heavy-duty conveyor rollers. And when hard maple is sanded on the lathe, it doesn't gum up sandpaper as cherry does.

Few woods are as easy and as pleasant to finish as maple. It has a moderately high natural luster, and you can quickly smooth its surface with scrapers or fine-grit abrasives. Some soft maples can be more difficult to work to a smooth surface free of fuzzy grain, and they may require more sanding with fine-grit paper than hard maple. A single coat of tung oil on maple tabletops, counters and cutting boards may be sufficient protection against stains from food and drink spills. But bare maple does have adequate porosity to accept stain and allow glue to bond. Also, because of maple's fine texture, you can finish it to a high gloss without using special fillers. Only a coat or two of light-bodied varnish is needed to build up a glassy smooth surface. And since maple is so hard, it supports virtually any finish without a great risk of denting or chipping. (For more on working with bird's-eye maple, see Bill Keenan's article on pp. 18-20.)

There are no chemicals in maple that threaten its utility. Although there are minute traces of tannin in maple bark, it is absent from the wood. Volatiles in common varnishes, lacquers and glues don't react adversely with maple to destroy their bond or affect drying time. In fact, given its fine texture, maple is excellent for painted projects because its featureless grain won't telegraph through the finish.

Limitations — Given maple's pleasant working characteristics and subtle beauty, there is little mystery as to why it is used in so many diverse applications. But it is not suited to every purpose and indeed has some significant shortcomings. First of all, since hard maple is not very stable compared to most other popular cabinetwoods, woodworkers should prepare for wood movement. Hard maple's average volumetric shrinkage of 14.7% (green to oven dry) is nearly 30% greater than that of black cherry (11.5%) and almost twice as large as that of Honduras mahogany (7.8%). Hard-maple spindles and tenons tend to loosen when exposed to seasonal fluctuations in humidity. Furthermore, hard maple has a rather pronounced tendency to warp because it develops severe stresses when drying. Its high volumetric shrinkage is compounded by a somewhat large difference between its 9.9% tangential shrinkage and its 4.8% radial shrinkage.

*Ordinary maple, **above, left,** is subtly beautiful, but bird's-eye figure, **above, right,** is probably one of the most sought after cabinetwoods in the world. Figured maple woods are freaks of nature resulting from abnormal growth. Curly figure, also called fiddleback or tiger maple, **below, left,** is often used in stringed instruments. Quilted figure, **below, right,** occurs most often in bigleaf maple.*

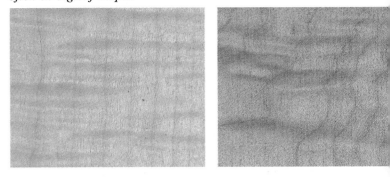

Maples				
Commercial Name/Species	Specific Gravity	Shrinkage(%)		
		T	R	V
Sugar, *Acer saccharum**	0.56	9.9	4.8	14.7
Black, *Acer nigrum**	0.52	9.3	4.8	14.0
Red, *Acer rubrum***	0.49	8.2	4.0	12.6
Silver, *Acer saccharinum***	0.44	7.2	3.0	12.0
Bigleaf, *Acer macrophyllum***	0.44	7.1	3.7	11.6
Box elder, *Acer negundo***	0.42	7.4	3.9	14.8

Specific Gravity = oven dry weight/green volume
T = Tangential shrinkage, green to oven dry
R = Radial shrinkage, green to oven dry
V = Volumetric shrinkage, green to oven dry
* Hard maple
** Soft maple

Another limitation is that maple has a low resistance to decay. Because maple lacks tannin or other strong chemical defenses often found in more durable woods, it is quickly attacked by fungi. On the positive side, though, the stains caused by fungi can produce a very attractive spalted pattern, which is actually prized for use in cabinetry and in turned decorative bowls. Spalted box elder can be especially nice. It is susceptible to attack by the fungus *Fusarium negundi*, which produces beautiful, coral-colored streaks, rather than the usual brown or blue-black coloration found in most spalted woods. Spalted wood, however, must be thoroughly seasoned as soon as possible after the staining occurs in order to force the fungi into dormancy. Otherwise, the wood will structurally deteriorate as the fungi multiply and literally devour the wood tissue. Unless producing spalted wood is your objective, maple should be dried quickly to remove all surface moisture, before the fungi can get established. Even when properly dried, though, maple is a very poor choice for marine or exterior projects of any kind. □

Jon Arno is a wood technologist and consultant in Schaumburg, Ill. Wood samples provided courtesy of A&M Wood Specialty, Inc., 358 Eagle St. N., Box 3204, Cambridge, Ont., Canada N3H 4S6.

This 18th-century Boston Bombé chest by Tom Lee, a graduate of the North Bennet Street School, Boston, Mass., illustrates the excellent color and grain patterns of true mahogany.

Mahogany
Classic-furniture timbers are getting harder to find

by Jon Arno

To build with mahogany is to share a woodworking experience with the skilled 18th- and 19th-century cabinetmakers who created some of the world's most cherished furniture. Unfortunately, fewer woodworkers are able to savor that experience today, because the true mahoganies, what the old cabinetmakers called Cuban and Honduras mahoganies, are in short supply. The trees, often growing more than 100 ft. high and as much as 40 ft. around, are found in ever smaller and more remote groves. Most of the original stands have disappeared; those that remain have been heavily logged. Usually only a few mahogany trees, two or three per acre, constitute a "stand," which makes logging inefficient and expensive. Harvesting is haphazard and often badly managed, with little thought given to ensuring adequate supplies for the future. Attempts to cultivate mahogany haven't been very successful: The tree is slow growing, requiring 60 years to reach economically

viable size, and many immature trees are destroyed by larvae of the widespread pyralid moth and ambrosia beetle. Also, the best of the highly figured lumber is often marked for use as veneer in production furniture shops or for interior decorative work, further depleting the supply. So mahogany, if you can find it, is expensive. For the real thing, cost can range between $5 and $10 per bd. ft. for clear, but plain-figured stock.

The true mahoganies come from several species in the genus *Swietenia*, but two species predominate: *Swietenia mahagoni*, the West Indies or island species, often called Cuban mahogany; and *Swietenia macrophylla*, the mainland species, found from east central Mexico to Bolivia, commonly called Honduras mahogany. With less true mahogany available, you're likely to find lumberyards stocked with substitutes, such as African mahogany (khaya) or even totally unrelated timbers, such as lauan, the so-called "Philippine mahogany" or Australian "Red" mahogany, which is actually a *Eucalyptus*. Some of the substitutes, such as khaya, sapele and andiroba, are members of the mahogany family, which includes about 50 genera and nearly 1,000 species, and are fine cabinetwoods in their own right.

The differences between the substitutes and the real stuff aren't always obvious, even to a practiced eye. It isn't until you begin working with the woods that the real differences become apparant. True mahogany is easily worked and shaped. Its exquisitely figured grain, hidden beneath the surface of roughsawn lumber, seems to come alive with a soft luster when planed. And stability, a virtue of true mahogany unmatched by any of its alternatives, may not be evident until months or even years after a project has been completed.

A historical perspective—The Spaniards must have begun harvesting mahogany almost as soon as they arrived in the New World. It was used in the construction of a cathedral in Santo Domingo begun in 1514. And the Spanish colonists quickly discovered the advantages of mahogany for shipbuilding: Strong, but lighter and more buoyant than oak, mahogany is an ideal ship timber. It also became important for its excellent bending properties, ability to be carved and high resistance to dry rot. Although it is not as impervious to decay and attack by borers as is teak (*Tectona grandis*), the heartwood of true mahogany is a popular choice for ship construction. It is so durable, in fact, that logs cut and left to rot in Santo Domingo in the late 1700s were salvaged more than 50 years later, with the heartwood still sound. The common seamen preferred mahogany, because unlike oak, it was slow to burn and didn't splinter as badly when hit by cannonballs.

Although the English were actively logging the coast of Central America as early as 1638, it wasn't until more than half a century later that mahogany—the English at this time called it "cedar wood"—reached England in quantity. But by 1725, mahogany was the preferred wood, along with walnut and oak, for the finest English furniture. Thomas Chippendale (1718-1779) used mahogany extensively, and his furniture became the leading edge of style. By the late 1700s, mahogany was also flourishing in America: Chippendale's designs were popular with British-trained American cabinetmakers. For the colonials, this style, with its imported look, had status.

Chippendale used high-quality mahogany, but he relied on the design of his furniture—its shell motif and claw-and-ball carvings—rather than on highly figured wood to achieve the furniture's rich appearance. With the introduction of the Federal style and its emphasis on simpler designs and straight lines, cabinetmakers began embellishing their furniture less and focusing more on the wood itself. Thus, the Federal style favored the more flamboyant and marble-like grain patterns that we now associate with the work of Thomas Sheraton (1751-1806).

Mahogany continued to be the premier cabinetwood in England and America through most of the 1800s. Its highly figured grain remained popular and contributed to the distinctive charm of the work of masters, such as Duncan Phyfe (1768-1854) in New York.

Thus, true mahogany is indispensable for the reproduction of period furniture, and although increasingly scarce, it continues to be the wood of choice for many woodworkers—a small wonder when you consider its characteristics. Few woods have as much going for them as true mahogany: Its durability, stability, structural uniformity and beauty provide a hard-to-beat combination. Because of this appeal, the woods of perhaps 100 or more species belonging to more than a dozen different genera and at least five unrelated botanical families have at one time or another been sold as "mahogany" (see the table at left). Some of them are fine cabinetwoods, similar to true mahogany in color, figure and density, and can sometimes pass as the real thing. But when it comes to true mahogany, pretty close isn't good enough.

Mahogany's characteristics—Among the true mahoganies, not even the closely related Cuban and Honduras species produce woods that are totally interchangeable. Both species vary considerably as a result of growing conditions, and some of the mahogany now coming out of South America differs substantially from that of the same species logged in Central America. The slower-growing island variety is usually a denser, heavier wood with tighter, more finely textured grain structure. But when less than ideal conditions produce slower growth, mainland mahogany, like the island variety, is also dense and finely textured.

Although the density may vary considerably from tree to tree, with specific gravity ranging from as low as 0.40 to more than 0.60 (oven-dry weight to green volume), the wood in a given board will have remarkably uniform density. As a rule, the mainland species density averages about 0.45. This makes it almost 12% lighter than black walnut (0.51) and a little too soft for applications that expose it to heavy wear, but it is surprisingly strong for its weight.

Few commercially important woods are as stable as mahogany: Tests conducted by the U.S. Department of Agriculture's Forest Products Laboratory indicate an average volumetric shrinkage of only 7.8% (green to oven-dry)—only about half the value for most popular domestic hardwoods. Sugar maple, for example, is 14.7%; black walnut, 12.9%; and white oak, 16.3%. Even black cherry, noted for its stability, measures 11.5%. Because shrinkage is small, mahogany dries with less tendency than most woods to check and warp.

Of at least equal importance to a wood's in-use stability is the amount it shrinks tangentially versus radially. When a wood's tangential shrinkage (shrinkage across the flatsawn board, i.e. perpendicular to the radius) is substantially more than its radial shrinkage, warp-producing stresses are magnified. Typically, most woods shrink about twice as much tangentially as they do radially. For example, black cherry has a tangential shrinkage of 7.1% and a radial shrinkage of 3.7%, producing a tangential/radial (T/R) shrinkage ratio of about 1.92. Black walnut is much better in this respect: With a tangential shrinkage of 7.8% and a radial shrinkage of 5.5%, its T/R ratio is only 1.42. But mahogany is even better:

The More Common Mahoganies		
	Common name	**Genus**
The mahogany family (*Meliaceae*)	American mahogany	Swietenia
	African mahogany	Khaya
	Sapele	Entandrophragma
	Andiroba (crabwood)	Carapa
	Rose mahogany	Dysoxylum
	Tigerwood	Lovoa
	Spanish cedar	Cedrela
The Lauan family (*Dipterocarpaceae*)	Philippine mahogany (Lauan Meranti)	Shorea, Parashorea Pentacme
Mahogany look-alikes		
Family name	**Common name**	**Genus**
Myrtaceae	Australian red mahogany	Eucalyptus
Guttiferae	Santa Maria	Calophyllum
Burseraceae	White mahogany	Canarium
Burseraceae	Gaboon (okoume)	Aucoumea

With a tangential shrinkage of 4.1% and a radial shrinkage of 3.0%, its T/R ratio is a low 1.36.

Working with the wood — This tolerance to swelling and shrinkage is of great practical benefit, but from the woodworker's point of view, the real joy of true mahogany is found in its working characteristics. These characteristics are largely attributable to its structure. Mahogany is a diffuse-porous wood and has a very uniform structure. Unlike other diffuse-porous woods, such as maple and birch, however, mahogany's pores are larger. In fact, they are similar in size to those of walnut, but are more evenly distributed, making mahogany more uniformly textured than walnut. Also, unlike walnut, mahogany is still available in long, wide, warp-free boards. Cabinetmakers like this, because they spend less time dressing the lumber and jointing boards to width, making mahogany an ideal choice for large casework. And because of its high stability, mahogany can be worked to close tolerances with little fear of joints working loose over time. Straight-grain mahogany planes smoothly and easily. There is some tendency for the more highly figured woods to tear out, but its not nearly as pronounced as with, for example, quartersawn cherry. There are harder cabinetwoods that can be easily worked with high-speed power tools, but few are as pleasant to work using handtools as mahogany, yielding fluidly to sharp cutting edges without excessive and tiring effort.

It's difficult to point to any specific characteristic to explain mahogany's special charm, but color is part of it. When freshly sawn, mahogany varies in color from yellow to pinkish red. It rapidly darkens to a warm, brown shade with highlights that vary from rich purple-red, most common in the island species, to amber-gold tints, occasionally seen in some of the lighter-color stock from the mainland. However, even the mainland species sometimes produce wood approaching the color of black walnut.

The island and mainland species produce mostly straight-grain woods, but interlocked, "ribbon" grain is not uncommon. Flamboyantly figured grain, such as fiddleback, blister, swirl, mottle and curly patterns, are available, but rare. Island mahogany generally is more figured, probably resulting from its slower growth. Unlike many woods that owe their unique figure primarily to some single, anatomical attribute, such as the large size of their earlywood pores or the dominance of their rays, the figure of true mahogany is like a composition, a "symphony" of subtle elements, each contributing to the wood's character without drowning out the others. On the tangential surface, the rays appear as short, dark, vertical lines approximately ⅛ in. long, forming horizontal, wavy bands across the board at ¼-in. to ½-in. intervals.

The vessels provide another striking component of the wood's figure. These tube-like structures are clogged with deposits that may vary in color from white to black in any given sample. When cut lengthwise, they pepper the tangential surface with vertical lines from about ¼ in. to 1½ in. long, depending upon how true to the grain the board has been cut. White vessel markings tend to be more common in the island species, but here again, either species will produce deposits that range from chalk white to carbon black.

Also contributing to the figure in a very subtle way are fine, pencil-thin, white lines that meander across the tangential surface. These are caused by concentric rings of parenchyma cells that form periodically as the tree grows, much like annual rings. This also is an important feature to look for in identifying mahogany, but these rings are not always easy to see once the wood has been finished.

Mahogany stains evenly and is complemented by shellac, varnish, oil or lacquer finishes, but because of the wide variation in color and figure, it's advisable to match woods for a piece carefully. The finish can alter or emphasize color differences between boards, so try the finish on a sample when selecting woods. Although mahogany will darken over time with exposure to sunlight, the deep hues, often associated with old furniture, result more from the darkening of the finish than from the wood itself. The appearance of true mahogany is enhanced by a certain almost-indescribable surface luster lacking in many of the mahogany pretenders, especially in the so-called Philippine mahoganies or lauans. Because this luster is more pronounced with dense mahogany, it is produced mostly in the island species, but both the island and mainland species finish beautifully. □

Jon Arno is an amateur woodworker and wood technologist in Schaumburg, Ill.

Mahogany look-alikes

The two most common substitutes for true mahogany are African mahogany and the Southeast Asian lauans, which are popularly called Philippine mahogany.

The English began to exploit African mahogany in the mid-1800s when American sources of true mahogany began to dwindle. African mahogany, or more accurately khaya, closely resembles the true mahoganies in most important respects. Khaya is cut from more than one species, but the most important is *K. ivorensis*. The wood comes mainly from West Africa, although subtly different species of khaya are widespread from Portuguese Guinea to Angola and from the Sudan to Mozambique. The colors of these woods span the full mahogany range, from light pinkish tan to reddish brown, but they seldom exhibit the amber-gold highlights found in some of the mainland American timbers. The grain is often interlocked and somewhat more coarsely textured, yielding a striped figure on quartersawn boards. Generally, khaya enjoys the same complex symphony of elements in its figure as the true mahoganies.

Although it is true mahogany's closest substitute, it is not identical. Though highly stable, khaya's average volumetric shrinkage of 8.8% is a full percentage point higher than true mahogany. Its tangential/radial (T/R) shrinkage ratio of 1.41 is also slightly higher, and on average, khaya is a little lighter and softer than true mahogany.

Philippine mahogany, or more accurately lauan, may have been introduced into Europe and America from Southeast Asia at least as early as 1800, but it had little impact on cabinetmaking until the 20th century. Since World War II, its use has skyrocketed, and lauan is now our most important tropical timber. This plentiful mahogany substitute is cut from numerous Southeast Asian species, but they are not at all closely related to the mahogany family, *Meliaceae*.

There are at least 70 subtly different species of lauan, and they produce woods ranging in color from ash gray to deep reddish brown. Many of them have interlocked grain, which gives radially cut (quartersawn) boards a beautiful mahogany-like, ribbon-striped appearance; on flatsawn surfaces, however, they are seldom as figured as true mahogany. The lauans are generally more coarsely textured, far less stable and usually softer than true mahogany. Specific gravity ranges from about 0.30 to as high as 0.70, so lauan can be almost as light and soft as basswood (.28) or heavier and denser than white oak (.60).

The softer woods from the so-called "white lauan" group make good secondary stock for interior components, while the darker "red meranti" (from Malaya) make attractive primary woods. There are a few lauan species that should be avoided: Mayapis (*Shorea squamata*), for example, has a high gum content that clogs sandpaper and prevents finishes from drying. Also, some species in the Balau group are extremely hard and cause cutting edges to dull quickly. For projects where authenticity or historical accuracy is not important, lauan has a lot going for it: It is inexpensive; comes in a variety of colors, densities and grain patterns; and is available in wide, clear boards. Lauan is one of the world's most important timbers, producing more plywood veneer than any other hardwood.

The table at the bottom of the previous page should help in sorting out some of the woods you might come across while in quest of "the real thing."   —J.A.

Tulip: Wallflower at the Hardwood Ball

Oft mistaken and maligned, it deserves a place on the cabinetmaker's dance card

by John Sillick

Straight and tall, *the dark trunk of a tulip tree stands out near Lake Ontario.*

I became an ardent fan of tulip, or yellow poplar, the night I ran a pile of it through my planer.

I had found a large fallen tree in the woods and dragged it to a neighbor who milled it. The log minus a shattered lower 8 ft. yielded about 700 bd. ft. I stickered and stacked it for a couple of months and then under the press of circumstance, got ready to use it for the shelving project that I did not wish to expend my oak or cherry for. Board after board came through the planer even and clean. I had expected some fuzzing but was excited to see the smooth shine of the surface. Boards 14 in. wide after air-drying in piles only 4 ft. high showed less than ⅛-in. cup (see the top left photo on p. 29). The shop was filled with a mellow sweetness as fresh-cut wood met the air.

The creamy yellow wood had a wide, even grain. Some boards had a slight olive tinge. I wiped on some cherry stain and was struck by the alchemy of it. Suddenly it looked like a cherry board. Trying a woodworker's "thumbnail" test, I expected the resistance of basswood or white pine, but found this board was much harder.

I wondered why tulip wasn't on everyone's list as a favorite wood. I found two reasons for tulip's secondary status today. First, tulip is widely perceived as a poplar species with all the faults of that wood. Second, the olive coloration of some tulip boards puts some people off. But with understanding, neither trait should continue to dog this deserving and available wood.

Exploring the tulip mystery

After my planing discovery, I looked up this wood variously called yellow poplar or tulip and discovered how ignorant I was about *Liriodendron tulipfera*. I encountered a mystery of mistaken identity and misinformation, which has limited appreciation and use of a worthy hardwood.

Tulip has a curious history. This large, productive tree was much appreciated in colonial times. Easy to mill and dry, it worked superbly with hand tools to be fashioned into gun stocks, coffins, stairways, flooring, tables and cabinets. It was used to line wells and to produce woodenware, for it imparted no taste. It was considered neither too soft nor too weak.

Peter Kalm, an 18th-century Swedish botanist who was a student of Linnaeus and friend of Benjamin Franklin, became a great admirer of the tulip tree when he made a pilgrimage to America. He recounted seeing a barn made from the wood of a single monster tulip tree.

Since the demise of the chestnut, tulip has become the most common tree in the Appalachian forest and is the largest hardwood tree in the United States.

What's in a name?

True poplar is light, prone to distortion and molds poorly. Trying to sand planer fuzz from a stack of poplar boards is a good exercise in patience. Yellow poplar has nothing in common with true poplar except an initial yellow color and the way the leaves of both species tremble in a light breeze. But tulip is routinely sold as poplar and generally is mistaken as a member of the poplar family.

Liriodendron tulipfera (literally, "lily-tree bearing tulips") is actually a magnolia but has had a variety of names. Yellow poplar is its official common name, but it is also called canoe-wood (a reference to the immense canoes that were charred and

Photos: William Sampson

dug out of its massive clear trunks), white-wood, white poplar, tuliptree and tulip poplar. In the United Kingdom, it is dubbed canary whitewood. To season this kettle of confusion, tulipwood is also the name given to the tropical timber *Dalbergia oliveri*, which is unrelated to domestic tulip. Tulip's willingness to accept stains has earned it the name chameleon wood and allows it to be mistaken for cherry when it's stained.

Where and how does it grow?

One sawyer, who cut 5,500 ft. of nice tulip for me, argued strongly that tulip was the same wood as the poplar tree that stood by his drainage ditch. In fact, tulip will not grow in wet locations, preferring hilly coves and upland soils.

Tulip seedlings prefer lots of sunlight. In our woods, young trees appear only where trees have been harvested, and the canopy is open. The best stands appear on cut-over land where tulips will pioneer the new forest. Our stands of tulip by Lake Ontario are an anomaly of our micro-climate. The tree's natural range is Pennsylvania through Georgia, mostly east of the Mississippi. Two states, Indiana and Tennessee, claim it as their state tree.

Tulip can grow as fast as Douglas fir and can live 200 years. Although heavily lumbered, giants are still encountered. A tulip with a girth of more than 24 ft. was recently harvested in North Carolina. A stand of tulip at its growth peak can produce a 1,000-bd.-ft.-per-acre gain in one year. A tulip can reach a height of 50 ft. in only 11 years. At 50 years old, it can be 120 ft. tall with a diameter of 24 in.

In a woodland setting, tulip trees stand out dramatically with their broad, remarkably cylindrical trunks. In our woods, 80-year-old trees stand clear 50 ft. to the crown, towering above their contemporaries (see the photo on p. 27). When Thomas Jefferson was building Monticello, he went to the woods for his Greek columns and brought in tulip trunks.

Tulip is also becoming a popular ornamental tree. The tree blooms in spring with large white tulip-like flowers, which reveal its magnolia kinship and are very popular with bees. In summer, the tree has beautiful large four-pointed leaves, which resemble the profile of a tulip flower. The leaves each unfold from an envelope during the growing season. In winter the tree decorates itself with seed pods.

Tulip is remarkably free of disease and suffers little from pest damage. Ice storms do wreak havoc with its branches, and stands should be carefully thinned so that canopies do not spread excessively.

What's the wood like?

Working with tulip (see the box below) quickly shows its obvious differences with poplar. Most poplars are light with a specific gravity of about .34, about the same density as white pine or basswood. Tulip is variably reported as .42 to .45, which is close to cherry (.50). The diffuse-porous structure of tulip is such that it is more resistant to denting than we would expect. It is at least 25% more compression resistant than white pine. Tulip's 15,900 psi tensile strength rating is twice that of the poplars and exceeds even hard maple.

Although not often noted, tulip exhibits interesting figure in its usually regular grain. Patches of bird's-eye-like ovals and quilting are often seen, although not as densely as found in maple. Ray fleck is as common in tulip as it is in maple or cherry.

Tulip is our second most widely exported hardwood. Only the combined oaks exceed it. Almost half of the tulip we send overseas goes to Japan. Methods are being developed to finish tulip in the deep reds and black that are popular in the Orient. Tulip is also finding a niche as a replacement for some rain forest lumber.

Working with tulip shows its versatility

Strong and flexible, thin strips of tulip can be bent in relatively tight circles without cracking, as demonstrated by the author.

Tulip dries quickly and is stable, finishes like a dream and planes and molds well. It also holds nails well (though it is often hard enough to require drilling for finishing nails). The National Lumber Standards Committee accredited tulip as a construction material in 1978.

In the lumber trade, tulip is sometimes called the "money tree" because tulip logs produce so much more usable stock than other species. Sawyers report that a tulip log will yield 10% more than other logs of comparable size.

Although tulip is routinely described as "soft and weak," it is surprising to see how well it turns on the lathe. I trimmed a room in tulip in an old house and turned plinth blocks for the corners of the doors and windows. If a wood has any tendency to tear during turning, it will be evident during such faceplate work. The blocks were quick to cut, needed very little sanding and had enough strength to maintain fine molded profiles. It shapes well, as shown in the bottom left photo on the facing page, and even has been used as a tone wood for musical instruments such as dulcimers (see the bottom right photo on the facing page).

This wood is also remarkably flexible. Thin strips can be bent into surprisingly tight circles without signs of cracking, as shown in the photo at left.

Tulip is marketed as "unselected for color," and the buyer can expect a variety of tones. The black and purple streaks that sometimes show up are thought to result from improper log storage or lack of air circulation in drying. This is found in less than 10% of tulip. Such boards can be used as secondary wood in construction or be taken advantage of as accent wood.

The tulip I like best is the pale green heartwood. It is hard, sands very smooth, its pores stain evenly and the wood quickly turns a warm brown in full sunlight. Green-colored tulip stains a better brown if it gets a suntan first.

Tulip's wide grain and even acceptance of stains invite finishers to simulate cherry and walnut. The color that pleases my eye, however, is a golden brown, such as produced by Minwax Golden Oak. —*J.S.*

From *Fine Woodworking* (September 1993) 102:65-67

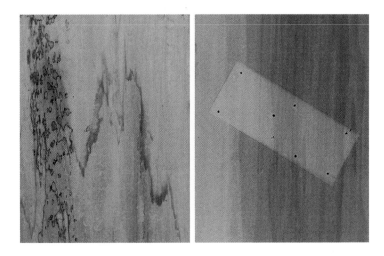

Clear, flat and wide—Yellow poplar, or tulip, is known for producing wide, clear boards, and it dries remarkably flat. A framing square resting on this board shows less than 1/8-in. cup over 15 in.

Sensitive to sun and spalting—Tulip quickly darkens in direct sunlight, as shown by the shadow on the board at far right. A shadow like this can be obtained in less than an hour in summer sun. The board at near right is an example of spalted tulip.

The ignorance that currently clouds tulip is another advantage, for it means the wood can be had cheaply. Clear tulip can sometimes cost as little as one-half the price of clear pine. I recently bought a few truckloads of tulip logs and had them milled. The total cost ran less than $250 per 1,000 bd. ft. Although the boards were cut from the second log in the tree, many of them are furniture quality; about a quarter of the 8-in. boards are clear 14 ft.

Tulip's more unusual aspects

One factor that retards wider use of tulip is the perception that its color is unattractive. Most tulip sapwood boards are a creamy yellow; the heartwood frequently has a yellow-green tint. Occasionally, boards have a wild purple streaking. But as noted earlier, tulip stains well, and browns easily mask the yellow and green.

However, there is no real need to stain tulip because this wood is extremely photosensitive. The yellows go light brown in a matter of hours in direct sunlight, and the green tint quickly turns a warm cherry brown in an afternoon. The speed at which the sun works on tulip is remarkable (see the top right photo). But artificial light does not seem to color the wood appreciably. Damp tulip wood also spalts quickly in warm weather.

In the face of the growing hardwood demand, tulip (or as the Hardwood Export Trade Council suggests, American tulip-wood) has great potential. It's vigorous growing, available, economical, pleasant to work with and attractive to look at when it is finished. Even so, the "Queen of the Forest" remains the Cinderella of the workshop. But tulip is just too deserving not to be going to the ball soon. □

John Sillick makes and repairs furniture in Lyndonville, N.Y.

Easily shaped, tulip works well for these raised-panel shutters made by Shane Secrist of Newfane, N.Y.

Versatile wood—Tulip shows its range of uses in a dulcimer built by Nils R. Caspersson of Holley, N.Y., and a blanket chest built by the author.

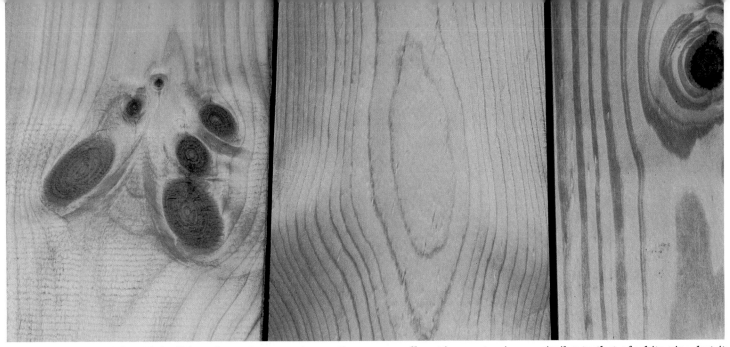

Eastern white pine, left, with its light color and even grain, contin- ues to be the cabinetmaker's first choice in pine because of its easy working and even finishing characteristics. The light color of west- *ern yellow pine, center, is very similar to that of white pine, but it also exhibits some of the contrast between latewood and earlywood that produces the showy figure of southern yellow pine, right.*

Pine
Capturing the special charm of a common timber

by Jon Arno

Pine is so relatively inexpensive, readily available and easy to work that it is often dismissed as a wood for beginners to practice on until they're experienced enough to work with more expensive hardwoods. This theory is wrong. Pine is a very respectable cabinet wood with a long tradition in American furni- ture-making. And although some species of pine are easily worked, others can be fairly difficult to handle and a nightmare to finish.

While there is no such thing as "good" pine or "bad" pine, gen- erally speaking there is a right pine for any given project based on the wood's structural properties or its traditional use. To get the most out of pine, therefore, you must know something about the limitations and applications of the more than 30 native North Ameri- can species. Fortunately, for practical purposes, these species can be divided into three main groups: white pine, western yellow pine and southern yellow pine, as shown in the photo above.

Although white pine is structurally the weakest and least durable of the three groups, it has the best working characteristics. Eastern and western white pine are virtually interchangeable and are ideal woods for colonial New England pieces. Sugar pine, a type of white pine, is a pleasure to work because of its uniform, fine texture and sweet aroma, but it is inappropriate for period reproductions due to the large, dark resin canals that produce flecks in the grain pattern.

The southern yellow pine group contains the hardest and heavi- est of the pines. These pines have showy figures with high contrast

between the soft earlywood and the hard latewood. This group is most frequently used as construction timber, but is authentic for some antebellum furniture as well.

Ponderosa and lodgepole are the dominant species of the western yellow pine group, and are the species most commonly found at lumberyards. These pines have a tamer figure, with more earlywood and thinner bands of latewood than southern yellow pine, and are softer and easier to work. In fact, unfinished western yellow pine looks similar to white pine, but the abrupt transition between earlywood and latewood requires different finishing techniques.

Grades of pine—With experience, it is not difficult to distinguish the various pines by sight and feel, but normally they are clearly labeled with a grade stamp (see sidebar on p. 33). Because of the great de- mand for pine in the construction industry, there is a premium on long, clear and structurally sound boards. Clear white or sugar pine, when you can find it, can cost as much as walnut. This economic reality often forces woodworkers to use the lower grades of wood. Usually clear stock is not that essential; knots that are tight and struc- turally sound can add charm and character to some furniture styles, as shown in the photo on p. 32. Just make sure the knots are at least 1 in. from the ends of the boards, where they won't interfere with joinery. Avoid knots ringed with a black line, as they will almost sure- ly work loose or fall out.

From *Fine Woodworking* (December 1989) 79:90-93

If you need clear pine for repairing period pieces or reproductions, you can get fairly sizable sections from lower grades of stock. Pines produce branches in whorls 18 in. to 24 in. apart along the main trunk, which results in beautifully figured clear wood between the whorls, as shown in the photo below. My rule of thumb is to buy plenty of the lowest grade of wood that will yield at least 50% usable material for a given project. When I need long, clear pieces, I buy the top grade for just those pieces, provided I can get both grades in the same type of pine. Unless the piece is going to be painted, don't mix pines from the different groups because they don't generally finish the same way, and grain patterns and colors will vary considerably. You should also buy your stock from lumberyards that allow customers to select their own wood. Woodworkers can usually find the right kind of light, soft pine even in a pile that has already been picked over by construction contractors, who tend to prefer the stronger heartwood that is too resinous and bland for furniture. If you only need short, clear pieces, you can use boards with loose or missing knots.

Working with pine—Pine's scent is one of the most pleasant fragrances in the world, but this benefit only compliments the primary pleasure of working with a wood that machines with so few problems. You do need sharp cutting edges and sawblades to prevent tearout with a soft wood like pine. Pine is also resinous enough to gum up cutting edges, so clean the blades frequently. But the resin has little effect on most glues; glue joints will be stronger than the wood itself. In addition, pine's spongy texture absorbs shock and, while pilot holes are needed for screws, nails can be driven into all but the hardest southern yellow pines without splitting the wood.

Even though pine is a soft wood, you can build furniture for rough, daily use by taking a tip from woodworkers of an earlier era and bulking up the design. Thicker stock makes for rugged components and stronger joinery, which traditionally has included everything from dovetails to butt joints and nails. Because pine has always been a timber of choice for utilitarian pieces, the joinery has tended to be simple, cheap or easy. Mortise-and-tenon and dovetail joints were preferred in colonial days as alternatives to scarce and expensive nails and screws. Pegged joints were frequently used, but as iron and steel became more readily available, square-cut nails and screws proved to be a more convenient choice. The Tremont Nail Co., Box 111, Wareham, Mass. 02571, manufactures a line of historically accurate square-cut nails and other fasteners.

When cutting joints like dovetails or mortises and tenons, you have to compensate for pine's spongy, easily compressed texture by cutting the pieces to fit a little snugger than you would if you were working with hardwoods. Also, minimize test fitting the joints to avoid excessively compressing the wood before final assembly. Tenons should be cut as large as possible and slightly longer than those used with hardwoods. A mortise cut in ¾-in. stock should be no wider than ¼ in. Using stock a full 1 in. thick or heavier will not only leave more material for the walls of the mortise, it will also allow for a thicker tenon. Cut dovetails with wider pins and at a slightly greater angle than you would for hardwoods—a 1:5 ratio should work well. This angle will reduce the likelihood of failure due to compression of the wood. However, the greater the angle, the greater the chances that the corner of the tail will split, so don't go overboard.

In developing your designs, remember that early American pieces were generally built with stock of various thicknesses rather than with today's standard ¾-in. stock. It was easier to get odd sizes of stock years ago when the woodworker could order virtually any thickness from the local sawmill. But even today it's worth the extra effort to plane down thicker stock or add edge moldings to achieve a thicker appearance.

Applying finishes—Perhaps the greatest challenge in working with pine is to select an appropriate finish and apply it properly. As with any other wood, preparation is the key to the quality of the final finish. Because pine is usually predimensioned—hardwoods are commonly bought rough—you might think that sanding with 120- or 180-grit paper would be sufficient. These fine abrasives don't cut deep enough, however, to remove the chatter marks left by fast-feed, high-speed commercial planers. The results are blotchy lines across the boards when stain is applied. I have found that belt sanding with 80-grit prior to assembly and then finishing up with progressively finer-grit paper yields dependable results. For more authentic reproductions, handplane the wood, and then use a scraper to remove any planing marks.

Further surface preparation will depend on the type of finish to be applied, and there are many choices. As a common utility wood, pine was often left raw to develop a natural patina, or simply rubbed with linseed oil or beeswax to protect the surface. Other finishes have ranged from shellac to varnishes to paint, each with its own peculiar problems due to the basic nature of pine. Pine's aggravating characteristics include the wood's natural resins, solvents that will dissolve many finishes, and showy figures caused by a large variation in grain density, ranging from as low as 0.28 specific gravity for the soft earlywood to as high as 0.78 for latewood. If pine is not sanded properly, the variation in

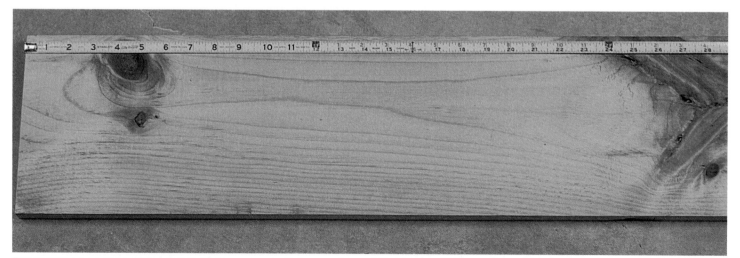

Depending upon the width needed, 18 in. or more of clear eastern white pine could be cut from this piece of #4 Common bought at the local lumberyard. By selective cutting, even boards with missing knots can provide beautifully figured, high-grade lumber.

This cabinet of #4 Common ponderosa pine, the cheapest grade available, was stained, but not sealed, to emphasize the figure.

grain density can result in wavy surfaces and uneven absorption of stains and finishes.

Shellac is one of the primary weapons in combating pine's finishing problems. As a final coat, shellac tends to spot or cloud when exposed to moisture, and has generally been superseded by harder, more durable varnishes. However, shellac is alcohol based and therefore not affected by pine's natural turpenes, so it can be used to seal knots and prevent the turpenes from bleeding into the modern topcoat varnishes. Turpentine- or mineral spirit-base finishes may not harden or dry if they are contaminated by the turpenes. A single coat of 3-lb. cut orange shellac works well as an undercoat; an additional coat serves as a very heavy-bodied sealer that compensates for pine's grain swelling tendency by building to a glassy-smooth surface. Shellac can help control color variations and stain penetration as well when used by itself or in conjunction with other finishes, as will be explained in the following discussion.

Oil and/or beeswax are common finishes on early American pieces. Oil finishes, unprotected by varnish, oxidize, absorb dust and grime, and eventually turn almost black. Beeswax or clear finishes on eastern white pine develop an orange patina known as pumpkin pine. Because time is an essential ingredient in developing this mellow appearance, pumpkin pine is hard to duplicate. A technique I have used to simulate this patina is to first wipe on a tint coat, made by dissolving ¼ oz. of raw sienna oil pigment in a quart of mineral spirits. When this is dry, seal the surface with several coats of orange shellac rubbed out with 0000 steel wool. The shellac further softens the color and creates an authentic, traditional look, since the finish was used as early as the late 1600s.

To achieve the darker look of oxidized oil or to make yellow pine resemble white pine, staining is necessary. Applying stain directly to yellow pine will result in a reversal of the grain contrast as the soft earlywood absorbs most of the stain and very little stain penetrates the hard latewood. To temper this high contrast, apply a wash coat of diluted shellac, one part of 3-lb. cut white shellac to two or three parts alcohol, prior to staining. The shellac penetrates into the earlywood and reduces its porosity, while a light sanding, once the shellac is dry, removes most of the sealer from the latewood. Now stain penetration of the earlywood is reduced, but the latewood will absorb the stain at nearly its original rate, so the color contrast between the two areas will be less obvious. Because stain penetration is decreased, you may have to use a darker stain to achieve the desired results. To reduce yellow pine's natural hue

and make it look more like white pine, the stain should be made slightly redder by adding about ½ oz. of burnt sienna pigment per quart of stain. A coat of orange shellac applied over the stain, but prior to the final varnish coat, will also give this finish a warmer tint.

Distressed finishes—Although I prefer a reproduction piece to look as it did when it was new, it is possible to simulate centuries of use by distressing edges, feet and work surfaces by rubbing them with sand or otherwise denting and abrading selected areas. By applying the finish before the piece is distressed, a more natural antique appearance can be duplicated. Once the piece has been abused to taste, apply a final coat of either black paint or dark brown stain and immediately rub it off, but leave some of the pigment on the wounds and in corners. The previously applied finish makes this rub coat, designed to simulate the grime of ages, easy to lighten with rags and turpentine if the contrast first appears too vivid.

While pine is often stained, historic evidence indicates that paint was a more traditional finish. Some of the fancier pieces were painted in several tones, with lighter tints on panels and darker, complimentary colors on frames. Also, pine was often painted to simulate the natural figure of more prestigious woods. A base coat was applied and then mottled, sometimes in conjunction with another tint or pigment, using a dry stiff-bristle brush, rags, feathers, combs or crumpled paper to achieve a grain-like appearance. Although with paint you don't have to worry about what species of pine is used, the knots should still be sealed with shellac to prevent their resins from bleeding.

Generally, early American pigments were somewhat loud, and it is helpful to visit museums to get a sense of the colors that were popular for certain period pieces. Milk paint was the primary vehicle for these pigments and its lack of opacity and tendency to raise the grain gave it a character all its own. While milk paint is still available (Van Dyke's, Box 278, Woonsocket, S.D. 57385; 605-796-4425 or The Old Fashioned Milk Paint Co., Box 222, Groton, Mass. 01450; 508-448-6336), a reconstituted, syrupy mix of non-fat dry milk colored with universal pigment or acrylic artist's pigments will achieve comparable results. This homemade variety is not moisture resistant, but it can be protected with a coat or two of varnish. Also, making your own milk paint allows unlimited choice of colors. Although the colors aren't authentic, flat latex paints can be used. Since they tend to raise the grain on raw wood, they simulate the look of milk paint better than oil-base paint, but a satin varnish topcoat is needed to provide a little luster.

A scrubbed pine or limed look can be achieved by rubbing a thin, almost transparent coat of oil-base white paint on raw wood and sealing it with satin varnish. This finish compliments even the racy figure of yellow pine. The paint tends to soften the grain's contrast, while the wood's natural yellow tones mellow out the paint's stark white pigment to achieve a rich, creamy beige finish. (For a further discussion of limed finishes, see "Creating a Limed Finish," *FWW* #79, pp. 82-83.)

A very striking appearance can be achieved by layering coats of different color paints and then sanding through to expose the lower layers at points where normal wear would occur. Any combination of two or more colors can be used. Apply two coats of the first color and then a coat of clear varnish between each succeeding coat of different color paint. This allows for a greater margin of error when sanding down to expose a previous layer. A final coat of satin varnish will enhance durability and soften contrast. ☐

Jon Arno is an amateur woodworker and wood technologist in Schaumburg, Ill. For more information on various types of pine, see "The Great American Pines," FWW #46, pp. 62-64.

Grade stamps: understanding the language of pine

Until early this century, woodworkers in eastern North America could buy pine with relative confidence that they were getting white or yellow pine from the vast pine forests of New England, the Great Lakes region and the South. While there are subtle differences between the southern yellow pines and the northern yellow pines, there is only one eastern white pine. The wood of this pine, *Pinus Strobus,* is so much softer and uniformly textured that it was the preferred species for cabinet work and interior trim and was easily distinguished from other pines.

As the eastern forests became exhausted, supply shifted to the west, introducing not only two more white pines, western white and sugar pine, but also the western yellow pines, predominantly ponderosa and lodgepole. Further compounding the situation, these western yellows proved to be softer and have a milder figure than the yellow pines of the east, making them very acceptable for most interior trim and finish work. Although unfinished western yellow pine looks a lot like eastern white pine, staining yellow pine emphasizes the grain variation between earlywood and latewood much more than it does with white pine.

It is possible to distinguish the western yellow pines from true white pines by subtle differences in the weight, color and texture or by a faint, dimple pattern commonly found on the flat sawn surface of ponderosa pine. But the far easier approach for distinguishing pines is to look at the grade stamp, which provides five categories of information that indicate the grade or quality of the material, the species or group of species, the moisture content when surfaced, the certifying association and the processing mill number.

Grading standards have been established by regional lumber associations, which also help their members market products. There are currently nine organizations in the United States that have been certified by the American Lumber Standards Committee Board of Review and 10 more in Canada, but for purposes of identifying species, it is only important to be able to break them down into three regional groups corresponding to the natural ranges of North American pines. For this purpose the initials of their trademarks are often descriptive enough. For example, WWP stands for Western Wood Products Association (1500 Yeon Building, 522 S.W. Fifth Ave., Portland, Ore. 97204-2122; 503-224-3930), while SPIB represents the Southern Pine Inspection Bureau (4709 Scenic Highway, Pensacola, Fla. 32504; 904-434-2611) and NELMA identifies the Northeastern Lumber Manu-

facturers Association (272 Tuttle Rd., Box 87A, Cumberland Center, Maine 04021; 207-829-6901). These non-profit organizations are generally very helpful, and they offer brochures, usually for a nominal charge, on grading rules and procedures as well as other information on the lumber industry. The American Lumber Standards Committee Board of Review (Box 210, Germantown, Md. 20874; 301-540-8004) also offers a facsimile sheet that contains information on all of the 19 approved agencies, as well as samples of each agency's grade stamp.

Identifying lumber grades: Understanding the grading systems used for pine is complicated by the similar but not identical guidelines used by each of the associations throughout the country. And although these various grades are generally comparable, the situation is further complicated because the nomenclature used to describe

A piece of premium-grade eastern white pine processed by NELMA-approved-mill no. 107 would bear this stamp. S-Dry indicates surfacing was done at 19% MC or less.

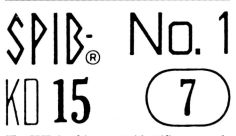

The SPIB in this stamp identifies not only the agency, Southern Pine Inspection Bureau, but also the species, southern pine. This stamp would be used by mill no. 7 on a #1 grade board, kiln dried to 15% MC or less before surfacing.

This grading stamp of the Western Wood Products Association would be used on a #2 grade lodgepole pine board that was surfaced with 15% MC or less at mill no. 12. WWPA can further pinpoint the origin of the material through the mill number if needed.

the grades varies by species and area of the country. For example, grading for Idaho white pine is expressed as Choice & Btr, Quality, Sterling, Standard or Utility. This compares roughly to C & Btr, D, #2 & Btr, #3 Common or #4 Common grades used for the other western pines. Corresponding grades for southern yellow pine are C & Btr, D, #1, #2 and #3 while NELMA uses C Select, D Select (or more commonly D & Btr), Finish, Premium, Standard and Industrial. For a better understanding of these grades, you can order a copy of the grading rules from the agency in question.

In many cases, the abbreviations used on the grade stamps are self-explanatory, but a few require interpretation. IWP stands for Idaho White Pine, one of the nicest of the western pines and almost indistinguishable from eastern white pine. Two Ps used back to back designate ponderosa pine. In recent years, however, there has been a trend toward mixing species and a lot of ponderosa is shipped with lodgepole, designated as PPLP. Another commonly encountered stamp is S-P-F that stands for Spruce-Pine-Fir and comes almost exclusively from Canada; however, some of the Eastern mills are starting to use an S-P-F Eastern stamp. As the mixed-species stamps become more prevalent, it becomes more difficult to determine exactly what type of wood you are dealing with, so the association trademark becomes the only clue as to the species involved.

While the association's trademark, included as part of the grade stamp, normally provides all the geographic information needed to close in on a probable species, you can probe still further by asking the association for information about the mill number in the grade stamp. By locating the mill, you can establish specific areas of origin.

Determining moisture content: The moisture content of the lumber at the time it is surfaced is also specified in the grade stamp. Three different levels are specified: S-Grn indicates the moisture content (MC) was above 19% when surfaced; S-Dry or KD-19 means surfaced dry at 19% MC or less; and KD-15 or MC-15 denotes 15% MC or less. The drier the lumber is when surfaced, the more dimensionally accurate it will be when purchased. Also, there is a greater tendency for lumber surfaced green to be twisted, warped or bowed.

Although the usefulness of these markings is becoming diluted, they are still very helpful in identifying at least the major group to which a particular pine belongs. Armed with this knowledge, the woodworker can make an intelligent choice of pine for furniture-making or repair work. —*J.A.*

Perhaps the largest tree ever felled by a human being, this Douglas-fir was brought down by George Carey (on the ladder) and his crew in 1895. The tree, reputed to be 417 ft. tall., grew on Vancouver Island, British Columbia.

Douglas-Fir: It's Not Just for Studs Anymore

A *tough softwood makes a great furniture wood*

by Jon Arno

If you're like me, the first images conjured up by the words *Douglas-fir* are of 2x4 studs, 2x12 joists and racy-grained plywood. There's plenty of validity to that stereotype, but there's more to the story. While its strength-to-weight ratio makes it the ideal construction timber, Douglas-fir is a remarkably diverse species, which will also yield plenty of furniture-grade wood.

What is Douglas-fir?

Douglas-fir has been (and sometimes still is) called Oregon pine, Columbian or British Columbian pine, Douglas spruce and red fir. Regardless of what it's called colloquially, there's little question that Douglas-fir is a member of the pine family (Pinaceae) along with spruce, larch, (true) fir and hemlock (see the photos at right).

On the genus level, though, it's something of an anomaly. Despite its vernacular name, Douglas-fir is not a true fir (genus *Abies*). First classified in 1803 as a pine, *Pinus taxifolia*, it was switched to the fir genus as *Abies taxifolia* in 1805. Later in the 19th century, the great naturalist John Muir referred to it as Douglas spruce, but it was never formally placed in the spruce genus, *Picea*. In 1889 it was given its own genus, *Pseudotsuga*, which translates as "false hemlock," and named *Pseudotsuga taxifolia*. Most recently, in 1950, its name was changed to the present designation, *P. menziesii*, honoring its discoverer, Archibald Menzie, a surgeon and naturalist who collected the first samples for scientific study in 1793.

There are only five species worldwide recognized as *Pseudotsuga*, and only two of these are native to North America. One of our domestic species, big-cone Douglas-fir (*P. macrocarpa*), is a small tree occupying a rather limited range in Southern California. It's not a significant timber species. The other, *P. menziesii*, is North America's most plentiful species of softwood and accounts for about one-fifth of our total reserve of softwood timber: Over 120 billion cubic feet of Douglas-fir is growing in the United States and Canada today.

The wood of Douglas-fir varies considerably throughout its vast growing range. Extending from Canada to Mexico and from the Rockies to the Pacific coast, Douglas-fir has successfully adapted to diverse growing conditions. In the mild, perpetually moist climate of the coastal Pacific northwest, second-growth plantings of Douglas-fir attain sawlog size very rapidly, producing a rather stringy and harshly figured wood. One tree recently cut on Washington state's Olympic Peninsula was 170 ft. tall and 3 ft. dia., but only 72 years old! While examples of this kind of growth certainly support the argument that Douglas-fir is a renewable natural resource, the wood produced by these rapidly grown trees just isn't the same. Bright orange in color, with wide annual rings and a rather coarse texture, it's an inferior construction or furniture wood.

The wood from old-growth trees, however, has a mellow brownish color with yellow to pale-orange highlights and a pleasant, pinstripe grain pattern on radially cut surfaces. Trees a thousand years and older, 8 ft. to 10 ft. across and well over 300 ft. tall, can still be found on good growing sites in Oregon and Washington. The unofficial record—substantiated only by the photograph on the facing page—is of a colossal specimen felled by lumberjack George Carey on Vancouver Island in 1895. This tree is reported to have measured 417 ft. tall and 25 ft. dia. If true, this would have been the tallest tree known to man, surpassing the loftiest living redwood by more than 50 ft.

There is yet another variety (botanically speaking, the same species, but with morphological differences) of *P. menziesii* indigenous to North America. A somewhat stunted variety that's native to the interior of the continent, its range extends from Alberta southward through the Rocky Mountains into Mexico. Because of the extent to which it has adapted to the more arid conditions of this region, some botanists suggest that this Rocky-Mountain variety should be considered a separate species, *P. glauca*. The two varieties cross-pollinate (or intergrade), however, and this has prevented the interior variety from attaining separate-species status. It is, nonetheless, a noticeably different tree. Seldom exceeding 100 ft. tall, its foliage is a lighter, bluish-green color.

The wood of this variety—often peppered with small knots—exhibits considerable variation in both texture and density. In the

Inset photo at right: Courtesy of Western Wood Products Association

Douglas-fir can be a renewable resource, as this 65-year-old stand (far right) shows, but the quality of second-growth timber pales beside old-growth. The bark of young Doug-fir is smooth, gray and thin, but turns brownish red, thick and deeply fissured as the tree ages (above right). The three-pronged bracts that protrude between cone scales (above left) are unique to Douglas-fir.

Photos this page except where noted: Ed Jensen

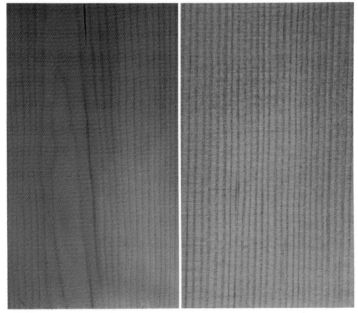

Flatsawn (left) and quartersawn (right) Douglas-fir exhibit very different characters. The proximity of the growth rings on quartersawn stock makes the extreme density between earlywood and latewood much less troublesome to work.

north, where the trees grow slowly but receive periodic moisture throughout the year, the wood tends to be dark red, fine textured, hard and exceptionally stable. Toward the southern end of its range, however, in Arizona and New Mexico, where less-frequent rains cause spurts of rapid growth punctuated by periods of relative dormancy, the wood tends to have proportionately wider bands of earlywood, which make it, overall, much softer, weaker and somewhat pinkish-yellow in color.

Beyond the stereotype: fir for furniture

But what about the wood of typical first-rate Douglas-fir? By this I'm referring to the old-growth wood from the Pacific Northwest. As softwoods go, Douglas-fir is downright tough. It's heavier and stronger than either yellow poplar or butternut, two hardwoods commonly used in the furniture industry, and it is nearly as dense as cherry. Also, like cherry, it is a very stable wood with a naturally warm, pinkish-brown color when freshly cut, shifting to a rich, subtle orange as it ages. Its resistance to abrasion, while not on par with maple or oak, is among the best of the softwoods, and this trait, along with its color, strength, stability and affordability, make it our most popular softwood for interior flooring.

The character of any wood greatly depends on how the tree has been cut. This is especially true for Douglas-fir because of the dra-

Working Doug-fir

by Curtis Erpelding

My first crude attempts at furniture were made with construction-grade Douglas-fir. I liked to think that those pieces resembled the modern pine Scandinavian furniture I admired in books and magazines. Still, I remember looking at my rough pieces and imagining my peers' skepticism, "When are you going to start working with real wood?" Fir was for building houses, supporting weight, easy to cut and nail. At best it found its way into floors, door jambs, window casings and trim moldings. It performs these jobs admirably, but, as I've gradually come to appreciate, it's capable of so much more (see the photo on the facing page). As with any hardwood, though, getting to know Doug-fir's particular idiosyncrasies will make working it less frustrating and more rewarding.

Machining properties: Douglas-fir generally machine-joints and planes well, although the face of flatsawn lumber is susceptible to tearout. Dampening suspected problem areas with a sponge prior to machining can help, as will using sharp blades, a light cut and a slow but steady feed rate.

When cutting profiles with a shaper or router, it's always better to climb cut (or back cut) if possible. *Climb cutting* means feeding the work in the direction of the cutter's rotation. This is a potentially dangerous operation, though, because the workpiece will want to fly forward—out of your hands—if you're using a shaper or router table. On a shaper, it would be foolhardy even to attempt this operation without a power feed; on a router table, you still need to use great care (a power feed would be preferable here also). If you are using a hand-held router, the router will try to self feed; you have to restrain it. When you're climb cutting with a hand-held router, you should take a number of light passes rather than one pass to finished profile to avoid having the bit catch and pull your router across your work.

Handplaning vs. sanding: When preparing a surface for finishing, I prefer to handplane vertical grain and to sand flatsawn boards. Vertical grain can certainly be sanded too, but the plane is faster and gives a superior surface. The disadvantage of sanding Douglas-fir (whether flatsawn or quartersawn) is that you're likely to get a bumpy effect because of the difference in hardness between earlywood and latewood. It's extremely difficult, however, to plane flat grain cleanly and without tearout because of the constantly changing grain direction. Wetting the surface of the wood, as when using a power planer, will help some. A well-tuned plane with a finely honed blade is a must, but it's still not an easy go.

A handplane with a blade angle of 45° to the work is normally recommended for softwoods, including Douglas-fir. In contrast to its positive effect on planing hardwoods, increasing the blade angle to 50° or 55° (as you might if you make your own planes) actually has a slightly negative effect on controlling tearout in Doug-fir. Doug-fir also responds poorly to a scraper, although areas can be leveled out somewhat in preparation for sanding.

Douglas-fir has a propensity to lift and splinter when the grain runs out to an edge. Handplaning rather than sanding an edge can help to control splintering. When sanding an edge, wrap the sandpaper around a block so that the edge of the paper can't catch on a point of dark latewood and pull up a splinter. For the same reason, if you're using a palm sander, orient it so the turned-up edges of the sandpaper held by the sander are in line with the edge you're sanding.

Despite all precautions, though, edges still seem to splinter and usually when least expected. Perversely, they always seem to surprise me on my last pass with sandpaper prior to finishing. Luckily, splinters are easy to repair. If a splinter is still intact (and hasn't lodged under your fingernail or in your palm) it can easily be glued back into place and clamped with masking tape. When the splinter is missing or so damaged that it can't be replaced, the edge can still be built back up with five-minute epoxy. Run masking tape along one face to form a dam, and work the epoxy into the damaged area. When the epoxy has cured, file and sand it to match the contour. The clear repair will become practically invisible.

Photos: Courtesy of Oregon State University—Department of Forest Products

matic contrast in density (and color) between its earlywood and latewood. The garish appearance of Doug-fir plywood is a result of the exaggeration of this contrast, which occurs when the log is rotary cut. When flatsawn, this fluid, meandering pattern is far subtler and more attractive—though still bold—resembling figured oak.

At the opposite end of the spectrum from rotary cut is quartersawn Douglas-fir, or VG (vertical-grain) fir as it's called in the Pacific Northwest (see the photos on the facing page). When it's quartersawn, the radial surface of the wood shows, displaying neatly parallel lines of light and dark grain (earlywood and latewood). The effect is so dramatically different from either flatsawn or rotary cut that the wood seems to have undergone a complete metamorphosis, having changed quickly from a splashy madras sportcoat into a formal, pinstripe suit.

The contrast between earlywood and latewood gives the woodworker a number of design possibilities, but it also poses some pragmatic problems both in machining and finishing the wood. In machining, the varying degrees of drag on bit or blade (due to the differing density of the wood) sometimes causes chatter or tearout. Also, blades must be kept especially sharp or crosscut edges may fray, creating a ridge of needle-sharp splinters. And being stabbed by a Douglas-fir splinter can be a prolonged, unpleasant experience, because even a minute sliver will cause a wound that will fester and heal exceptionally slowly. Although the exact cause of this reaction is unknown, it's suspected that a terpene in the wood is a histamine sensitizer. (See the sidebar below for an in-depth look at working and finishing Douglas-fir.)

From practical and economic perspectives, Douglas-fir has a lot to offer the furnituremaker, which is something those in the Northwest have known for awhile. It's time woodworkers in other parts of the country added it to their palette of furniture woods. Until recently, it's been readily available in virtually any width, length and thickness, and at a relatively moderate cost. Old-growth Douglas-fir has become a bit scarcer and pricier in the last few years, due to both log exports and logging bans, but there are still vast forests of the timber. Woodworkers should embrace rather than deny the fact that the old-growth forests are a finite resource and should treat this great wood with the same veneration furnituremakers of old had for Cuban mahogany and Brazilian rosewood. As long as it's thought of as merely a construction timber, high-volume appetites will continue to devour the remaining stands of these centuries-old giants. Conversely, if woodworkers give Douglas-fir its due, elevating its status in the hierarchy of woods, it should be around for many years to come. □

Jon Arno is a wood technologist and consultant in Troy, Mich.

Finishing: Most softwoods have either a pale-yellow to white color, like pine, hemlock and spruce, or a reddish-brown color like red cedar and redwood. Douglas-fir is unique among the softwoods for its orangish color, and in my finishing, this is the color I try to preserve and enhance. Staining Doug-fir is completely out of the question as far as I'm concerned. I can't imagine what I'd possibly try to make it look like, and it seems an insult to try to make something that's fine in its own right look like something it's not.

To my eye, oil is the definitive finish for fir. Yet a straight oil finish on fir tends to take too long to build and looks too dark and dry. To avoid these shortcomings, I use several coats of dilute shellac or lacquer first, which seals the wood and allows the subsequent oil coats to build faster without overly darkening the wood. The object is for the sealer to penetrate the wood rather than build on the surface. A sealer and three coats of oil will give the same surface luster as six or more coats of oil alone. I prefer lacquer to shellac as a sealer because of shellac's tendency to remain sticky if contaminated with water. I dilute one part regular lacquer with three parts thinner and brush on two coats, sanding with 320-grit or 400-grit sandpaper between coats. Allowing the sealer to dry for one day before oiling is sufficient.

I prefer a light-bodied oil like Watco to tung oil, which dries and builds too quickly for my taste. The first coat is brushed on and allowed to sit about half an hour—long enough to penetrate but not to become tacky—before wiping off. A day later, a second coat is rubbed on with steel wool and wiped off immediately. Subsequent coats are applied in the same way at one day intervals. Try not to wipe off the oil too thoroughly because you want to leave a very thin film that will polymerize. Polymerization is responsible for the low luster and depth that are the hallmarks of a good oil finish. Using a clean, dry rag may defeat your purpose by removing all the oil. A moderately (not saturated) oily rag is better. Make sure you dispose of the rags properly to prevent spontaneous combustion.

After three coats of oil, the wood starts to acquire a glow; the color deepens rather than darkens, and its signature orange color and graphic grain pattern start to give this most utilitarian of softwoods an exotic panache. For a soft, pale, ethereal effect, skip the oil and apply several coats of wax over the sealer instead.

In the real world of budgets and deadlines, it's not always possible to use our favorite, perfect finish, and humbler alternatives must be substituted. Several coats of sealer alone can provide an adequate finish that's resistant to dirt and fingerprints and kind to the natural color of the wood. Lacquers, varnishes and polyurethanes can all be used on fir, though I don't like the coated, superficial look they impart. There are other finishes for floor and marine applications, but I've chosen to ignore these, both out of prejudice and ignorance. After all, we're talking about fir and furniture, and it's about time we invite this neglected orphan into the family of fine furniture woods. □

Curtis Erpelding is a professional woodworker and designer in Port Orchard, Wash.

Photo: Steven Young

Clean design and crisp joinery distinguish Curtis Erpelding's work in Doug-fir. To enhance its orange color, he sealed this piece with dilute varnish sealer, and then finished it with four coats of Danish oil.

These pecan trees grow on a nut-producing plantation in Georgia. The pecan is the largest of the U.S. native hickories, but its trunk usually doesn't yield long boards.

Hickory and Pecan
America's muscle woods

by Jon W. Arno

I've always been a bit surprised that hickory and pecan aren't often used in furnituremaking, even though lots of these beautiful woods are harvested in this country. In fact, the only hardwoods harvested in greater quantities are oaks, poplars and maples, all common furniture woods. About the only time you hear any reference to hickory is in relation to ax handles or sporting goods.

Timber dealers sort the eight most valuable hickory species into two groups, true hickory and pecan hickory, each of which refers to four distinct species. True hickory is one of the heaviest and strongest of our domestic woods. It is remarkably springlike and very resilient when exposed to repeated bending and shock. Even in an age of synthetic materials, hickory maintains its international reputation as the first choice for tool handles, and it is also used for sports equipment, pallets and crates. Despite its iron-like hardness, you can steam-bend hickory easily and you can machine its creamy white sapwood and light-tan heartwood to a crisp edge. And this close-grained wood finishes well and doesn't require fillers. Pecan hickory has the same attributes as true hickory, although it isn't quite as hard and dense, and therefore it isn't quite as strong. But pecan is easier to work and its reddish-brown heartwood often has a more mellow figure.

In this article I'll tell you a little more about these attractive woods and their working characteristics, and I'll help you identify them (see the sidebar on the facing page). I think you'll find that hickory, and particularly pecan, *Carya illinoensis* (from trees like those in the photo above), are worth a closer look before you plan your next furniture project.

History of a tough family—True hickories and pecan hickories are from the same genus, *Carya*, which is commonly called hickory. This genus belongs to the Juglandaceae family, which also includes the walnut genus, *Juglans*. Although this ancient angiosperm family was once distributed around the world, all species of hickory and walnut were annihilated in ancient Europe by glaciers. Walnut was reintroduced into Northern Europe a couple of millenia ago through the trade of nuts, but hickory was never re-established. Thus, hickory never had a chance to become part of the European cabinetmaking tradition.

Considering 17th-century America's abundance of walnut, oak, maple, chestnut and cherry, you can understand why colonial craftsmen chose these familiar furniture woods and ignored the hickories. The North American Woodland Indians taught the settlers to eat the sweet hickory nuts, and the displaced Europeans also learned to use hickory for ax handles, wagon spokes and archery bows.

Pecan, *C. illinoensis*, on the other hand, became popular in the French settlements in the lower Mississippi Valley for the distinct and still-popular French Provincial style furniture. With its cabriole legs, scalloped skirts and framing, beaded edges, and considerable hand-carved decoration, it's a wonder this style found a new medium in pecan. Although the pecan hickories are the softest of the hickories, none of them are as easy to carve as walnut and chestnut, which the French used in Europe.

Hickories are bargains—True hickory and pecan hickory are widely available from sawmills and sawyers at prices ranging from

From *Fine Woodworking* (March 1991) 87:78-80

$1 to $2 per board foot. Hickories grow throughout eastern North America, from southern Canada to central Mexico. But genuine pecan, (*C. illinoensis*), with a botanical name meaning "the hickory of Illinois," is primarily a Southern species native to the lower Mississippi Valley. Since the development of the papershell variety of nuts, however, pecan has been cultivated throughout the Gulf Coast states, from Texas to Northern Florida and Virginia. In fact, Georgia, which was once totally void of this species, now leads the nation in pecan nut production. Unfortunately for the woodworker, orchard-grown genuine-pecan trees produce short lengths of lumber.

According to the U.S. Forest Service, there are more than 40 billion bd. ft. of standing hickory saw timber in the United States. But hickories are exotics almost everywhere else in the world. Of the 15 species of hickory worldwide, 3 (which are of little commercial value) grow in China and the rest grow in the United States. The eight domestic species of hickory, shown in the chart on the next page, are commercially valuable, and great quantities of true hickory are cut for tool handles, target bows, skis and firewood. The hickory genus, however, suffers from identity problems here in its native range, because both true hickory and pecan hickory are often bundled together and marketed as "mixed hardwoods." Here you'll find both hickories mixed with other woods like oak, ash and sometimes elm, all of which are used in pallets and crates. Since sawyers may not know what hickory species they're cutting, customers can't count on uniformity from shipment to shipment or from board to board. If you're after genuine pecan, you will probably have the best luck in the South, where most of the pecan nut plantations are located. However, this isn't a guarantee, because true hickories crossbreed with pecans and air-borne cross-pollination creates a hodgepodge of hybrid species. This causes botanists to say the hickories are highly unstable.

Working with hickory—Both true and pecan hickories are ring-porous or semi-ring-porous woods, with large earlywood pores and smaller latewood pores. However, like walnut, hickory's mellow figure is caused by the somewhat gradual transition between earlywood and latewood. This also means that the wood can be planed and turned smoothly, because the cutter edge won't chatter

Identifying hickories

If you plan to buy any of the true hickory or pecan hickory species, you must be able to distinguish them from mixed hardwoods, like ash and elm; you might be able to do this with your naked eye. But to distinguish the true hickories from the pecan hickories, you'll probably have to look at clean-cut end-grain samples with a 10-power hand lens and compare them with the photomacrographs below.

White ash, *Fraxinus americana* (shown in the left photomacrograph), can be mistaken for hickory, especially if your samples are light-colored sapwood. White ash reveals an abrupt transition from large earlywood pores to dense, more lustrous latewood pores. The smaller pores in the latewood are surrounded by parenchyma, forming light-colored patches against the darker background tissue. Hickories, on the other hand, have continuous thin bands of parenchyma, forming fine white lines, that are parallel to the annual rings.

Slippery elm, *Ulmus rubra* (shown in the center, left photomacrograph), may be more difficult to distinguish from hickory than ash. With a hand lens, you can see elm also has light-colored wavy bands, which are formed by the latewood pores. In hickory, the bands and pores are separate. Also, elm's earlywood is a narrow strip that is usually just a few pores wide, and the transition from earlywood to latewood is very abrupt.

Separating true hickories from pecan hickories is difficult; as members of the same genus, they're very similar. However, shagbark hickory, *Carya ovata* (shown in the center, right photomacrograph), is ring-porous and reveals a more abrupt transition from earlywood to latewood than pecan. Pecan, *C. illinoensis* (shown in the far right photomacrograph), is typically semi-ring-porous and the transition is more gradual. Also, shagbark does not have bands of parenchyma in the earlywood; pecan does.   —*J.A.*

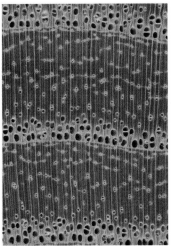

This 10-power photomacrograph of white ash endgrain shows abrupt transition from earlywood to latewood and light parenchyma around latewood pores. These traits distinguish it from the hickories.

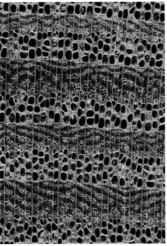

Slippery elm can be distinguished from the hickories by its latewood pores inside light-colored, wide wavy bands of parenchyma. The earlywood is seen as a narrow strip only a few pores wide.

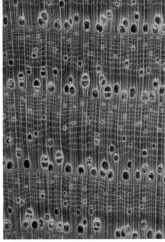

Shagbark hickory is ring-porous and distinguishable from pecan by an abrupt transition from earlywood to latewood and by thin bands of parenchyma that cross its rays only in the latewood.

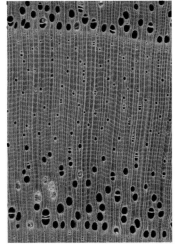

Pecan, unlike shagbark hickory, is typically semi-ring-porous and there is a gradual transition from earlywood to latewood. Its thin parenchyma bands are evident in both the earlywood and latewood.

Photos this page: R. Bruce Hoadley

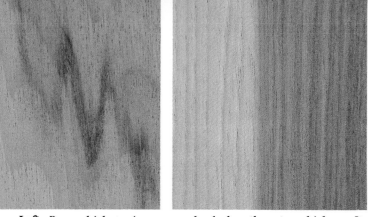

Left: Pecan hickory is commonly darker than true hickory. Its rust-colored heartwood mellows in time to a reddish brown with creamy white sapwood. Right: This sample of true hickory, which is the end scrap of 1-in.-thick by 6-in.-wide tongue-and-groove flooring, is lighter in color than pecan.

Hickories

Commercial Name/Species	Specific Gravity	Shrinkage (%)		
		R	T	V
True hickories				
Shagbark hickory, *C. ovata*	0.72	7.0	10.5	16.7
Shellbark hickory, *C. laciniosa*	0.69	7.6	12.6	19.2
Pignut hickory, *C. glabra*	0.75	7.2	11.5	17.9
Mockernut hickory, *C. tomentosa*	0.72	7.7	11.0	17.8
Pecan hickories				
Pecan hickory, *C. illinoensis*	0.66	4.9	8.9	13.6
Bitternut hickory, *C. cordiformis*	0.66	NA	NA	NA
Water hickory, *C. aquatica*	0.62	NA	NA	NA
Nutmeg hickory, *C. myristiciformis*	0.60	NA	NA	NA

Specific Gravity = Oven dry weight/volume at 12% moisture content
R = Radial shrinkage, green to oven dry
T = Tangential shrinkage, green to oven dry
V = Volumetric shrinkage, green to oven dry
NA = Information not available

Shagbark hickory has curly, shaggy bark and its small round nuts are edible and sweet, but difficult to crack. The hard, elastic, reddish-tan heartwood is lighter in color than pecan (*C. illinoensis*) and it's surrounded by a wide band of creamy yellow sapwood, especially on immature, second-growth trees.

Shellbark hickory prefers moist soil, and its range is much smaller than shagbark. Shellbark has less shaggy bark and its edible nuts are slightly larger than those from the shagbark, but otherwise the two woods are identical.

Pignut hickory is plentiful in the Appalachian foothills from Massachusetts to Georgia. The nuts are bitter, but they're used to fatten livestock. Pignut wood is the hardest of the hickories.

Mockernut hickory tolerates dry, sandy soil and it's found farther south than other true hickories. Its small, edible nut is in a thick husk, and its wood may vary due to different growing conditions.

Pecan hickory is primarily cultivated for its nuts, especially the papershell variety. Pecan is the largest of all the hickories, growing to 140 ft. tall and more than 6 ft. in diameter. Its dark reddish-tan heartwood is often streaked with dark brown or black, and it is semi-ring-porous with a more mellow figure.

Bitternut hickory is plentiful and widespread. It is sometimes marketed as pecan, but it's lighter in color. It grows farther north where the wood may have a flamboyant figure due to slower growth and a more abrupt transition between earlywood and latewood.

Water hickory is native to the coastal plains of the South Atlantic and Gulf Coast states, and prefers swampy soil. This smaller tree's nuts are tiny and bitter, but its wood is very similar to pecan.

Nutmeg hickory nuts are shaped like true nutmegs, hence this tree's name. Its wood has the favorable characteristics of pecan (it's dark and has a subtle figure), but it is easier to work. It may be the connoisseur's choice, if it can be found. It grows in pockets from Texas to the Carolinas, but it isn't plentiful and is seldom separated from other species in sawmills.

or lift and tear out porous earlywood tissue. Due to the extreme hardness of hickory, you get crisp, unfrayed edges when you shape, bore and saw it. And hickories contain proportionally more cellulose and less gum and lignin (the natural adhesive that bonds wood cells together and makes wood rigid and brittle); so sharp bits and blades won't friction-burn as readily as they do on some woods, such as cherry and maple. Despite being so hard, hickory's low lignin content makes it one of the world's most limber woods. The four true hickories are especially resilient and have a springlike elasticity.

Compared to walnut, hickory has a fine texture and considerably more surface luster, making it easier to polish and more appropriate for rubbed wax or oil finishes. Provided your hickory is seasoned adequately, it doesn't wool up when sanded, and you probably won't need fillers to achieve a glassy smooth finish if you coat it with heavy bodied varnish. These characteristics are common to all of the hickories, but there are notable differences between true hickories and pecan hickories.

True hickories—The four species of true hickories are harder, heavier and more elastic than pecan hickories. As with many dense woods, true hickories shrink considerably when drying, and so the wood is somewhat unstable. True hickories are generally lighter in color than pecan hickories, as shown in the samples above. But you can't always tell the two types of hickories apart by color, because growing conditions may produce true hickory with attractive, dark heartwood that can be streaked with rust-red or chocolate-brown highlights (see the sidebar). Old, slow-growing true hickories often yield beautifully figured boards, which tool-handle makers grade defective and hence price cheaper than pecan. But these old trees are rare and you have to look for this kind of wood.

Second-growth true hickory, which grows rapidly on fields that have been logged, has wide annual rings, light color and straight grain, and this wood is the handle maker's choice. Since this second-growth wood has proportionally more dense latewood, it is stronger. The demand for hickory tool handles is so high that only 25% of true hickory timber ends up as ordinary lumber. And much of the wood that doesn't meet the handle maker's requirements is sold as firewood or converted into chips for smoking meats. In fact, few cabinetmakers have had enough experience with true hickory to tell us about its working characteristics.

Pecan hickories—The pecan hickories are slightly softer and easier to work than any of the true hickories, but genuine pecans are still hard enough to be on par with white oak. Many of the characteristics that make pecan hickory less desirable for tool handles are what make it ideal for cabinetmaking. Genuine pecan is 20% to 30% more stable than the true hickories. Its average volumetric shrinkage (13.6%, green to oven dry) is less than white oak and sugar maple. As a result, properly made joints in pecan furniture remain snug and, provided the wood is seasoned carefully, warping and checking aren't serious problems. And with the exception of bitternut, pecan hickories are darker than true hickories and seldom need staining. Their natural, rust-tan color, shown in the left sample above, mellows in time to a rich and attractive reddish brown when finished with penetrating oil or clear varnish. Even though pecan isn't as elastic and resilient as the true hickories, it is still a first-class muscle wood compared to most of the other common, domestic hardwoods. □

Jon Arno is a wood technologist and consultant in Schaumburg, Ill. Wood samples provided courtesy of A&M Wood Specialty, Inc., 358 Eagle St. N., Box 3204, Cambridge, Ont., Canada N3H 4S6; and Constantine, 2050 Eastchester Road, Bronx, N.Y. 10461.

Ash's distinctive bark, with its neat, contrasty striations, makes the tree easy to identify at any season of the year. Its compound leaves, composed of leaflets on a central stem, are among the first to fall in autumn. A distinguishing characteristic of black ash is the leaflets' close attachment to the stem.

Ash
Counterfeit oak or quality cabinetwood?

by Jon W. Arno

At a recent antiques show, I found a dozen or so turn-of-the-century commodes labeled "oak." The general public and a lot of antiques dealers seem happy enough to identify every light-colored, open-grained wood as oak at a glance. The oak label serves as a convenience for pricing and dating such pieces, but it isn't always accurate. Two of the commodes at the show were of mixed wood construction (predominantly elm); the three nicest were unquestionably ash.

Most people may not have much reason to care. Ash and oak are both open-grained woods, with similarly attractive and somewhat racy figures. Furniture made from either wood has a look of solid quality. Yet I think ash outclasses oak in several important ways, at least from a cabinetmaker's viewpoint—the two woods have decidedly different characteristics. For starters, oak is a

member of the beech family, *Fagaceae,* which includes the oaks, the beeches and the chestnuts. Ash belongs to the olive family, *Oleaceae,* and is related to lilac and forsythia.

You don't have to be a botanist to quickly separate oak from ash. Oak has prominent rays that are easily visible on the flat-sawn surface, where they appear as bold lines called ray flecks. In some species of white oak, these flecks may be more than $\frac{1}{16}$ in. wide and well over 1 in. long, while in the red oaks they are generally smaller and darker. In fact, the rays are such a dominant feature in white oak that it's often specially quartersawn to expose them as broad bands or ribbons. These are extremely hard and dense, and in stained wood you could call their appearance either fantastic or outrageous, depending on your taste. I person-

Oak and ash are easy to tell apart. Oak has prominent rays, most pronounced when it's cut radially (top left), but also visible as a needlelike pattern on the tangential surface (bottom left). Ash's rays are hardly visible, allowing both radially and tangentially cut lumber to be mixed in the same piece of furniture. Brown ash is in the center, white ash on the right. The lower half of all samples has been oiled.

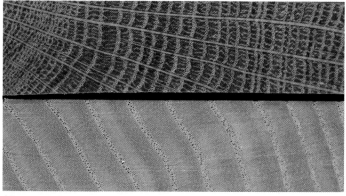

The rays, lines of cells extending from the pith to the bark, are much more prominent in oak (top) than they are in ash. Both woods are ring-porous: large cells produced in early spring are followed by more solid growth in summer.

ally don't like the effect, but if you do, score one point for oak, because no matter how you cut ash, it will not produce this pattern. Like all woods, ash has rays, but they are almost undetectable with the naked eye. As a cabinetmaker, I view this as one of ash's great virtues, because flatsawn and radially sawn boards can be used in the same piece with no surprises when the stain goes on.

Oak contains tannic acid. If you expose the wood to strong ammonia vapor, a chemical reaction will turn it dark brown. This staining process is known as fuming, and it won't work on ash. Personally, I use ammonia only on windows, but if fuming sounds like a good idea to you, score another point for oak.

Oak's acid content is a mixed blessing at best. A friend of mine once left a green piece of oak on his tablesaw overnight, and by morning it had permanently etched its shape as a black rust mark, which is still there after four years.

Ash's biggest advantage is that it is generally less dense than oak. If we cabinetmakers accept our two premier domestic hardwoods as having nearly ideal density—black cherry with a specific gravity of 0.47 (green to oven-dry) and black walnut at 0.51—we find that the various species of ash straddle this range, while the oaks are all somewhat denser. Ashes run from 0.45 to 0.55, oaks from 0.52 to 0.80. Ash is by no means a soft wood in comparison to pine, basswood, butternut, poplar or aspen, but it is relatively soft when you consider its ability to withstand pounding and stress. Ash yields an end product with great strength relative to both its weight and the amount of energy expended to shape or fashion it. And what could be nearer and dearer to a cabinetmaker's heart?

Because of these advantages, ash was one of several favored woods in Grand Rapids factories during the so-called "Golden Oak" era. Oak got all the publicity, but ash often was the dominant species in those utilitarian and now quaintly obsolete mixed-wood pieces: the dry sinks, commodes, cupboards and wardrobes that were cranked out by the thousands in the late 19th century for America's growing middle class. I'm grateful that nobody thought to call the stuff "Golden Ash"—the lack of publicity helps keep ash at a reasonable price.

While keeping a low profile in cabinetry, ash has established a worldwide reputation as the wood for baseball bats and as one of nature's most perfect materials for tool handles. For these purposes, second-growth trees with straight, evenly spaced grain are selected and specially graded. The white-ash sample shown on this page was cut from a friend's woodlot and wouldn't make a bad bat. Such ash has great strength-to-weight ratio and rigidity. Also, once the surface is smoothed, ash polishes well. Whether this is achieved by constant contact with human hands, as in the case of a tool handle, or by the deliberate effort of a woodworker, the end result is a definite plus.

Within each annual ring, ash has a honeycomb of porous earlywood followed by a layer of dense latewood, making it a sort of natural laminate. The American Indians discovered that they could separate the layers by soaking the quartered log and pounding it vigorously. As the earlywood broke down, thin strips of strong, highly flexible latewood peeled off, which the Indians used for basket splints and ribs in their canoes.

There are over a dozen species of ash native to North America, but only a few of them reach timber size. Those that do all produce ring-porous woods. There are, however, some subtle differences that relate not only to the species of ash, but also to the environment in which the tree grew. Generally speaking, the

From *Fine Woodworking* (March 1985) 51:49-51

strong, straight-grained wood resulting from second-growth timber, which is so desirable for tool handles and sports equipment, is not the best for cabinetmaking. First-growth ash, or ash that has grown slowly for whatever reason, produces the nicest furniture lumber. For one thing, the ratio of heartwood to sapwood is greater in slow-growing trees. For another, these trees produce relatively more earlywood than latewood each season, which means that their wood is lighter in weight, more porous, and far more interesting in figure.

In the lumber trade, most of the wood marketed as "white ash" comes from two species: white ash (*Fraxinus americana*) and green ash (*F. pennsylvanica*), both of which are plentiful throughout the eastern United States. Although on the average white ash might be a little denser and tougher than green ash, variations in growing conditions make the two overlap considerably. Another species, blue ash (*F. quadrangulata*), is of little consequence in the lumber trade because of its limited and sporadic range (around the Ohio and Mississippi River basins). It produces a wood that is almost identical to green ash, and it too is marketed as white ash. Blue ash gets its name from a blue dye extracted from the bark, which was once used for dyeing cloth.

The so-called "white" ashes make nice cabinetwoods once the project is complete, but three other species of ash are noticeably softer and easier to work: black ash (*F. nigra*), pumpkin ash (*F. profunda*) and Oregon ash (*F. latifolia*). To my way of thinking, black ash is the connoisseur's choice. Native to the Great Lakes states, New England and Canada, its environment is a harsh one, which forces slow growth that results in a lighter, less dense wood with exceptionally pretty flatsawn figure. The heartwood is a beautiful soft brown in color (in some parts of its range, black ash is referred to as "brown ash" by lumber dealers) and produces a natural "fruitwood" tone with nothing more than a coat of clear varnish. Because of its narrow annual rings, black ash was the preferred species for basketweaving, and like all the ashes, its stratified nature makes it one of the better woods for steambending.

Pumpkin ash, a similar species, is found in the South. It's less dense than the white ash species and extremely variable as a result of environmental conditions. Pumpkin ash growing in swampy areas will produce a buttress-like base that yields light, soft wood, tending to brittleness. On the West Coast, Oregon ash produces a reasonably good cabinetwood. Its specific gravity of 0.50 makes it somewhat softer than any of the white ashes.

Price and availability of the ashes depend a little on how creative you are. Like the old saying "Water, water everywhere, nor any drop to drink," ash is abundant, but my favorite grades for furniture usually end up as shipping crates and pallets, not in retail lumberyards.

Until recently, local lumberyards didn't have much reason to stock ash. Customers always seemed to be asking for maple, cherry, walnut and oak—and if not these, then some exotic timber. Today, at least in my area of Wisconsin, times are changing. Without much trouble, I can get select, kiln-dried ash at between $1.40 and $2.00 a board foot. The problem is, the mills aren't always careful to identify the species, and lumberyards therefore don't always know what they have. Most of the time it's white ash, and of such high quality that it lacks character.

To find my favorite, black ash, I look around at the beginning of the distribution chain, either buying direct from a mill or going to a pallet manufacturer. The last time I did this, about a year

Michael D. Durante

Turn-of-the-century pieces from the 'Golden Oak' era—like the author's commode above—often are not oak at all, but ash.

ago, I got lucky. The pallet manufacturer said: "Yeah, I got some ash, but it's just that soft brown stuff from up near Rhinelander; you can have it for forty-five cents a board foot...." "Well, maybe I can make it work," I muttered. I took all he had, about 200 bd. ft., stickered and air-dried it for a few months (with its low stump moisture content, ash dries well and easily), then had it planed for 10¢ a foot. Sure enough, it's a cabinetmaker's dream: beautiful, slow-grown northern black ash, at 55¢ a board foot. How sweet it is!

To conclude from all of this that ash is somehow an undiscovered, world-class cabinetwood to be ranked with walnut, cherry, rosewood and teak would be driving a point beyond its credible limits. Ash is nice in comparison to many woods, but it also has its faults. After praising ash for its laminate qualities, I should point out that the flip side of this feature is that the wood splits easily, as anyone who has spent much time chopping firewood knows (and appreciates). Ash is also very splintery, and unless your hands are calloused from constant shopwork, you may pick up some slivers when cutting and coarse-sanding it. Once shaped, however, it smooths out nicely. Given its extremely open grain, ash must be filled before you can finish it to the kind of glass-smooth surface required for some surfaces, such as tabletops. And, finally, ash does not weather well when exposed to moist, outdoor conditions. Powderpost beetles and other wood-eating bugs absolutely love the stuff. If resistance to the elements is important to your project, score one last point for oak, white oak in particular. It weathers well. Especially in antiques shops. □

Jon Arno is an amateur woodworker and wood technologist in Schaumburg, Ill.

I've known about sassafras since my childhood, growing up in the wooded hills of south-central Michigan. In fact, one of my earliest memories is of helping my uncle collect the roots of sassafras shrubs for making tea. He loved his sassafras tea, and it was a taste I soon acquired. He also taught me to pick the tender young leaves and chew them as a thirst quencher while we foraged in the woods for mushrooms and other late spring delicacies. It was not until much later, though, that I discovered sassafras was more than a shrub, that it would grow big enough to be a timber tree down in the southern part of its native range from Virginia to Arkansas (see the photo at left). Although not common, examples of this species that approach 100 ft. tall and 4 ft. dia. do exist.

From beverage to cooperage

Sassafras is a member of the laurel family, Lauraceae. There are only three species in the Sassafras genus: One grows in central China and another in Taiwan, but only our native species, *S. albidum*, is of commercial significance. Like other members of the laurel family such as cinnamon, bay and camphor, sassafras produces a natural oil, which has a fragrant, spicy odor. When the first explorers arrived along the East Coast of what is now the United States, they were quick to recognize the commercial potential of sassafras, and ship-

Sassafras is easily identified—Its leaves take three distinct shapes (boat-shaped, mitten-shaped and three-lobed), often on the same tree. In winter, it's recognizable for its branches, which grow nearly perpendicular from the trunk. Little more than a shrub in northern states, sassafras is a respectable timber tree farther south in its native range.

Sassafras
Fragrant wood that works sweetly, too

by Jon Arno

Photo this page: Peter Del Tredici

loads of the root bark were taken back to Europe. Sassafras tea, known as saloop in the tea houses of 17th-century London, ranked in popularity with coffee, true tea and cocoa until some now nameless physician announced that it was a reliable cure for venereal disease. At that point, the consumption of sassafras tea, at least in public, sort of dried up.

Although the oil distilled from sassafras bark has remained an important commodity for scenting soap and flavoring foods and medicines, the wood has never enjoyed much popularity in its own right. Most sassafras lumber comes to market mixed with other general-purpose hardwoods (formerly with chestnut and nowadays usually with black ash, *Fraxinus nigra*) and is used for applications such as pallets, loose cooperage and crating.

In appearance, sassafras and black ash have much in common. Like black ash, sassafras is ring-porous and open-grained, with an attractive figure and grayish tan color (see the bottom photos). With an average specific gravity of 0.42 (oven dry weight/green volume), sassafras is only slightly softer and lighter than black ash (0.45), but it is much weaker and less elastic. While black ash is excellent for bending, sassafras is exceptionally brittle. In fact, its modulus of elasticity is actually lower than that of basswood, which is otherwise our weakest commercially available, native hardwood. On the basis of strength, sassafras is vastly inferior to black ash and only borderline acceptable for use in light-duty furniture applications. Also, it tends to split easily, a frailty it shares to some extent with black ash and even more so with its companion, chestnut.

I discover sassafras

Over the years, I've shied away from sassafras because of its weakness. But several summers ago, I needed a substitute for chestnut to make some reproduction clock cases and happened to come across some unusually wide and attractively figured pieces of sassafras for only $1.50 per bd. ft. The color of the sassafras was a little closer to that of chestnut than the black ash I had on hand, so I elected to buy it and experiment with it. The clock cases turned out beautifully, and the sassafras was such a joy to work with that I became hooked on it.

Although not as pungent as the aroma given off by a steaming cup of sassafras tea, the faint scent produced when the wood is sanded is equally spicy and pleasant. Because sassafras is so brittle, sharp blades cut through it, leaving crisp edges. In contrast, ash tends to fray when crosscut, leaving a fine ridge of splinters where the blade exits. And sassafras virtually powders as it comes in contact with high-speed router bits, while ash requires a steady rate of feed or it quickly burns. Also, sassafras has a natural surface luster, so 220-grit sandpaper leaves the wood with a warm reflective glow that you would expect to achieve on most woods only after a coat or two of wax.

The sound of sassafras

Ever since that first experience with sassafras, my desire to work with it has left me searching for appropriate projects. Because of its great weathering properties and buoyancy, it has been used to some extent in boatbuilding and for other exterior applications such as fence building. But these pursuits have never been high on my menu of interests. After racking my brain and ransacking my library of project books for ideas, I finally decided to try it as a

Sassafras is a pleasure to work—It's soft, cuts cleanly and has a tangy aroma. It dents easily, though, and is brittle, so it's probably for the best that this handsome sassafras stepstool made by Kelly Mehler always has been used as a plant stand.

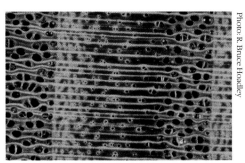

Photo: R. Bruce Hoadley

Sassafras or black ash? The strong figure and tawny color of raw sassafras (below right) recall black ash. Darker pieces of sassafras deepen to a cinnamon brown when finished (above right). Sassafras' pronounced grain pattern is due to its ring-porous cell structure, as shown above in the macrograph of its end grain.

Photos except where noted: Robert Marsala

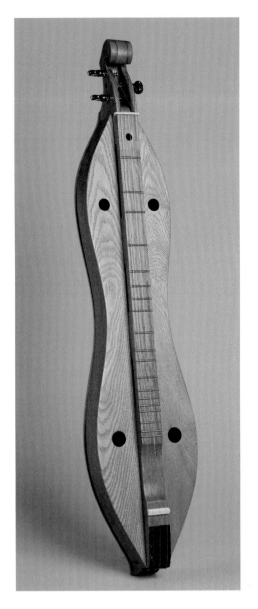

Sassafras that sings—For this Kentucky-style dulcimer in solid sassafras, Jon Arno used an indigenous wood to build an indigenous instrument. He thinks the wood's brittleness may be responsible for the bell-like tone the dulcimer produces.

soundboard wood in musical instruments. Bingo! The dulcimers I've made with it (see the photo at left) generate a bell-like tone that puts all my previous walnut, ash and cherry dulcimers to shame.

I can't offer a verified, scientific explanation why sassafras possesses such pleasant tonal qualities, but my personal theory is that it is due to the wood's brittleness. Even when cut into soundboards that are less than ⅛ in. thick, the wood is rigid and adamantly opposed to absorbing shock; this must translate the vibration of the strings into sound waves with much greater fidelity.

Sassafras has another attribute that is highly beneficial in dulcimer making: It undergoes little seasonal movement. This will appeal as well to anyone making other things to precise tolerances—drawers, jewelry box lids, cabinet doors. When it's compared to other domestic woods commonly used in instrument-making, sassafras performs well in this regard. With an average volumetric shrinkage of only 10.3%, fluctuations in humidity produce less in-use movement in sassafras than in most other woods. Also, as indicated by the ratio between its tangential and radial shrinkage (T/R=1.55), sassafras develops low drying stress and is not particularly prone to warping. Walnut, with a T/R ratio of only 1.42, is slightly superior in this department, but its 20% greater volumetric shrinkage offsets the advantage. Furthermore, walnut's renowned ability to absorb shock, while an advantage in gunstocks, leaves it with rather limp tonal qualities. In this musical application, sassafras is hard to beat. Of course, some of the softwoods, such as spruce, western red cedar and redwood are more recognized for their tonal qualities, but among our domestic hardwoods, sassafras might well be the best there is. □

Jon Arno sells and studies wood in Troy, Mich.

Working with sassafras

by George K. Rome

Since I first encountered sassafras a few years ago, I've used close to 1,000 bd. ft. of it for bookcases, kitchen cabinets, wet bars, toolboxes and jewelry boxes. It's delightful to work and versatile but with peculiarities and limitations as well as assets.

Being ring-porous, sassafras has a lot of figure. It takes stain well, and the grain pattern is close enough to red oak to pass as the same wood when stained. I've also pickled it pink and white, and it colors better than oak but tends to turn yellow far faster.

Unstained sassafras will turn a dark shade of brown when exposed to sunlight for a month or so, especially when it's been finished with shellac. The toolboxes I've made for trim carpenters, which get real exposure to the elements, turn a striking brown with a silvery greenish cast that is almost iridescent.

I get sassafras from Paxton Lumber (7455 Dawson Road, Cincinnati, Ohio 45243; 800-325-9800) where it's available only in 4/4 thickness. Rough sassafras boards tend to be extremely straight and flat with little internal tension. End checks are extremely common, though, and it's not unusual to lose a good foot off each end of a 10-ft. board. Several times, I've found hairline checks running the length of a raised panel after applying stain. The checks were totally invisible before the stain hit–I swear!

Aside from the checking problems, sassafras is a dream to work. It sands like balsa and cuts almost as easily. Unlike pine and poplar, it doesn't tend to clog sanding belts, but it plays hell with sanding drums on my drill press. It cuts beautifully on the tablesaw, where the wood's softness and lack of internal stress make for cuts that require little cleanup. It seldom burns, but its sawdust is so fine that it's as slippery as medium-density-fiberboard dust when it covers the concrete floor of my shop.

Sassafras gets dented easily by everything from normal clamp pressure to dried glue on the workbench. But a rub with a washcloth dipped in warm water followed by a pass with an iron at the cotton setting will remove most dents. Because of its softness, it's not a wise choice for use as base moldings or countertop edges. But because red oak will stain the same color, I often use oak for the parts of a piece that will receive the most wear.

I've worked with many domestic and exotic woods, and for my money, the only one that's as pleasant and easy to work as sassafras (aside from an occasional piece of mahogany) is black walnut. And we all know if the good Lord made a wood that was nicer to work than black walnut, he kept it for himself. □

George Rome, former owner of furniture manufacturing companies in Taiwan and China, lives in Louisville, Ky.

Desert ironwood dulls tools quickly but when turned or cut with sharp tools, looks like polished marble.

Ironwood: What's in a Name?
Dense, tough and long-wearing, there are more than a dozen contenders for the title

by Ken Textor

Corrective surgery on my definition of ironwood began several years ago during a tour of an aging lumber mill in northern Maine. Heavy sawn timbers were moved around that mill on rollers the guide said were made of ironwood.

The trouble was, the rollers didn't look like ironwood—at least, not ironwood as I knew it. The material I had always heard referred to as ironwood was a dark brown wood that was known most commonly as lignum vitae (see the box on p. 49). These rollers were definitely cream-colored with a light brown heartwood. Foolishly, I mentioned this to my elderly guide.

"Son," he said patiently, "all my life, we've called that ironwood. Some of the university folks call it hop hornbeam. I don't really care what anybody calls it, but those rollers have been there since 1932. To me, that wood's as good as iron." End of discussion.

Since then, I've found that when you mention ironwood to North American woodworkers, you're apt to be talking about at least four different woods. And if any old-timers or botanists are listening, you're up to 13 species in North America alone.

The four woods most frequently called ironwood in North America today are indeed hop hornbeam (*Ostrya virginiana*) and lignum vitae (*Guaiacum sanctum*, or *G. officinale*), as well as American hornbeam (*Carpinus caroliniana*) and desert, or sonora, ironwood (*Olneya tesota*).

During the first half of this century, a number of other woods were also called ironwood, including one most commonly known as inkwood (*Exothea paniculata*), another that was sometimes called white ironwood (*Hypelate trifoliata*), leadwood or black ironwood (*Krugiodendron ferreum*) and darling plum or red ironwood (*Reynosia septentrionalis*). Other North American

Rare and expensive, desert ironwood is best used for small projects such as this replacement chisel handle. The grain of desert ironwood is so fine it doesn't require a finish, though it will develop a patina.

Photos except where noted: Vincent Laurence

| **Hop hornbeam** | **Lignum vitae** | **American hornbeam** | **Desert ironwood** |
| *Ostrya virginiana* | *Guaiacum officinale* | *Carpinus caroliniana* | *Olneya tesota* |

woods sometimes referred to as ironwood include three species in the genus *Bumelia* (*B. swartz, B. lycioides, B. tenax*), casuarina (*Casuarina equisetifolia*), buckwheat tree (*Cliftonia monophylla*) and a rare cousin of the hop hornbeam, the western hop hornbeam (*Ostrya knowltonii*).

What makes a wood an ironwood?

Iron is, above all, heavy, and this is the first characteristic that you notice when handling most of the would-be ironwoods. The relative weight of a wood is expressed in terms of its specific gravity. This is simply a measurement of the wood's weight compared with an equal volume of water. For instance, to find the specific gravity of dried white oak, you would compare the weight of an average cubic foot of white oak with a cubic foot of water. White oak is lighter than water, with an average specific gravity of 0.68 as compared to the reference standard, water, at 1.00.

With a specific gravity ranging from 1.34 to 1.42, black ironwood is clearly the ironwood most true to its name. Desert ironwood, with a specific gravity of about 1.15, is a distant second. But the problem with black ironwood, as with most ironwoods, is its scarcity. Its growing range is confined to southern Florida, some islands in the northern Caribbean and parts of Mexico

Tough, but not impossible to work, hop hornbeam is a good wood for utilitarian applications such as this bench-vise screw.

and Belize. In researching this article, I made dozens of phone calls but was still unable to find a commercial source of black ironwood. As it turns out, black ironwood was available for small turnery and specialty items until sometime in the 1930s, but even then, supplies weren't always reliable. Today, about the only way to get your hands on some black ironwood is to know the tree and to know someone who has one in his or her backyard.

The same is true of white ironwood, red ironwood and inkwood, all of which have high specific gravities, good rot resistance, tremendous hardness and other iron-like qualities. They all grow in the same general areas as black ironwood, attaining heights of no more than 40 ft. with trunk diameters ranging from 12 to 20 in. Because of their small size and relative scarcity, these species never became viable as timber species. Without commercial value, they eventually became unavailable.

The *Bumelias*, casuarina and the buckwheat tree, for similar reasons, never really gained commercial acceptance. And the western hop hornbeam is just too scarce to be viable commercially.

Commercially available ironwoods

Probably the most commercially successful of the ironwoods is desert ironwood. Though it doesn't attain much more than shrub size, it's still generally available through specialty wood dealers. But because of its size and its slow growth rate, desert ironwood is relatively rare and, therefore, quite expensive: from $6 to $12 per pound, which works

| **Leadwood, black ironwood** | **Darling plum, red ironwood** | **Bumelia** | **Casuarina** |
| *Krugiodendron ferreum* | *Reynosia septentrionalis* | *Bumelia spp.* | *Casuarina equisetifolia* |

  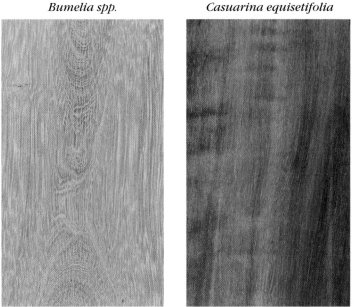

out to somewhere between $36 and $72 a board foot. Moreover, because of the strong demand for and relative scarcity of desert ironwood, some environmental organizations would like to see stricter controls on its sale, distribution and harvesting.

But even if price, availability and environmental concerns weren't a problem, desert ironwood would still be a challenge. Because of its density and high mineral content, tools have to be razor sharp to work it, and they'll need to be sharpened often to keep cutting (see the top photo on p. 47). With sharp tools, though, a marble-like finish is possible (see the bottom photo on p. 47).

Because of its expense and the size it's available in, desert ironwood is used mostly for smaller items, such as sculptures, letter openers and pen stands.

A couple of ironwood "lights"—Compared to most of the tropical ironwoods, desert ironwood and lignum vitae, the two hornbeams that go by the name *ironwood,* are positively lightweights. Their specific gravities are both about 0.70, and neither is particularly rot-resistant nor is as hard as any of its tropical and desert brethren.

For both of these woods, the ironwood name is the most important part of their appeal. Other more commonly available woods are heavier (live oak and some hickories), more rot resistant (black locust and Osage orange) and nearly as tough and hard (yellow birch and some hard maples). But they both have a long-standing reputation of wearing well, as the origins of the term *hornbeam* attest.

The name *hornbeam* predates *ironwood.* It came from an Old World cousin, the European hornbeam. For hundreds of years, the wood of this tree was favored for making yokes for oxen, its strength and durability put to the test daily. Yokes that survived were passed on from one generation to the next, and along with them, the reputation of the tree from which they were made.

Having worked with both American hornbeam and hop hornbeam, I can testify to their hardness, toughness and the comparative ease with which they work (see the bottom photo on the facing page). Just the same, I wouldn't go out of my way to buy more of either species, largely because there are more readily available substitutes with similar and even superior qualities. To me, their prime value seems to lie in their mystique as ironwoods.

Indeed, it seems those who are trying to market various woods are the ones most eager to label a wood *ironwood.* This is probably the heart of the ironwood name game: a matter of marketing, even among the early Colonials. After all, it's easier to sell a wood called ironwood than lignum vitae, *Carpinus caroliniana* or any of the rest.

For the bewildered woodworker, I have some simple advice: Stick with the local lore. As I learned on my tour through that lumber mill in northern Maine, there's not much you can say that will shake someone's faith in his or her ironwood. □

Lignum vitae: contender or pretender?

If we use specific gravity as the prime consideration in calling a wood ironwood, then lignum vitae, at 1.14, is clearly an ironwood. Moreover, although botanists don't recognize it as such, if you go into any boatbuilding shop in the southeastern United States and ask for ironwood, you'll most likely be handed a chunk of wax-coated lignum vitae. Lignum is notoriously unstable, famous for cracking and checking, hence the wax coating to moderate moisture exchange.

That said, lignum also possesses a characteristic that almost wholly redeems it: It's naturally self-lubricating, impregnated with oils that make it perfect for several specialty markets. One of these is lignum's main traditional use as a submerged bearing for a boat's propeller shaft. This is still its principal use. It's also still used for pulley sheaves and shells, caster wheels and various other turned, usually nautical, items in which great strength and low-friction are assets.

Lignum vitae is generally available today, but it costs about the same as desert ironwood ($36 to $72/bd. ft.) and, in fact, is more like desert ironwood than any of the other ironwoods. It dulls tools incredibly fast like desert ironwood, has an almost identical specific gravity, and cuts and takes a polish nearly the same.*—K.T.*

Ken Textor is a writer, boatbuilder and sailor in Arrowsic, Maine.

A healthy elm in full summer dress exhibits a vase-like profile and no yellowing of the leaves, which would indicate the presence of Dutch elm disease. Although thousands of American elms were planted along main streets in the 1800s, most towns have only standing dead trees left as a result of the disease. Still, isolated stately examples remain.

American Elm
Bold grain and tough disposition

by Ken Textor

W hen the elms on our property started dying, tree experts and woodworker friends suggested that we cut them down and burn them. "They're not even much good for firewood," one neighbor advised. But I couldn't accept that. Our seven towering elms had stood vase-like and majestic for more than 100 years (see the photo on the facing page), and it seemed a crime to cart them off as scrub brush.

Thus began my long and lively affair with American elm (*Ulmus americana*), a wood so steeped in American history, so versatile and so attractive that it's hard to believe it's still undervalued and overlooked. I've used the wood in everything from boatbuilding, to simple containers, to flooring. And I was pleasantly surprised at how handsome the wood looks in cabinets and furniture. To put elm in perspective, it's best to look at its early American uses.

Colonial encounters with elm

When the Pilgrims landed, elms were as common in North America as oaks and maples. American elm was one of a half dozen elm species that reminded the immigrants of similar trees of their homelands. But the "new" elm was definitely bigger, and it was a better wood source.

Elms were soon cleared from the land and put to work. American elm (also known as gray elm, white elm or water elm) was found to be extremely resistant to wear and splitting. Perhaps there's no equal in these departments, as anyone who has tried splitting elm for firewood will attest. Because of these qualities, farmers used elm to make tool handles and barn implements, such as milking stools, grain bins, troughs and coopered items. Elm was a particularly good choice for barn floors because it resisted hoof wear. I'm told it's still highly prized by the Amish for wagon wheel hubs. Because elm is such a tough hardwood, it was also used for utilitarian pieces, like the step in the photo below.

Interestingly, elm became an American icon not so much for its versatility as for its political significance. In pre-Revolutionary War Boston, a giant elm stood as a rendezvous for the rabble-rousing Sons of Liberty who planned their redcoat taunting in its shade. One night, the redcoats summarily chopped the tree down and defied the colonists to do something about it. Angry residents vowed to nurture new "Liberty Trees" with British blood. One hundred years later, during the nation's centennial celebration, every self-respecting patriotic town planted elms along its Main Street.

Elm's variety and decline

My elm trees were among those planted during the centennial. Unfortunately, in the intervening years, the American elm met a foreign invader far more dangerous than British soldiers: Dutch elm disease (see the story on p. 53). It alone was, and still is, responsible for destroying millions of trees, making the tree and its lumber today almost as scarce as chestnut.

A forester told me there are still a number of elm stands in the Midwest. But whether they're true American elm is unclear. Lacking a microscope, I found that color is the best way to tell American elm from the more common slippery and winged elm species. American elm is light brown to brown while slippery and winged are more distinctly red. There are also four other varieties of elm: cedar, wych, English and rock. For more on these varieties, see R. Bruce Hoadley's book, *Identifying Wood* (The Taunton Press).

Challenges in milling elm

There was no scarcity of wood when my elms died. Of the seven trees sent to the sawyer, nearly 2,000 bd. ft. of lumber came back. Logs 48 in. dia. were common, but there were some problems.

Many sawyers were reluctant to mill elms, particularly if they were border trees. Several sawyers told me that line trees often have old iron nails and wire embedded in them that could endanger millworkers or destroy sawblades. I resolved this to the satisfaction of at least one sawyer by passing a metal detector over the log beforehand. But there were other problems.

Trees grown in the open have more inherent stresses than trees grown in the forest. This is because winds constantly sway open-grown trees back and forth, building tension into the fibers. Wind shakes were evident in my elms, which had lined a salt marsh on the Maine coast. During sawing, many of my planks took on a significant sweep, cup or split long before they started drying.

Properties and appearance

With an average specific gravity of 0.50, American elm is quite dense compared to white pine (0.35) but less dense than other hardwoods like black walnut (0.55). Stability is not elm's strong suit. When dried to 6% moisture content, its approximately 3½% radial shrinkage and roughly 7½% tangential shrinkage are moderately high, making elm susceptible to warping and checking. I dried my elm planks in the barn for two years, and a few deformities became more pronounced while others disappeared.

Once stable, elm is fairly easy to saw, rasp, sand and bore. When it's cut, the wood exhibits a distinctive barn odor. Elm works well

Elm's interlocking grain makes splitting and surfacing difficult. The grain reverses in cyclic spirals as you move outward in a log. The inherent stresses in a cupped board will often cause it to crack as it's passed through a planer due to roller pressure. **This board was flattened with a handplane.**

Toughness and resistance to wear make elm particularly well-suited for simple, traditional pieces, such as this step or footrest. Early American farmers valued elm for utility items like milking stools and other barn implements. It's not uncommon to find antique tables and wagon-wheel hubs made of elm.

in steam-bent applications, glues nicely and resists splitting when nailed or screwed. The wood's weakest properties are its surfacing and shaping qualities. For jointing and cutting dadoes, you're best off using sharp blades and high-speed power tools.

Interlocking grain—Elm is hard with coarse, interlocking grain that causes tearout while surfacing. But it's exactly these difficulties that give elm its striking figure, especially on pieces of crotch. Waves of light latewood pores create zigzag patterns on the tangential surface. Elm's interlocking grain is formed when successive layers of wood grow first in left-hand spirals, then in right-hand spirals. For more on this, see R. Bruce Hoadley's book, *Understanding Wood* (The Taunton Press). Add the tension of growing in the open, and a trouble-free pass through the planer becomes a luxury. In fact, when planing problems develop, I usually achieve a better surface using a handplane or scraper.

Once planed, elm shows its beauty. The grain displays a tweed or herringbone look on flatsawn lumber (see the top photo on p. 51).

Moreover, the grain captures light and refracts it like a hologram. This iridescence livens up its otherwise muted light-brown tones. Occasional darker brown streaks (mostly found in trees infected with Dutch elm disease) break up the color uniformity.

Naturally, with all my newfound inexpensive lumber (it cost 25 cents per bd. ft. for sawing), I felt free to try elm in all kinds of applications. I found elm turned very easily. The wood came off in smooth, small shavings. However, the surface did need sanding to be smooth. Likewise, carving went fairly well though the twisting grain has to be respected with sharp tools.

Elm's workability shortcomings and a 10% to 20% waste factor did not prevent me from using it in furniture and kitchen cabinets (see the photo at left below). In addition, I found elm particularly well-suited for use in small, open boats. When steamed, the wood bends easily and without the splitting that often occurs with oak. Although elm is rated only slightly resistant to decay, a sailboat that I built with elm approximately 10 years ago shows little sign of rot (see the top right photo below).

Decent bending characteristics convinced the author to use elm to frame his sailboat. Discovering that early boatbuilders used elm nearly as much as oak, Textor replaced the vessel's ribs and her transom with elm. Paint and marine varnish help protect the wood against the elements.

Random-slat cabinets allow elm's grain patterns full rein. The iridescent figure comes alive under a clear varnish, especially on the upper-cabinets. To help combat wood movement from Maine's wide humidity shifts, Textor stiffened the door backs with battens.

Elm furniture, when shellacked or varnished, often takes on an amber hue. In the case of this baby's changing table made by Tico Vogt, subtle brown streaks and herringbone grain patterns are visible through the finish.

Availability and finishing

Once I had used my entire stock of elm, I started looking around for more. It was a tough search (see the sources of supply box). Most lumberyard stock comes from dying elms bordering old farms. Elm is more plentiful in the Midwest than in the East, but it is not as widely distributed as oak and maple. Elm usually costs two to three dollars per bd. ft.

Finishing elm requires care. Because of its open grain, the surface of elm may need filling. But I found filling cut down on the wood's iridescence. Instead, I prefer one coat of an oil-based varnish over several coats of shellac. The shellac seals the surface and, with only one varnish coat, yellowing is minimized. If you prefer an amber look, you can finish with several oil/varnish coats, as shown in the bottom right photo on the facing page.

Despite American elm's decline, it may make a comeback. For now, there are plenty of dead trees waiting to be harvested. ☐

Ken Textor is a writer, boatbuilder and sailor in Arrowsic, Maine.

Sources of supply_____

Badger Hardwoods, Route 1, Box 262, Walworth, WI 53184; (800) 252-2373

Colonial Hardwoods, 7953 Cameron Brown Court, Springfield, VA 22153; (800) 466-5451

Groff & Hearne Lumber, 858 Scotland Road, Quarryville, PA 17566; (800) 342-0001

Heidler Hardwood Lumber, 2559 S. Damen Ave., Chicago, IL 60608; (312) 847-7444

Maurice L. Condon Co., 250 Ferris Ave., White Plains, NY 10603; (914) 946-4111

Willard Brothers Woodcutters, 300 Basin Road, Trenton, NJ 08619; (609) 890-1990

(Veneer only)

Albert Constantine & Son, 2050 Eastchester Road, Bronx, NY 10461; (800) 223-8087

Certainly Wood, 11753 Big Tree Road, East Aurora, NY 14052; (716) 655-0206

Dutch elm disease: cause and cure

Stories of American elm and Dutch elm disease are inextricably entwined. But as for the disease's name, it is somewhat misleading. For their part, Dutch scientists were among the first to research the disease and come up with possible cures when it arrived in Europe from Asia in the late 19th century. In any case, some progress has been made on two fronts: developing a treatment for infected elms and developing a disease-resistant hybrid of American elm.

The disease is actually a fungus carried from tree to tree by a beetle. The insect and the fungus arrived in the United States in the 1920s by way of a shipment of European elm logs that were bound for American sawmills. In the bark of those imported logs were eggs of the European elm bark beetle. When the eggs hatched, Pandora's box was opened.

The fungus (ceratocystis ulmi) gets into the water-transporting layer of the tree's bark and cuts off the supply of water to the leaves. Various strains of the disease evolved and a particularly virulent strain went after American elms.

Treatment by trimming and spraying: If you catch an elm in the early stages of the disease, you can usually save it. Premature yellowing leaves near the tree's crown signal the presence of the disease. Such limbs should be cut out right away. Once trimming is done, you should have the upper reaches of the tree sprayed with an insecticide to kill the beetles and their eggs. Simultaneously, you should have fungicide injected into the water-carrying layer of the tree at its base. (Only licensed tree surgeons should carry out these operations because of the chemicals involved.)

If the disease is caught early, vigilant treatment often succeeds, but any trees beyond saving should be cut down and disposed of. If not, the trees will breed more beetles and more fungus that will likely kill off neighboring trees within a mile or so.

Disease-resistant hybrids: The Elm Research Institute (ERI), founded in 1967 by arborist John P. Hansel, began a massive education program run in cooperation with the Boy Scouts and other organizations. The institute has developed the American Liberty elm, which is identical to the American elm in appearance, growth habits and hardiness.

The Liberty elm is ideal for urban sites because, once established, it tolerates pollution, drought and salt. The trees have also survived repeated injections of Dutch elm disease. A sapling-planting program called Johnny Elmseed has been under way for several years. For more information on elm preservation, write ERI, Elm St., Harrisville, N.H. 03450 or call (800) FOR-ELMS (367-3567). —*K.T.*

Elm-lined Gillet Ave. as it appeared in Waukegan, Ill., in the summer of 1962 before the trees were ravaged by Dutch elm disease. Identified in 1932, the disease is actually a beetle-borne fungus.

Like a cancer of the tree world, Dutch elm disease spread unchecked, destroying millions of American elms. This photo was taken from the same spot as the photo at left just 10 years later.

The Demise of American Chestnut

Tragic loss of a great American timber

by Jon Arno

A t the conclusion of one of my recent wood-identification seminars, a shy and obviously puzzled young man came up to me with a 2-ft.-long 1x6 of grayish buff-brown wood. Before approaching me, he had fumbled through my set of samples on the table by the podium in search of a match that would save him from asking the inevitable question, "Do you know what kind of wood this is?"

Because the sample was so beautifully clean and clear, determining its identity stumped me for a minute. But one peek at the endgrain through the hand lens revealed the familiar flame-shaped pore pattern of American chestnut, *Castanea dentata* (see the two photos of the samples on p. 56). Chestnut was once a major American timber, but millions of acres of the trees were destroyed by a blight early in the 20th century. Although my sample set contained American chestnut, there was little mystery as to why this fellow was unable to make the match. My only sample was a remnant of an old barn beam—wormy and streaked with black from the reaction between tannin and steel cut nails—but it was a treasure to me just the same.

As the young man's shyness subsided, I learned that this magnificent piece of chestnut came from his grandfather's shop. And since his grandfather had passed away recently, he wasn't willing to part with this board; its value to him went well beyond the rosewood, walnut and money I was prepared to offer in exchange. Later, it occurred to me just how brief each generation's collective experience is. Only a few decades ago, any schoolboy would have recognized chestnut at a glance. It seemed to be everywhere: the split rail fence he climbed on the way home, the spice rack on his mother's kitchen wall, even the chest of drawers from which he plucked his socks in the morning. And now it is gone; it's almost as if it had never been.

The tragedy of the blight

First reports of the chestnut blight came from the New York Botanical Gardens in 1904. The lethal Asian fungus (*Endothia parasitica*) that caused it probably was introduced on nursery stock brought to North America from the Orient sometime in the late 1800s. Radiating out from New York at a pace of about 20 miles per year, this unstoppable scourge had decimated the entire native range of American chestnut from New England to Georgia and west to eastern Missouri by the late 1940s.

Because the fungus does not destroy the root system, the term *extinction* cannot yet be applied. Chestnut still exists throughout its native range as sporadic thickets of sprouts coming off of ancient stumps. These sprouts may attain diameters of 2 in. to 4 in. and heights of 20 ft. Some may even bear fruit before they too succumb to the blight, but as a North American timber species, the status of chestnut has now been reduced to that of a shrub. To be sure, there are isolated specimens (see the photo at right on the facing page) that are of great interest to botanists seeking specimens that may have natural resistance. Reports of a healthy tree discovered in Oakland County, Michigan, made it into a suburban Detroit paper not long ago. Also, small woodlots planted by early settlers outside of chestnut's native range can be found that contain healthy specimens spared by their isolation. And there is a small grove in western Wisconsin as well as other occasional plantings all the way to the Pacific.

The demise of any species, fauna or flora, weakens the fabric of life on earth, but the loss of American chestnut represents a tragedy of epic proportions. Prior to the blight, chestnut may have been the single most important species in America's Eastern mixed-hardwood forest. Although not the largest of our native trees, in the forest it had attained heights of more than 100 ft. and diameters in excess of 6 ft. and often yielded clear logs up to 50 ft. or longer. The nuts (see the photo at left on the facing page), technically a seed, were as sweet as the European species (*C. sativa*) and plentiful, coming by the bushels from every tree in multiples of two or more to the burr. The annual food production per acre from mature stands of chestnut rivaled (in some cases surpassed) that of cereal crops such as wheat or even corn. "Chestnuts roasting on an open fire" were traditional holiday treats, and the nuts were also an important ingredient in stuffing. The remainder of the crop served as fodder for livestock or as a mainstay in the diet of native wildlife, thus ultimately coming to our table as meat from the butcher's shop or the hunter's bag.

But what about the timber?

As plentiful as chestnut was, it was never a prized cabinetwood of the caliber of walnut or mahogany. It was too common, too utilitarian and, frankly, it was lacking in some important functional properties. For instance, with an average specific gravity of only 0.40 (oven dry weight/green volume) which is identical to that of yellow poplar (*Liriodendron tulipifera*), chestnut was much too soft to serve as the primary wood in truly rugged and durable furniture. Its ring-porous, open-grain surface (shown on this page in the background) presented some finishing problems, and its propensity to split, while a benefit to the shingle maker, made it risky to use for wide panels or structural members bearing weight across the grain.

Chestnut never was a pretentious choice for glamorous woodworking. It was a plebeian wood, a cheap and plentiful performer of common tasks. Its outstanding weathering properties made it an ideal telephone pole, a somewhat spongy but long lasting railroad tie and an exceptionally durable coffin. It was also used extensively

Photo this page: Susan Kahn

Chestnut trees once covered nine million acres of America. *The nuts (above) were a major cash crop in Appalachia, and the timber was used for everything from telephone poles to furniture. But around 1900, a fungus spread across the country and within 50 years had destroyed this resource. A few groves, like the one at right in Trumpelo County, Wisconsin, survived because of their isolation.*

for sash and trim, siding, beams and doors. Chestnut was also a popular choice for the substratum of veneers. With an average volumetric shrinkage of only 11.6% (green to oven dry), it was quite stable relative to other woods used for that purpose such as red gum *(Liquidambar styraciflua,* 15.8%) and even yellow poplar (12.7%). Given its stability, its soft, easy working characteristics and the fact that it was plentiful in the Connecticut river valley and southward through most of the original Colonies, it was commonly used as a secondary wood by some well-known Early American cabinetmakers. For example, chestnut can be found hidden away as the drawer sides and interior parts of some of the finest 18th-century work of the Newport, R.I., masters John Townsend and John Goddard.

As secondary woods go, chestnut has a lot of charm, and its absence leaves a gaping hole in our line-up of domestic species. A secondary wood can be bland, but chestnut isn't. Its ring-porous nature gives it a pleasant figure on the tangential surface, and its mellow light-brown color darkens just enough under a clear coat of varnish to produce a warm, attractive hue without the use of stain. In addition, a great deal of chestnut found its way into small,

functional articles that seem to have a knack for surviving, such as sewing boxes, knife trays, spice chests and clock cases. It is not difficult to find items made in part or completely out of chestnut; however, because the wood has a faint resemblance to oak, examples of it are sometimes mislabled in antique stores. To identify chestnut in existing pieces, look for an unfinished surface to see if the wood has a natural grayish, buff-brown color. Then, if it also has an oak-like figure, but is surprisingly lightweight for oak and seems to lack oak's dominant ray flecks, there is a good chance it is chestnut.

For today's woodworkers, acquiring chestnut is, of course, a problem. If you watch the classified ads and browse sawmills, a trickle of chestnut can be found. Because of its great weathering properties, standing deadwood remained sound enough to harvest for many years after the blight. Also, lumber resawn from the beams of demolished barns and buildings finds its way into today's market as expensive, wormy-chestnut paneling, but this is an unreliable and finite source. Of the dozen or so species of chestnut worldwide, the European species, *C. sativa,* is most similar to the American variety, both in terms of the flavor of the nut and the

Photo above left: Larry Brewer; photo above right: Dale Hindale
From *Fine Woodworking* (January 1992) 92:70-73

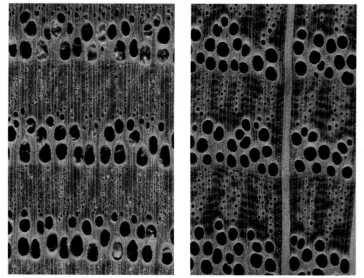

How to tell chestnut from oak: *Chestnut, as shown in the background on p. 54, has a buff-brown color with an open-grain figure similar to oak, with which it is often confused. However, chestnut is substantially lighter and softer than oak, and oak's rays are clearly visible on all surfaces while chestnut's rays are difficult to see without magnification. For final verification, examine a smoothly cut section of endgrain with a 10-power hand lens. As shown in the photos of chestnut (left) and oak (right) above, the larger pores in both woods are concentrated along the outside of the annual rings. But chestnut's larger pores tend to form wavy bands with flame-like bursts radiating away from the annual ring (see the photo at left).*

stature of the tree. Because of these similarities, I think the insights provided by the European craftsman, Rudi Wolf (see the sidebar at right), are of special interest because they present a hands-on account of a woodworker who still has a plentiful supply of chestnut. Sadly, the blight was introduced into Italy sometime in the 1930s and apparently the European species is not significantly more resistant than ours was.

Some hope for the future

I would like to conclude this eulogy to the American chestnut by saying that it has been so much a part of the American scene that it will be forever fondly remembered. But I can't. As evidenced by the shy young man at my seminar, few generations will pass before it is as forgotten as the flavor of mammoth meat. But there may be hope. Like strains of flu in human populations, plant diseases are known to lose their virulence. Recently, scientists have isolated a less-lethal (hypovirulent) strain of the fungus that can be injected into a tree, like a vaccine, to protect an individual specimen, but it's not a workable solution for large numbers of trees. Also, there are Asiatic species with exceptional resistance such as Chinese chestnut, *C. molissima,* and plant breeders are hard at work searching for hybrids that capture this feature without carrying that species' genes for small stature and poor timber form. Perhaps a hybrid will be found, a chestnut that is almost as good as the one we will, by that time, have forgotten. For woodworkers today, however, it is only through the shared experiences of Old-World craftsmen like Rudi Wolf that we can "savor the flavor of mammoth meat." ☐

Jon Arno is a wood technologist and consultant in Schaumburg, Ill. For more information on breeding and other research projects aimed at re-establishing the American chestnut, contact The American Chestnut Foundation, 401 Brooks Hall, PO Box 6057, West Virginia University, Morgantown, W. Va. 26506-6057.

Chestnut: A European perspective

by Rudi Wolf

Fifteen years ago, I settled in the south of France, in a mountainous area called the Cevennes, which is part of the Massif Central. Coming from Holland, a flat land beneath sea level, it was quite a change for me. I had prepared for my new life by studying to be a woodworker for six months at a state school for jobless adults. When I arrived in this mountain village, I introduced myself as a carpenter, although I still had much to learn about the trade.

One of the first things I learned was that working for local people meant working with the local wood—chestnut. Chestnut *(Castanea sativa),* shown in the top photo on the facing page, has been one of the most important cultivated trees in the south of France and in the whole Mediterranean area for thousands of years. It seems that a century ago there were more than 300 varieties adapted to all types of geographic and climatic situations. The trees produced nuts that could be used fresh, dried or for cooking; for making a kind of marmelade; to fatten up pigs or to feed to goats to increase their milk production. And then there was the wood.

Chestnut it should be: People in this region grew up with chestnut and would not accept a door or window made of oak. Even when I tell them that I have fine oak planks in stock, which were cut 12 years ago and are well seasoned, their inevitable reply is "Chestnut it should be." Chestnut is used for anything and everything: construction timbers, beams and roof planks, floors, doors, windows, shutters, tables, cupboards, matted chairs, bee-hives and barrels. The wood is also used to dam the river to provide a summertime water reserve in case of fire, and even the young shoots are split into thin strips and used for weaving baskets.

Unfortunately, in recent times many trees have died from the same blight that destroyed the chestnuts in America, and so the chestnut's economic importance has declined. But the blight has not been as bad here, and healthy trees are still plentiful. My 90-year-old neighbor, a farmer, can still distinguish about 20 to 30 varieties of chestnut on the basis of subtle differences in the nuts.

In spite of how commonly used chestnut wood is, I couldn't find it at the commercial lumber firms in town. I had to go inland to the smaller local sawmills where the newcomer, as I once was, tends to get the worst wood. It took me years to learn to recognize the wood's subtle characteristics. Healthy chestnut is whitish yellow and quite solid. Lower grades tend to be brownish in color and somewhat softer. Common defects are, of course, rot and wormholes and a kind of yellow discoloring caused by mildew. But worse yet is the "roulé" or "roulure," which is when the annual rings separate (not to be confused with heart split or dry split). In severe cases, a plank becomes like a bundle of matchsticks, and it is not uncommon to scrap 30% of each board by sawing out the roulé. When the wood is freshly sawn, it is sometimes difficult to see the defects, but I eventually learned to look carefully when buying my wood.

This roulé problem is undoubtedly the reason why modern industrial woodworkers won't touch the stuff—it's just too much trouble. But for the older people in this region, chestnut is an integral part of the traditional way of doing things. They are very proud of the knowledge that's been handed down from father to son about how to use chestnut because, after all, its their tree, their wood.

Working in the old ways: Some years ago I told my elderly neighbor that I wanted to buy a ladder. He sounded a bit angry when he said, "Don't throw your money away!" He told me that I should wait until winter, go to the north slope of the mountain and cut a pole of chestnut from a 12-to 15-year-old tree. Next, he said to saw the pole lengthwise, make mortises in both pieces and insert dry, split rungs of knot-free chestnut. He assured me that when the green wood dried and shrunk, the rungs would be secure. To prove this, he showed me some ladders that he had made more than 20 years ago. In spite of the fact that they were always left outside in the wind and rain, they were still perfect.

Last year a farmer commissioned me to make a "pastieire," which is a large slope-sided box or trough used to kill and butcher pigs. Upside down, the box makes a table on which the pig is secured and bled. Then the box is turned over and used as a kind of shallow bathtub as hot water is poured on the dead beast so that the hairs can be rubbed off the skin. I couldn't find the high-quality chestnut planks needed for the job, and so I proposed another type of wood. But no, he was willing to wait a year for chestnut.

Restoration work on local houses and furniture has also taught me much about how chestnut was used and how to work with it. When restoring the doors and paneling in the old houses around here, I usually discover beautiful, old chestnut after removing several coats of thick, brown paint. The doors and shutters in the center photo at right are copies of the doors that orignally graced this old shop front. When restoring old woodwork or furniture, it is sometimes necessary to darken new chestnut to match the old wood. An untreated plank of chestnut will turn a soft brown after a few years, but I've found that by putting the wood in my goat's stable, the coloring process is speeded up. This is probably caused by the dung's ammonia vapors reacting with the tannin in the chestnut.

One year I made several little stools with fancy carved tops like the one in the bottom photo at right, which I had planned to sell to the tourists. Chestnut is similar to oak, only a little more brittle, and although you can't cut fine details when turning or carving, shallow bas-relief is possible. Unfortunately, tourists didn't buy the stools because there were cheaper, mass-produced stools on the market. However, to my amazement, the usually frugal local farmers came looking. Turning the stools around in their hands, they commented on the quality: "Strong construction, and you used grafted chestnut on the top. Easier to carve, isn't it?" For them, the price was no problem. They know about good construction because they use their own hands to make most of life's necessities.

Slowly, the importance of the chestnut forest is diminishing. The blight plays a role, the people's changing lifestyle another. Now they are planting Japanese varieties that are not affected by the blight, but these new, heartier varieties just aren't the same. As an integral part of the culture, the chestnut is disappearing from the scene here as it did in America. ☐

Rudi Wolf is a woodworker in southern France.

Photos this page: Paul Starosta

Large, healthy chestnut trees, like this one on the plateau of the Larzac in France, are still plentiful in Europe. However, the same blight that destroyed the American chestnut is slowly spreading through Europe.

Chestnut has long been the wood of choice for doors, windows and interior paneling in the mountain villages of Cevennes, France. The chestnut doors and shutters on this old shop front are copies of the originals. The old window frame above the doors is made of wild cherry.

Wolf made chestnut stools with bas-relief designs, like the one shown here, to sell to tourists. As it turned out, the tourists preferred the cheaper, mass-produced souveniers, but the locals appreciated the quality and bought Wolf's stools.

Catalpa, often planted as a yard ornamental, boasts large clusters of white flowers in June and develops long cigar-like seedpods that make it instantly recognizable in winter. The lumber, below, is similar in appearance to chestnut or brown ash, but is more stable and easier to work. Catalpa's softness, however, makes it prone to dents and wear.

Photo: Michele Russell Slavinsky

Catalpa
Not just a shade tree, but timber

by Jon Arno

Ask any 10 woodworkers you know, even those who pride themselves on their experience with rare woods, what they think about catalpa. Probably all 10 will be able to describe the tree with its unusual, cigar-shape seedpods, beautiful white flowers and heart-shape leaves. You might even get a story or two about how they once tried to smoke a seedpod or how much fun it was to climb the catalpa tree in the backyard when they were kids.

When you get down to business though, most of them will probably confess they are unaware catalpa is used for lumber. Fence posts maybe, but lumber no.

If any of them have used catalpa wood, there is a good chance they liked it so much they have been reluctant to spread the word. Catalpa, given the supply situation, is a secret they would just as soon see kept. Why? Because catalpa is a very fine cabinet-wood, and at least at the present, it isn't that expensive. It is, however, hard to find.

Depending on your luck, you might be able to get kiln-dried, S2S catalpa in a common grade for as little as $1 per bd. ft. at a local lumber supplier. A few of the well-stocked mail-order houses carry it, listed for as much as $4.75 per bd. ft. But the more typical place for a woodworker to find some catalpa is at the local sawmill, where it comes in a log or two at a time and is quickly bought by the first few woodworkers who see it. The only other way to come by the wood is to cut down the tree and air-dry it yourself. With very little care, it will end up as good as any you could buy.

There are two species of catalpa native to the United States. Either tree might be called catawba locally or be known as cigar-tree or Indian-bean, because of the shape of the seedpods. Southern catalpa, *Catalpa bignonioides,* is found in Gulf Coast states from the Florida panhandle west to Louisiana. Used locally for fence posts and occasionally for lumber, this small tree is not commonly found outside its native range.

The other catalpa, *Catalpa speciosa,* or northern catalpa, is a much larger tree capable of heights in excess of 100 ft. and diameters well over 5 ft., although mature specimens that are 70 ft. to 80 ft. tall and 3 ft. to 4 ft. in diameter are more typical. For more than a century now, northern catalpa has been a widely planted ornamental, especially in the Midwest. It is a fast grower and very hardy, provided it gets adequate moisture. It is also very cold tolerant. I have seen catalpa growing as far north as Minneapolis, where winter temperatures of 30°-below are more frequent than most of the residents care to think about.

Well, if catalpa is so hardy and so often planted, why isn't its wood more plentiful? First, plantings tend to be a tree here and a tree there, or at best, in a windrow or woodlot of a few dozen trees. Trees grown in the open like this branch out quickly instead of reaching up, and as a result, they produce little quality timber. Also, no sawmill gets a lot of the logs at any one time.

Catalpa is also scarce because the only region of the country where, even charitably speaking, the tree could be said to form pure stands is in its native range. In the case of northern catalpa, the native range is one of the smallest of any North American hardwood. Until man began to transplant it, northern catalpa was found only along a narrow band of bottomland near the confluence of the Ohio and Mississippi rivers from around Louisville, Ky., to Memphis, Tenn., with a few small pockets in the surrounding states. The fact that this narrow range was on the path of westward migration has helped the tree spread, but it is still not plentiful anywhere.

What makes all of this important to woodworkers is that catalpa is a wonderful cabinetwood, both visually and in the ease with which it can be worked. Its ring-porous structure makes for a very bold figure on the flatsawn surface, somewhat resembling oak and ash (see pp. 41-43). Because catalpa does not have prominent rays, its quartersawn wood is not as loud and unpredictable to stain as the oaks, and it is much, much softer.

Perhaps the one native hardwood that most resembles catalpa is chestnut. Unfortunately, few woodworkers today have the chance to work with chestnut either. Catalpa, with an average specific gravity (SG) of only 0.38 (oven-dry weight/green volume), is even softer than chestnut, which averages 0.40SG. Virtually all of the oaks are in the tool-dulling range above 0.55SG.

Although catalpa is darker in color and not quite as stringy as chestnut, it is on the splintery side and may fray a little when crosscut. This is an insignificant handicap when you consider how soft and easy it is to work and what beautiful results its open-texture, wavy figure provides. And like chestnut, catalpa has excellent weathering properties. All of these characteristics make it an ideal choice for many cabinetmaking and carving projects, especially outdoor sculpture.

As similar as chestnut and catalpa are, the two are not closely related. Chestnut, like the oaks, is a member of the beech family, *Fagaceae.* Catalpa belongs to the trumpet creeper or bignonia family, *Bignoniaceae,* and is one of that family's few large representatives in North America. Most of catalpa's close relatives inhabit the tropics, and many of them are vines rather than trees. However, several tropical members of the family produce valuable timber, such as primavera, surinam and calabash.

The beautiful white flower of catalpa is one clue that its genetics diverge from those of chestnut. Another clue more meaningful to the woodworker is catalpa's strong scent, which unlike the tannin smell of chestnut, is impossible to put into words. Whether it is pleasant or not is a question I haven't resolved for myself yet, but once you've cut into a piece of catalpa, the musty-spicy odor won't soon be forgotten.

Catalpa is not perfect. Its extreme softness and open grain make it a poor choice for any piece of furniture that will get heavy wear. In this respect, its working qualities remind me of butternut, and like butternut, it is a pleasure to shape and fit. A woodcarver will quickly note that catalpa is more uneven-grained than butternut, which makes controlling cuts a little more difficult. But, the surface left behind is silky smooth to the touch. Catalpa sands better than butternut, too, but be sure to use a block or the soft, porous wood may be abraded away, leaving the harder wood in each annual ring raised. The finish is magnificent when first rubbed out. Once you have experienced the pleasure of catalpa, there is a tendency to use it for everything, but it is so easily dented it really should be reserved for display pieces that are often seen but seldom banged around.

While not germane to woodworking, catalpa packs few BTUs and makes very poor firewood, which I mention mostly to discourage the practice of burning it. Because catalpa is an ornamental species that sooner or later outgrows its available space, mature trees are often cut down by homeowners who are indifferent to the wood's subtler properties. More than once I have rescued a carving blank or two from a neighbor's woodpile.

If a catalpa tree in your neighborhood has outgrown its welcome, it could prove to be more than just "neighborly" to help take it down in exchange for some of the choicer pieces.

You can hack out turning blanks and carving blocks with a chainsaw, and most of them will dry alright. As with any other wood, it is a good idea to coat the endgrain with glue or paraffin as soon as possible. As you do, you'll see another feature that makes catalpa a prime wood: The tree is almost all dark heartwood, with the lighter sapwood seldom more than two annual rings wide. If you cut the wood into boards, make sure the pile is well stickered, weighted down and protected from soaking rain. Because of catalpa's excellent weathering properties, degrade caused by staining is not much of a problem. Fresh-cut catalpa can be very wet, however, and may take longer than you expect to dry. Weigh a sample periodically. When the weight stabilizes outdoors, the wood will be down to about 15% moisture content.

Shrinkage in drying is low and relatively uniform. Catalpa, in fact, is one of the most stable hardwoods in North America. With an average radial shrinkage of 2.5% and a tangential shrinkage of 4.9%, drying tension and warping is minimal. In contrast, elm has a radial shrinkage of 4.2% and a tangential shrinkage of 7.2%, and beech is even worse. By comparison, air-drying catalpa is a breeze. It is sometimes even possible to dry whole log sections in one piece. The wood is weak enough that drying stresses can distribute themselves evenly throughout the wood instead of forming prominent checks.

After air-drying, bring the wood indoors for a while in the winter to reduce its moisture content further. In a month or so, you will be able to share one of woodworking's best-kept secrets firsthand. And by the way, I wouldn't be telling you all this if I didn't have several hundred board feet in inventory and a line on a few logs still on the stump. When I see what looks like an unwanted shade tree in somebody's yard, I can be a very neighborly sort of guy. □

Jon Arno is an amateur woodworker and wood technologist in Schaumburg, Ill.

Gnarly Monterey cypress overlooking the Pacific in Pebble Beach, Calif., is typical of woods regularly harvested by woodworkers. The wood is not hard to dry and trees are large enough to produce bowl blanks and instrument soundboards.

Backyard Exotics
World-class figure from neighborhood trees

by Jon Arno

In a previous issue, *Fine Woodworking* asked readers to share their experiences with unusual woods they had harvested right in their own backyards or in wooded areas near their homes. The topic seemed offbeat, so it was a little surprising when scores of readers wrote, identifying more than 80 different species. Most of the respondents were carvers or turners, who thrive on small chunks of wood. You just don't find long 1x2 FAS, or even No. 2 common boards when scavenging windfalls and orchard thinnings.

The obvious explanation for this pursuit is frugality—finding a cheaper way to feed our tablesaws, planers and other cast-iron pets. Many readers indeed confessed that their first foraging attempts were aimed at acquiring cheap supplies of the more prestigious timbers: walnut, cherry, oak and maple. However, they quickly found the project to be almost addictive, despite the backbreaking chainsaw and ax work, the hauling and storage problems and the sloppy chore of end coating each piece, sticker-stacking the pile and babysitting the project for months to ensure the wood is drying quickly enough to prevent mildew, but slowly enough to prevent checking or warping. No wonder commercial dealers don't mess with offbeat species.

Finding woods to harvest is easy. Mother Nature quickly fills in virtually any patch of land in a temperate or tropical climate with all varieties of native woody species. In the upper Midwest where I live, elm, cottonwood, ash, box elder and other species with wind-borne or bird-transported seed will soon establish themselves. The letters we received indicate nature is more generous to some parts of the country. Woodworkers in the Deep South, especially in semi-tropical Florida and in the east-central hardwood belt, enjoy a bewildering array of species much greater than those of us in the North. Even in the arid Southwest, however, beautiful species like mesquite *(Prosopis juliflora)* and desert willow *(Chilopsis linearis)* rival the finest commercial timbers.

My truly memorable finds have been in the backyards of suburban America, a virtual mother lode of exotic woods. Over the decades, no expense has been spared to landscape our neighborhoods with jewels of the botanical world. Orchard owners thinning or replacing their stock frequently dispose of walnut, olive, pecan, apple and cherry. One reader surprised me by turning up an unbelievable variety of exotics in Milton, Mass. Bill Nesto went foraging at what he called "the tree zoo," the nearby Arnold Arboretum, after a hurricane hit the area and found a cork tree, Kentucky coffee tree, pagoda tree, smoketree, Japanese snowball and several other species. Now I'd like to share some of my favorite comments from the wood foragers who wrote to us.

Jon Arno is an amateur woodworker and wood technologist in Schaumburg, Ill.

From *Fine Woodworking* (March 1988) 69:88-91

Blackjack Oak: One local wood that I've enjoyed using is known as blackjack oak *(Quercus marilandica)*. It's usually used for fence posts or firewood, because it checks and cracks badly and warps in unbelievable positions. Its grain is interlocked, somewhat like elm, but its color is a beautiful reddish orange with brilliant black streaks.

—*Rick Parker, Gentry, Ark.*

Chaparral Woods: The plants of the Southern California Chaparral make national news nearly every fall, as they fuel the brush fires pushed down the coastal canyons by the dry Santa Anna winds. During the rest of the year, these plants are largely overlooked, even though the plant community includes numerous members of the **rose, sumac, heath, sunflower, buckthorn, oak** and **pine** families. The only harvesting equipment needed is a bowsaw (you won't find anything big enough to warrant the chainsaw noise) and a good botanical guide for the region. The wood is generally dense due to slow growth in a rather arid environment. The main trunks seldom exceed 4 in. to 5 in. in diameter, making them ideal for woodcarving, turning and other small projects. One of my personal favorites is **laurel sumac** *(Rhus laurina)*, which grows up to 8 in. in diameter. The wood is tan with occasional green and red hues. Although moderately soft, it carves well and holds fine detail.

—*Joe N. Smith Jr., Del Mar, Calif.*

Laurel sumac

Many large, blackjack oaks are destined to become firewood or fence posts despite their reddish-orange colors and black highlights, because the wood tends to crack and warp.

Chinaberry: My most unexpected pleasure was obtaining a Chinaberry tree almost 30 in. in diameter. This tree *(Melia azedarach)* was introduced into the United States many years ago, and is, I believe, one of the few mahogany species growing in this country. The wood has a reddish color with marked grain. It dries without checking and is easy to work for small projects. Bandsawn boxes are especially showy because of radial changes in grain across short spans. Chinaberry trees grow very fast, but are short-lived. About 30% of my tree had rotted, but drying appears to stop the rotting. I've set aside a 6-in.-thick plank that I'll make into a tabletop if it doesn't happen to rot in the next five years.

—*John M. Wilson, Aiken, S.C.*

Fruitwood: Thanks to the generosity of my friends, I've decided that fruitwoods are the prettiest wood for the spoons and other tableware I make. Collecting is easy and fun; friends prune their trees or know someone who's cut down a fruit tree. I put a classified ad in my husband's farm newsletter and found ranchers pruning old orchards planted by homesteaders. I've harvested usable flitches of **apricot, apple, pear** and **greengage plum**. I can't decide if I like the fruitwoods because the grain is so pretty, they finish so well or they smell so good when you work them.

—*Rosemary Rupp, Pendleton, Ore.*

Peach: About 18 months ago, I harvested some peach trees from an old orchard and ended up with 50 small logs, about 2 ft. long and 4 in. in

diameter. These were air dried under the house for eight months, sawn into ¼-in.-thick planks and stickered in the house. When I planed the pieces, I ended up with a lot of chips because the figured grain chipped so badly. Eventually, I built an abrasive planer that dependably produces ⅛-in.-thick stock. The wood is very stable. There's been no checking or splitting during the drying process, but the planks have bent longitudinally along the heart axis, probably the result of flatsawing. I suspect quartersawn boards would be more stable. The wood seems somewhat brittle, but nonetheless works well with either hand or power tools. The color is golden brown and nicely figured.

—*Jerry Spady, Oak Ridge, Tenn.*

Los Angeles Trees: When I started to investigate local woods, I was astounded by the incredible variety available in the city of Los Angeles. The best for me is **bluegum**, *(Eucalyptus globulus)*. I do lose a lot of it in the drying, but what's left is wonderful timber. It has a

Eucalyptus

Indian laurel

cool, yet friendly feeling. The pink color fades rapidly, but some sections retain a nice, reddish-brown color. Another marvelous street tree, although it shrinks and warps badly, is **Chinese elm** (*Ulmus parvifolia*). The wide sapwood is similar in color and pattern to American elm or ash. The heartwood is a reddish brown with slightly darker stripes. It's also very hard and tough. Another wood I like is **indian laurel** (*Terminalia alata*), which is lighter and softer and much easier to season. The wood finishes to a high luster and exhibits a nicely variegated pattern of light and dark browns.

—*Alden Smith, Los Angeles, Calif.*

Manzanita: I located a large manzanita (*Arctostaphylos*) stump while searching for firewood in a burned-over section of Los Padres National Forest near Santa Barbara, Calif. The hard, dense, reddish-colored manzanita intrigued me, so my father-in-law and I cut it off at ground level and hauled it home. From the start I realized that making useful

Small, gnarly manzanita trees often fall victim to seasonal brush fires.

Photo: Jerry Blanchard

boards from the stump would be difficult. The chainsaw dulled almost instantly—apparently the combination of natural drying and the very hot fire had actually hardened the wood. The wood was extremely hard and brittle to machine. I was able to obtain some small, very thin boards from which I built a jewelry box. The wood is a brilliant red-brown color with a nice contrasting maple-colored sapwood. It polished up brilliantly. One caution: The wood is a protected species in California, however, due to its graceful form and relative scarcity.

—*Lyle Erman, Redmond, Wash.*

Mesquite: This species has a beautiful brownish-red color. With tangential cuts, the yellow sapwood often produces a pleasant variegated effect. If you leave the bark on and seal the ends, you can usually obtain air-dried boards with few cracks. The wood is hard and somewhat brittle. Mesquite (*Prosopis spp.*) grows mainly as a shrub in the more arid parts of west Texas. Even though ranchers are usually glad to get rid of it, harvesting it is still hard work. It is very difficult to find limbs long and straight enough to make

Mesquite

boards. If the shrub lives long enough and ample water is available, trees 10 in. or larger in diameter develop. I know of a firm in San Antonio that harvests trees nourished by the San Antonio River and its tributaries and kiln dries the wood to produce beautiful flooring.

—*Martin E. Riley, Arlington, Tex.*

Osage-Orange: If osage-orange (*Maclura pomifera*) grew in an isolated region of the Amazon, I'm convinced it would sell for $10 a bd. ft. Although most experts call it osage, in the southeastern and lower southwestern parts of the United States where it grows in abundance, it's known as bois-d'arc, pronounced "bowdock." Seldom tall, and almost never straight, the trees grow in profusion along creeks and ditches, competing with other moisture-loving trees for sunlight. It sports vicious thorns, especially in fast, new growth. Mature trees produce a green fruit about the size of an orange, with a quilted surface. The wood is heavy, hard and tough, and the heartwood, which makes up most of the log, is virtually immune to insects and rot. The wood's across-the-grain strength, even when green, may be the highest of any domestic wood. Its bright yellow color darkens over time to a golden orange shade. Contrast between winter and summer growth is a positive feature, enhanced by rather wide bands of fast-growing rings. The wood dries with little shape change.

—*James P. Rozelle, Marietta, Ga.*

Russian Olive: This species is planted as an ornamental tree in some parts of North Dakota, mainly in government-sponsored shelterbelts. The wood is almost as dense as black walnut, has about the same working characteristics when sawn, planed or turned, is often

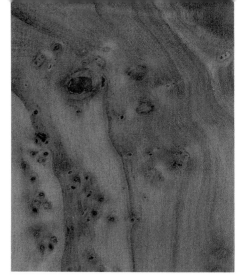

Russian olive

heavily grained and polishes well. The Russian olive *(Elaeagnus angustifolia)* tree is fairly large. I've collected some beautiful burl sections up to 18 in. in diameter from roots. When finished with a penetrating oil, it becomes deep tan with dark, chocolate-colored grain.

—*Dr. Lloyd Best, Wahpeton, N.D*

Toyon: One of my favorite woods, toyon *(Heteromeles arbutifolia)* is usually just a shrub, but I've obtained trees as large as 24 in. in diameter. The wood is very beautiful and hard, sometimes curly and marbled with blacks and tans. I've also obtained small burls. Toyon seems to end-check very little and dries well without much shrinkage. Another beautiful tree in this area is **Monterey cypress** *(Cupressus macrocarpa)*. My friend Earl Bushey uses it for musical instrument soundboards and furniture. Occasionally you find curly sections, but they can be hard to plane without tearout.

—*Jerry Blanchard Pebble Beach, Calif.*

Oysterwood: Cuban oysterwood *(Gymnanthes lucida)* is very hard, about 78 lbs. per cubic ft., and in the Florida

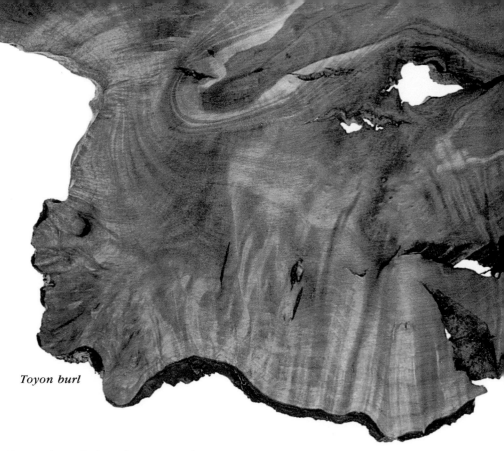

Toyon burl

Keys, at least, it doesn't grow very large—10-in. dia. is the largest I've found. I put white glue on the endgrain after cutting the pieces and it cures very well. The pith, however, always cracks, so getting a board for something larger than a jewelry box is close to impossible.   —*Charles W. Waggener Lake Worth, Fla.*

There is no limit to the possibilities. A successful forager can pluck and nibble, at will, from nature's larder. I'm convinced the native woods ignored by the commercial lumber industry offer some of the most beautiful, wildly figured woods in the world. And, as Jerry Blanchard wrote, "The point is wood isn't something we need to find in cuboid pieces on hyped-up store shelves, replete with sticky tags and high prices," it's growing all around us.   □

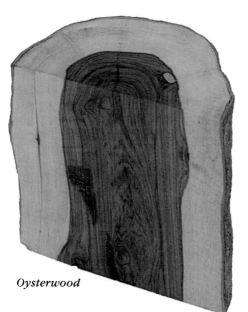

Oysterwood

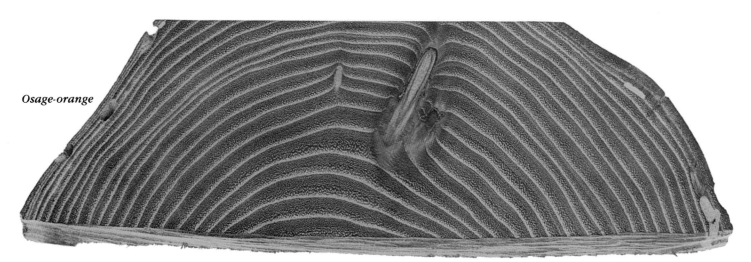

Osage-orange

Mesquite: A Hardwood with Character

Why we love these twisted, cracked and buggy little boards

by D. Herbert Nordmeyer

Mesquite thrives *in the scrublands of Texas and New Mexico. The harsh climate, plus the depredation of grazing cattle, produces a short, twisted log and lumber with plenty of character.*

Photos this page : Ken E. Rogers and Herb Nordmeyer.

W hen I talk about mesquite, I'm likely to hear such comments as "Mesquite, that's barbecue wood," and, "I've been fighting mesquite all my life." Recently, I mentioned mesquite to an intarsia artist who replied that people who use the wood are worse than religious fanatics. With remarks like these being made in the center of the mesquite tree's range, is it any wonder that most woodworkers have never heard of mesquite lumber? Those of us who know and love this hardwood dream of the day it replaces cocobolo. We think it is a wonderful and beautiful wood that's rich with character, and we want to tell the world about it.

The honey mesquite *(Prosopis glandulosa)* is native to northern Mexico and southern Texas; therefore, it is not exotic in the conventional sense. Mesquite originally grew near streams and rivers. When grass fires set by Indian hunters were controlled, the mesquite spread onto the prairies. It then spread north with the cattle drives and today continues to be spread by cattle that eat the beans.

Over much of its range, mesquite is cursed by ranchers, fought by the government, cut for firewood and shredded for barbecue chips. Yet, unlike the tropical exotics, the mesquite continues to spread. Around 1950, there were 44 million acres of mesquite in the United States. By the late 1980s, we had about 78 million acres.

Only in its native range or in ideal soil does one find mesquite of a size suitable for lumber. Until recently, there were no sawmills in the mesquite regions of Texas, and mesquite logs are too heavy to transport long distances to be milled. Most commercial sawmills cannot handle mesquite logs, which are often no more than 2 ft. long, so the would-be sawyer must build his own mill or modify some commercial model. Currently, mesquite lumber is available in small quantities from about a dozen sawyers (see the sources of supply box on p. 67). One source, San Pedro Mesquite of Benson, Ariz., is slicing mesquite veneers.

The mesquite is a tough tree that thrives in an extremely harsh climate, and people respond emotionally to it. After fighting the mesquite for years, ranchers and other Texans find this scruffy tree to be a worthy adversary. When these people discover the beauty of the wood, they fall in love with it.

The virtues of mesquite

Mesquite wood displays fascinating, fantastically twisted grain patterns. The mesquite tree typically develops multiple trunks after cattle graze off the terminal bud. These trunks spread sideways for several feet, and then they begin to grow vertically again. Further grazing and wind storms knock the trunk down again. Consequently, much of the tree consists of crotch wood and reaction wood, twisted and intergrown.

Mesquite wood is hard, dense and dimensionally stable (see the chart on p. 66). Not only does mesquite shrink less than other hardwoods, but the ratio between radial and tangential shrinkage is very close to unity, which means there's less warp in flatsawn boards and fewer problems when joints are exposed to humidity changes. Because it is about twice as hard as hickory, mesquite resists scratches and abrasions, and it makes excellent tabletops and flooring.

The color of mesquite wood varies with the region in which it was grown and with the soil type. In general, freshly cut mesquite heartwood is a reddish-tan to reddish-brown, with yellow and black highlights. Exposure to light usually intensifies the reddish-brown color. Within this generalization, the color of the wood can range from the lightness of pecan to purple.

Mesquite lumber has many defects, which we like to call "char-

Photos: Ray Dumas

Delights from the touring Wyndham Mesquite Collection include Kindred Spirits (above) *by Charlie Boren of Burleson, Texas,* and Vesuvius (right) *by Joel Lee of Reagan Wells, Texas.*

Friends of the jewel of the Southwest

by Ken E. Rogers

Los Amigos del Mesquite is an organization of more than 300 persons from eight states and six countries. The members are united by their obsession with the mesquite tree, which many of them call the jewel of the Southwest. One cannot get together with more than a couple of the amigos without the conversation turning to the most recent mesquite project or to some new technique for working and finishing the wood.

Los Amigos del Mesquite holds a meeting every September with a program that includes visits to mesquite sawmills and workshops, scientific papers on the tree and its uses, technical demonstrations and a trade show. The event features mesquite barbecue and jelly made from the mesquite bean.

Three years ago, the organization sent blocks of mesquite to well-known woodworkers, turners and carvers throughout the country, asking each to create an object that brought out the best in the wood. The resulting collection of 23 pieces, known as the Wyndham Mesquite Collection, will tour the Southwest until September of 1993.

For more information about Los Amigos del Mesquite, contact Ken E. Rogers at the Texas Forest Products Laboratory, P.O. Box 310, Lufkin, Texas 75901.

Because of its hardness and dimensional stability, mesquite is an excellent substitute for tropical hardwoods, as in this rolltop desk by Jim Butcher of Bulverde, Texas.

acter." The defects include wind shakes, borer tunnels and bark inclusions. Most mesquite craftsmen fill the defects with epoxy, either black or mesquite-colored. Some craftsmen fill defects while the mesquite is green or air-dried, but I get superior results by waiting until the wood has been kiln-dried to 8% to 10% moisture content. Many people assume that the epoxy fillings are natural mineral streaks. Some sawyers have been known to charge extra for character; I am regularly accused of selling the clear lumber and making works of art from the rejects.

Mesquite is not oily, so it glues well with ordinary yellow glue or with epoxy, and it accepts all types of finishes, including paste wood fillers, lacquers and varnishes. A common finishing technique in southern Texas is to sand smooth and apply several coats of tung oil. Under lacquer, the rich look of mesquite may take six months to develop. To counter this, one furniture builder applies tung oil and after it has dried a minimum of three days, applies a

lacquer finish. The wood can be bleached and stained to cut back its reddish color if that's what the customer wants.

The trouble with mesquite

Mesquite wood is not readily available. When I built my sawmill four years ago, the Texas Forest Service estimated that about 5,000 board feet of mesquite lumber were being sold each year. Now there are at least three mills that each produce more than that, but even so, our industry is microscopic.

Not many woodworkers know about mesquite. Some of my mail-order customers are displaced Texans (Texans are the only people who buy Texas souvenirs). Others are woodworkers seeking a replacement for exotic hardwoods. Once I sell some wood into an area, others see it and decide to try it.

Mesquite boards are small, rarely longer than 6 ft. nor wider than 6 in. Once in a while, you can find clear eight-footers that are a full 12 in. wide, but this is rare. Normally, the larger the board, the more serious its character. There is no uniform grading system. What one sawyer calls grade 1, another may call grade 3 and another may call premium grade.

Powder-post beetles love mesquite sapwood. Beetle-control methods include microwaving, heating to 140°F for 24 hours and freezing to 0°F for 24 hours. Some people believe that several coats of polyurethane will keep the beetles out while others believe in a soaking in dilute boric acid. All of these methods work occasionally, but the only certain way to prevent reinfestation is to cut off the sapwood.

How to buy mesquite

Now that you have been introduced to mesquite, how can you resist buying a few hundred board feet (see the sources of supply box)? Before you buy, ask about the grading system. Expect to pay $10 per board foot for mesquite lumber that is essentially clear on both sides and more if you need planks wider than 8 in. or longer than 6 ft. Expect $3 to $4 per board foot for sound lumber with defects on both sides. If the price is under $3, the wood is probably green or contains excessive sapwood and bark.

Working with mesquite wood will be an experience you'll never forget. And you can save the scraps for a Texas barbecue. □

Herb Nordmeyer makes mesquite furniture and craft objects in Knippa, Texas. He also operates a mesquite sawmill and sells mesquite lumber by mail order.

Properties of mesquite							
Species	Density (lbs./ft.^{3})	Compression parallel to the grain (p.s.i)	Compression perpendicular to the grain (lbs./in.^{2})	Side hardness (lbs./in.^{2})	Radial Shrinkage (%)	Tangential shrinkage (%)	Volumetric shrinkage (%)
Mesquite	45	8220	3360	2336	2.2	2.6	4.7
White oak	37	7440	1070	1360	5.6	10.5	16.3
Pecan	41	7850	1720	1820	4.9	8.9	13.6
Black walnut	34	7580	1010	1010	5.5	7.8	12.8
Cherry	31	7110	690	950	3.7	7.1	11.5

The fact that radial shrinkage about equals tangential shrinkage means the wood dries flat, without warping, and stays flat when the humidity changes. Compared to other hardwoods, mesquite is denser, harder and more stable. Low volumetric shrinkage means the wood does not shrink much when drying.

Working with mesquite

by Leslie Mizell

At first glance, the texture of mesquite wood is somewhat rough, with worm holes, checks and cracks, and defects that would warrant throwing away any usual wood. But this is all due to the extreme climate in which mesquite grows, which causes it to yield beautifully figured grain. The arid environment makes mesquite a slow growing tree and the density of the lumber is near a third greater than that of red oak.

Normally, these features would be undesirable when designing a high end piece of furniture and would lend the wood usefulness only in rustic settings, but for me, these only add expression to the piece.

I've worked with a lot of different woods, but the first time I tried mesquite I could only guess about how difficult the task would be. From the reddish color of the wood and its weight, I assumed that it would be like bubinga: gummy stuff that chips and tears. To my most pleasant surprise, the opposite was true.

Because mesquite trees grow in such an arid environment, the wood dries with very little movement and absolutely no gummy moisture. The wood can virtually be ripped with a crosscut blade without pinching. The only problem is an occasional separation of grain, which makes some boards useless until you glue the splits closed.

Mesquite is probably one of the best carving woods. Its density allows me to carve the finest details with no tearout. I don't necessarily try to select the straightest grain for carving, I just use what I think looks the best. Even using wild grain patterns, the wood chips off the edge of the carving tool with ease.

When it comes to sanding, there's absolutely no doubt about it, mesquite wood sands easier than any wood I've ever touched. A rasp can do wonders on sculpting a piece, and a single piece of sandpaper can sand a mile of mesquite. I use a small piece of 80-grit on a dowel or block to do fine rasping and then finish it with 220-grit. I guess it's the dryness of the wood that lets the sandpaper cut so easily and last so long.

From here the piece is ready to finish. I begin with a light coat of linseed oil diluted with mineral spirits, which I let dry overnight. Next I apply diluted sanding sealer and top-coat with a few coats of diluted lacquer. I use it heavily diluted so as not to leave a built-up finish. I want a finish that looks like oil but which still gives protection to the piece, so it will stand daily use. Finally, I steel-wool it with #0000, and then I wax it.

The long drive to a mesquite sawmill inspired Leslie Mizell to design and build his Texas Chippendale chair, which features the lone star carved on the back splat, a crest-rail armadillo and the silhouette of the Alamo at the base of the splat.

At this point, the wood colors range from honey-brown to pink, and may appear to be mismatched, even though these colors may all appear in the same board. Now the magic begins: I set the finished piece in direct sunlight, which allows the ultraviolet rays to blend the colors of the wood. It begins to happen within a few minutes. The wood darkens and eventually becomes a deep, rich, beautiful red. This will also happen in indirect light, but will take a lot longer. A full day in direct sunlight can make a tremendous difference.

Leslie Mizell makes furniture in Cleveland, Texas.

Sources of supply

ECC Shop, Inc., Evan J. Quiros, 2105 Galveston St., Laredo, TX 79040; (512) 723-7151

Hardwood Lumber Co. of Dallas, 10551 Goodnight Lane, Dallas, TX 75220; (214) 869-1230

Mesquite Lumber and Crafts, Herb Nordmeyer, Box 68, Knippa, TX 78870; (512) 934-2616

Mesquite Production Company, Route 1, Box 68-B, Hondo, TX 78861; (512) 426-3000

Mesquite Products of Texas, PO Box 88, Bulverde, TX 78163; (512) 438-3118

Mesquites Unlimited, Cameron Harrison, Route 4, Box 322, Wichita Falls, TX 76301; (817) 544-2262

Frank Paxton Lumber Company, PO Box 17968, Austin, TX 78760; (512) 443-0777

Jim Prewitt, PO Box 269, 111 General Cavasos Blvd., Kingsville, TX 78363; (512) 592-5948

San Pedro Mesquite Co., Benson, AZ 85602; (602) 622-4307

Wallace Seabolt, Route 2, Box 171A, Alleyton, TX 78935; (409) 732-5663

South Texas Molding, PO Box 549, Alamo, TX 78516; (800) 444-2881

Texas Kiln Products, Route 2, Box 1710, Smithville, TX 78957; (800) 825-9158

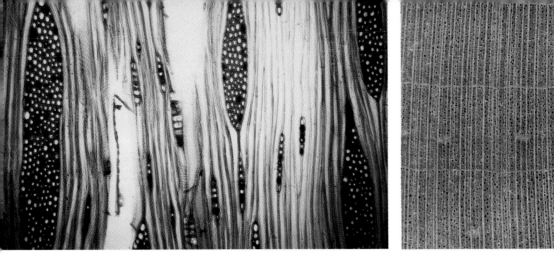

Left: Soft maple's grayish cast may distinguish it from hard maple's creamy white to light reddish-brown color, but a microscopic check is reliable. Magnified 10 times, hard and soft maples look similar. The rays in this red maple sample (soft) look like fine, evenly sized and evenly spaced lines. Far left: Magnified 250 times, you see that ray width (seriation) is up to eight cells wide in this sugar maple sample (hard). Rays are only up to five cells wide in soft maple.

Adventures of a Wood Sleuth

Making a positive ID settles each case

by Bruce Hoadley

When I was a student majoring in wood technology, I accepted my wood anatomy and identification curriculum as just one more of the many academic requirements for professional competence. I knew my wood-identification skills were important in many phases of wood technology, but I gave little thought to ever using this expertise outside my chosen field. During these subsequent years, however, I have been fascinated by the parade of wood-identification problems that have come my way from all walks of life. Of the calls and letters I receive asking for assistance in identifying wood, only the occasional inquiry is directly related to my own profession as a wood technologist and then it usually involves some routine problem in lumber sales or manufacturing technology. Most of the requests come from the unrelated fields of science, commerce and law. In some cases, identifying the wood is the only matter of concern; in others, identifying one or more wood samples is but a small piece of a much larger and more complex problem.

The anecdotes that follow are offered as a sampling of the surprising breadth of wood-identification applications in the real world. They also serve to illustrate a few of the principles, techniques and anatomical features that are involved in identifying wood.

Commercial lumber questions—As might be expected, disputes between vendors and customers concerning the species of hardwood or softwood lumber arise from time to time. If I were to single out the most frequent controversy in this category, it would be whether soft maple has been substituted for hard maple in a lumber shipment.

Typically, the customer suspects that the lumber is not hard maple because an unusually large number of pith flecks is evident on the tangential surfaces of boards after they are dressed. Pith flecks are found regularly in soft maples (shown in the above, right photomacrograph); however, they are occasionally numerous in hard

maple. Therefore, hard and soft maples are separated more reliably by examining the rays with a microscope (see the above, left photomicrograph), rather than with a hand lens.

In one instance, I examined a total of 12 tangential sections from 3 boards, and the largest rays were 4 and 5 seriate (the width of rays measured in cells). Only 2 rays were 6 seriate, and gray-colored mineral streaks were also evident. Therefore I concluded that the lumber was indeed soft maple, as claimed by the customer. In all other instances of this hard vs. soft maple controversy, however, I was able to find many rays that counted 8 or more seriate in every tangential section sampled, indicating that the lumber was hard maple, as claimed by the supplier.

Another commercial-shipment question stands out in my mind because of the personal embarrassment it caused me. In the midst of a busy day, I received a call from an engineering firm that was participating in the renovation of a large warehouse. Douglas fir *(Pseudotsuga menziessi)* had been specified for the structural posts, but upon receiving the shipment, the firm suspected that another species had been supplied.

The project was on a tight construction schedule, and before proceeding, the contractor wanted confirmation that the timbers were Douglas fir. I assured the caller that checking for Douglas fir was a simple matter and that I would be happy to do so as soon as samples were sent to me. Unfortunately, all I said was "samples," without specifying their size. For the next two days I awaited delivery, but none came. Finally, on the third day, a trucker appeared at my office with a dolly laden with 20-in. lengths of 12x12s. I felt myself flush with embarrassment as I realized the unnecessary time and cost of shipping such large chunks when I only needed splinters, which could have been mailed in an envelope.

In examining the pieces, the reason for concern became obvious. The wood didn't look much like Douglas fir. Some pieces (like the one in the left photomacrograph on the facing page)

From *Fine Woodworking* (May 1991) 88:70-72

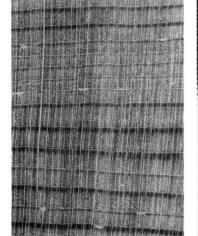

Right: This slow-growth Douglas fir endgrain, magnified 10 times, shows narrow, inconspicuous latewood, giving an even-grained appearance. Normal-growth Douglas fir has uneven grain from wider growth rings and conspicuous latewood. *Far right:* Magnified 150 times, you can see Douglas fir's spindle-like fusiform rays, which contain single horizontal resin canals, and spiral thickenings in longitudinal tracheids (the main cell type in softwoods).

were so slowly grown—there were 80 rings per inch in a few portions—that they appeared even grained, lacking the usual distinct, uneven-grained rings so characteristic of Douglas fir. The heartwood color was more yellowish brown than the familiar reddish brown of Douglas fir heartwood, and some of the pieces had only a trace of the characteristic Douglas fir odor.

Nevertheless, tangential sections examined microscopically confirmed that every piece was Douglas fir. Each sample had spindle-shaped fusiform rays (shown in the above, left photomicrograph) and abundant spiral thickenings (helical ridges along the inner surface of the cell wall) in the earlywood tracheids (non-living cells that function as food conductors and give support), as shown in the above, right photomicrograph. In reporting the results, I assured the firm that the wood was the correct species, but urged that the material be checked to determine whether the structural grade requirements had been met. Since then, I have been very careful to give clear instructions regarding the size of samples to be submitted for identification.

Identifying wood in furniture — Compared to identifying a single sample of wood or even a series of 20 or 30 samples, checking all the woods in a major furniture collection is a challenging task. Such an assignment presented itself when I was invited to assist in identifying more than 200 pieces of case furniture in the Garvan Collection and related collections at the Yale University Art Gallery. Here the task had an added challenge: the samples had to be taken inconspicuously and with a minimum of damage to the objects. I had to read as much as possible from the surface characteristics of the wood and assess such physical features as weight, color, evenness of grain and prominence of rays. Fortunately, woods such as beech or oak have conspicuous rays, and old stain or paint can actually help highlight ray size and distribution.

In sampling primary woods (the visible exterior woods in a piece of furniture), small fragments can be removed from an inconspicuous spot, such as under a glide caster on the bottom of a foot or under a drawer lock at the edge of the original mortise. Using the methods shown in figures 1 and 2, it was often possible to inconspicuously remove the necessary section for microscopic examination directly from the piece at a point of wear or minor damage, and it was sometimes possible to take tiny sections directly from the inside faces of shrinkage checks, which usually occur precisely along a radial plane.

The routine in surveying a piece of furniture is first to decide visually which components are of the same wood, and then to establish a sampling plan to microscopically verify a representative number of samples of each apparently different wood type. Although microscopic checking most often simply confirms the initial visual identification, occasional surprises do turn up.

For example, I quickly glanced at the side panels in a chest and thought they were hard pine because of obvious uneven grain. I decided to examine a radial microscopic section for confirmation and, anticipating hard pine (shown in the top, left photomicrograph on the next page), expected to see dentate ray tracheids (which appear like uneven cell walls with tooth-like projections that reach into the cell cavity) and pinoid cross-field pits (which are multiple, variably sized oval- to football-shaped pits that are elongated diagonally across the field). I was startled to find myself staring at hemlock, like that shown in the top, right photomicrograph on the next page, which has smooth-wall ray tracheids and cupressoid cross-field pits (which are oval with oval apertures that are narrower than the border on either side). I had followed my intuition and had failed to check for resin canals, which are a hallmark of pine. Resin canals are easy to see with a hand lens and

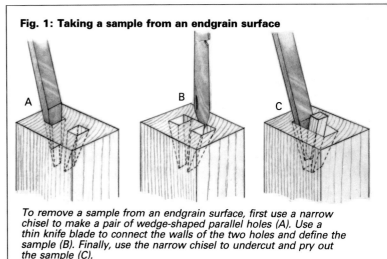

Fig. 1: Taking a sample from an endgrain surface

To remove a sample from an endgrain surface, first use a narrow chisel to make a pair of wedge-shaped parallel holes (A). Use a thin knife blade to connect the walls of the two holes and define the sample (B). Finally, use the narrow chisel to undercut and pry out the sample (C).

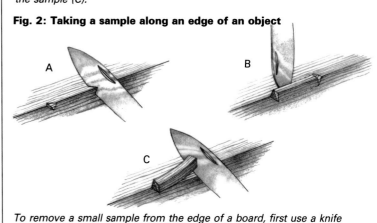

Fig. 2: Taking a sample along an edge of an object

To remove a small sample from the edge of a board, first use a knife to notch a pair of stop cuts (A). With the knife tip, score the edges of the sample to guide the split (B). Finally, engage the knife edge in the bottom of one of the stop cuts and gently pry the sample free with a slight twisting motion of the knife (C).

they were not present. Catching these occasional surprises is a sobering reminder that visual impressions alone can be quite deceptive and that microscopic follow-up is a comforting safety net.

The Garvan Collection experience made me especially alert when identifying woods with surface features obscured by old finish, stain or accumulated dust and dirt. A painted Windsor chair is the ultimate test in wood identification. The layers of earlywood pores in ring-porous species such as oak and ash are usually detectable, and the conspicuous rays of oak and beech will often show through even the muddiest of finishes. The diffuse-porous hardwoods are especially deceptive and sometimes impossible to identify.

Maple, and particularly soft maple, was perhaps the most commonly used wood for turnings, so it is usually assumed that legs and similar turnings are maple. But a surprising number are not.

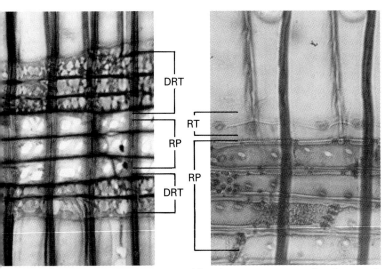

Left: *Under 275-power magnification, you can see Southern yellow pine's uneven-wall, dentate ray tracheids (DRT), which are found in all species of hard pine. It also has oval or football-shaped pinoid pits in the ray parenchyma (RP).* *Right:* *This photomicrograph of Eastern hemlock, magnified 550 times, shows the smooth-wall ray tracheids and oval-shaped cupressoid cross-field pits in the ray parenchyma.*

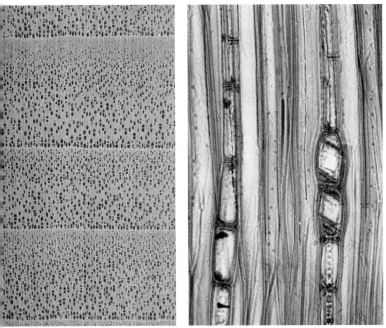

Left: *Quaking aspen's rays are so fine that they are nearly invisible when you look at them with a hand lens; in fact its rays are uniseriate (a single cell wide).* *Right:* *This photomicrograph (magnified 250 times) shows crystals in the longitudinal parenchyma cells in black walnut.*

Microscopic examination of a tangential section normally puts the question to rest. For example, the stout turned legs of 17th-century chairs are often found to be aspen (shown in the bottom, left photomacrograph), as quickly revealed by its thin uniseriate rays.

Perhaps the greatest single surprise in the case furniture of the Garvan Collection was a chest that had been labeled butternut. It certainly looked like butternut in surface color and figure. But the routine microscopic sampling paid off, as the sections revealed gash-like pitting on the radial walls of the vessels and large crystals in many of the longitudinal parenchyma cells, shown in the bottom, right photomicrograph. These features reliably confirmed black walnut.

Lawsuits—I have been a consultant and expert witness in lawsuits in which wood or wood products were involved and wood identification was in some way critical to the outcome. The most difficult single problem that I have ever encountered resulted from an accident in which a window washer fell when his ladder suddenly broke. The man suffered head injuries that left him permanently incapacitated.

The ladder was sold as having hemlock rails. I identified one rail as Western hemlock, an acceptable species for ladder rails. The other was apparently fir, individual species of which are usually considered indistinguishable on the basis of wood tissue alone. Confusingly, the ladder code allows noble fir *(Abies procera)*, but not other species, and so it became critical to know which fir species was used.

Crystals in the ray parenchyma cells were extremely sparse. Fortunately, I remembered a journal article on work done at Forintek Laboratory in Vancouver, B.C., Canada, that established a correlation between the ray-parenchyma crystal count and various fir species. I made crystal counts and then consulted the paper. The low number suggested that the wood was not *A. procera*, but probably *A. amabilis* or *A. lasiocarpa*.

As a check of my own work, I submitted a sample of wood to Forintek Laboratory. Their findings were similar. Next, I tried a color spot test that gives a purple coloration on subalpine fir *(A. lasiocarpa)*, but not on Pacific silver fir *(A. amabilis)*. The wood sample from the ladder gave no reaction. Ray-cell contents are reported to be clear or pale yellow in *A. balsamea* and *A. lasiocarpa*, but dark brown in other Western firs. The contents of ray cells in the questionable ladder rail were dark brown.

I concluded that the ladder rail was probably Pacific silver fir, and that its extremely low density (0.25 specific gravity) and weakness were principal contributing factors in the ladder's failure.

Just for fun—Wood identification need not always be serious or important. For a change of pace, I sometimes find myself identifying wood just for fun. This is not to say that the task is always successful or easy.

A friend once dropped off a small sack of assorted woods to "check out when you get a minute." When time permitted, I laid them out on my bench. I didn't recognize a single one. With a razor blade I cleaned up an endgrain surface on each for a closer look with a hand lens. They were all hardwoods, but strangers every one. A few looked like dipterocarps, perhaps lauan or meranti. I called my friend to ask him the source of such an exotic assortment. The reply was that they were crating boards from a Japanese motorcycle. I threw in the towel. □

Bruce Hoadley is a professor of wood technology at the University of Massachusetts in Amherst and a contributing editor to FWW. *Photos by author. This article is adapted from his new book,* Identifying Wood, *published by The Taunton Press, 63 S. Main St., PO Box 5506, Newtown, Conn. 06470-5506.*

Paulownia

A transplanted hardwood that grows like a weed and works like a dream

by John H. Melhuish, Jr.

Paulownia trees are a miracle of growth. Even in areas with poor soil, the trees can grow to be nearly 60 ft. tall, like the one shown in the photo above, in a relatively short time. You can gauge this growth by the inset photo, which shows a woman standing next to a one-year-old tree. Despite this rapid growth, the wood is easy to dry and can be worked within a few weeks of harvesting.

Paulownia, a light-colored hardwood revered for centuries by Japanese craftsmen because of its workability and beauty, may someday be the wood of choice for many American woodworkers and an economic boon for loggers in the Southeast. Not bad for a tree that apparently slipped into the United States accidentally, in the form of seeds used for packing material.

I first became interested in paulownia wood while working for the U.S. Forest Service on projects to reclaim land that had been strip-mined. Loggers and environmentalists were enthusiastic about the paulownia development in mined-out areas. The trees grow at an astounding rate, from seed to 10-ft.-tall in six months (see the inset photo at right), and they grow best in areas with poor-quality soil. I, along with other researchers, feel that it is important to find good uses for the lumber once the trees have outgrown their usefulness as soil stabilizers on the strip-mined lands. Because few American craftsmen have worked with the wood, I asked some local woodworkers to try it. You can see some of their results in the photos on p. 73. So far the results of our early woodworking experiments have been promising.

A stable wood with a long tradition

Paulownia is a lightweight but very strong, very stable wood that's easily worked with sharp tools. It has a satiny surface that stains and finishes very well and an open grain that resembles oak or ash (see the bottom left photo on p. 73). The color of the wood itself varies according to where the trees grow and when they are har-

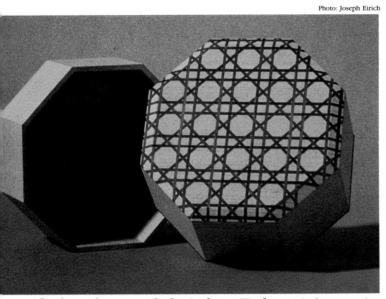

Photo: Joseph Eirich

The box above, made by Isaburo Wada, a sixth-generation Japanese craftsman, demonstrates paulownia's stability. The precisely fitted top takes eight seconds to lower itself on a cushion of air.

vested. Darker-colored stock is produced in the warmer southern states where the trees grow very fast. The slower growth in the more northern states produces a lighter color and finer growth rings, which are preferred by wood buyers. The color of stock from both regions is better if the stock is harvested in January or February, when the sap is down.

In addition to the local woodworkers' experiences, we have also been impressed with the beautiful paulownia objects crafted by the Japanese. Traditionally, paulownia was used to build *kotos* (harps) because the wood's specific gravity is about 0.28 (compared to 0.40 for yellow poplar and 0.60 for white oak), and this low density contributes to the wood's superior acoustical quality. Also paulownia has long been incorporated in high-quality furniture such as the *tansu* (a wedding chest). The wood for a bride's tansu often was harvested from a paulownia tree planted by the woman's father at the time of her birth.

Because the wood is virtually unaffected by changes in humidity, the Japanese could build to very tight tolerances, which is especially important when making ceremonial containers and other special boxes. According to tradition, every important or sacred object in Japan is housed in a custom-built box. Some items are enclosed in a series of boxes, each one documenting when the object was passed from one generation to the next. Paulownia is preferred for the best boxes because the wood can absorb a great deal of water before any moisture soaks through, and it's so stable that the lid can be mated to the body of the box with a piston-like, virtually waterproof fit (see the photo above).

Also, compared to other fast-growing hardwoods, paulownia is relatively easy for a craftsman to dry without elaborate equipment. The lumber air dries with a minimum of bow or twist and virtually no cupping, casehardening or honeycombing (although small surface checks occur occasionally). One recent study concluded that "the high dimensional stability and fast drying rate of paulownia lumber make this species the easiest-to-dry commercial wood currently growing in the United States."

A stowaway takes root

But, it was the tree's easy-to-grow nature that was largely responsible for the species development in this country. A native of China, paulownia probably came to the United States in the mid-1800s. One popular theory is that in the days before styrofoam peanuts,

paulownia seeds, which are very tiny and light (1.75 million seeds per pound), were used as packing material to cushion dinnerware shipped from the Orient. The wispy seeds escaped and took root when the china was unpacked. The trees probably first appeared along the Potomac River in the Washington, D.C., area but have since spread as far as the Pacific coast. However, Kentucky, Tennessee, West Virginia and an area as far north as Ohio and as far west as Illinois are most likely to produce high-quality wood.

The value of paulownia in the United States was not recognized until 1970 when Japanese wood buyers driving through Virginia noticed the trees growing wild. The trees had been nearly eradicated in Japan by a viral disease, so the buyers were especially excited to discover the old-growth trees and began extensive searches by helicopter to locate all of them. Single trees sold for $3,000 and up; one prime specimen reportedly sold for $20,000.

Because of the potential economic value, tree farmers have begun establishing paulownia plantations in the eastern United States. The seedlings thrive in disturbed sites such as road cuts, surface mines and other poor or marginal land. The trees have deep taproots, prefer well-drained and south- or west-facing locations and can grow to more than 60-ft.-tall, with trunks that are 1 ft. to 2 ft. dia. and larger. The leaves of juvenile trees are sometimes 3 ft. wide, but they are somewhat smaller on adult examples. The showy trumpet-shaped flowers of the adult tree are usually violet-colored and appear in the spring, before the leaves emerge. The flowers form 10-in.-high stalks, which resemble delicate reindeer antlers. In the fall, seed pods resemble bunches of grapes.

Much more research is needed to ensure that the trees produce good lumber. The fast-growing tops of the tree, for example, are susceptible to winter kill in the cooler growing zones. This can cause the tree to produce many spreading branches, which decreases the quality of lumber unless special pruning and other silvicultural techniques are used. High-grade paulownia lumber currently sells for about the same price as walnut, but it's unclear if those prices will remain stable or if overseas buyers will consider the new trees as valuable as old-growth paulownia trees, nearly all of which have been harvested.

My hope is that paulownia will grow in importance as wood technologists and craftsmen continue to use it for construction, furniture, crafts and musical instruments. I encourage you to try it. In some areas it may be known as Kiri, princess tree, empress tree, royal paulownia (the species was named in honor of Anna Paulovna, daughter of Czar Paul I of Russia and wife of King Willem of the Netherlands), or elephant-ear tree. The first time you see a young paulownia, you'll likely favor the elephant-ear title because of the tree's floppy leaves. ☐

John H. Melhuish is a retired researcher for the U.S. Forest Service, Northeastern Forest Experiment Station and lives in Berea, Ky. He would like to express his appreciation to B.J. Truett and M.E. Melhuish for their assistance in preparing this article.

Sources of supply

Many mills and lumber companies in the South have paulownia lumber. Here are a few to contact.

Parks Log Co., Inc., PO Box 403, Highway 64 E., Fayetteville, TN 37334; (615) 433-5595.

Bailey and Sons Timber Co., Route 1, Hornbeak, TN 38232; (901) 538-2174.

H and H Logging, 198 S. Fork Terrace, Glasgow, KY 42141; (502) 646-2779.

S. B. Hackney Lumber Co., Route 6, Lebanon, TN 37087; (615) 444-3480.

U.S. craftsmen discover paulownia's virtues

by Warren May

My first experience working with paulownia was last year when I had several locally grown logs slab sawn at a nearby mill. Surprisingly, after air drying the green wood in my shop for only three weeks, the paulownia was dry, stable and ready to fashion into my speciality—Appalachian dulcimers (see the bottom photo at right).

The small logs were given to me by U.S. Forest Service researcher John Melhuish, who proposed that my shop investigate the commercial possibilities of this local wood. I was intrigued from the start because I had been hearing rumors about Paulownia for some time. I first became aware that such a wood existed about 10 years ago. I came across it on a price list from one of my suppliers of musical-instrument wood. One of my employees at the time was from a sawmill family here in central Kentucky, and he told me that every sawyer he knew was looking for these trees (presumed to be the male of the *Catalpa*) because the elusive golden wood would yield vast sums (by the pound) on the export market.

Once we started working with paulownia, the excitement, curiosity and information about this strange wood grew daily. People brought us articles about paulownia from newspapers and magazines and our super light, good sounding dulcimers caught on. Every cut-off scrap was saved to give to visiting woodworkers, collectors and hobbyists. This wood had an almost magical quality surrounding it. No wonder it has been prized so highly for centuries in the Orient.

In our shop we have found paulownia wood to be very light, but firm. It joints, planes, scrapes and sands very well, without the fuzzing or tearout that occurs in some pines or soft grades of mahogany (see the photo below). Carving and sculpting paulownia with sharp tools is a real joy. The grain pattern of the smaller trees was very strong with some curl around select knots, which I maneuvered into sound holes on many of my dulcimers. When bending the ⅛-in. strips for my dulcimer sides, I found that they needed to soak in water for only a few seconds before they practically melted around my forming jigs.

Several dulcimers later, paulownia continues to be user friendly. A few of the dulcimers were given as gifts by the state of Kentucky to Japan and China. My father-in-law has made sculpted-inlay jewelry boxes using the easily shaped small pieces for contrast with walnut and cherry. And one of my woodworkers has built wonderfully functional, lightweight briefcases of paulownia, with a urethane finish for durability (see the top photo). We have also finished paulownia with lacquer and with a linseed oil/polyurethane mixture with topcoats of either lacquer or varnish. The first coat of finish firms the surface quite well for additional coats.

Certainly paulownia is not the perfect wood for every project. It is very soft compared with other hardwoods, light in color and has a very strong grain pattern. Sanding without a block may cause an uneven surface, and it lacks the weight of traditional hardwoods. But user satisfaction and high-public interest coupled with the fact that one can harvest this tree and use almost every inch of it within a matter of weeks really does make paulownia worth its weight in golden color. □

Warren A. May owns and operates a woodworking shop in Berea, Ky.

Photo: Dick Burrows

Paulownia's light weight makes it an ideal choice for a briefcase, like the one above, built by John Kennedy of Berea, Ky. And Warren May's paulownia dulcimer, below, takes advantage of the wood's excellent acoustical qualities.

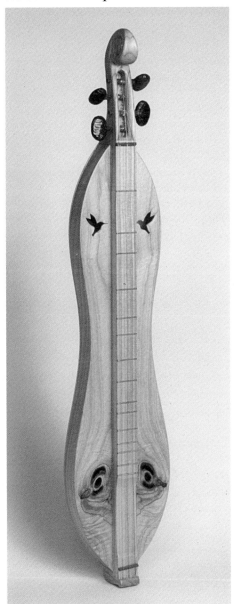

Paulownia can be easily worked with sharp tools, and can be planed to a satiny surface that needs little or no sanding before finish is applied.

Wood Identification
Reading endgrain with a hand lens

by Jon Arno

Wood identification is becoming increasingly difficult in today's complex and global lumber trade. Foreign species are especially troublesome, but with the popularity of terms such as "white woods," "spruce-pine-fir (S-P-F)" and "mixed hardwoods," the identity of even common domestic species is easily lost between stump and lumberyard.

Most woodworkers can identify a variety of woods by eye or by a combination of features, such as density, color, figure and even smell. But mistakes are inevitable, because almost every wood has a look-alike. However, the woodworker who really wants to identify domestic and exotic cabinetwoods can do so most of the time. For less than $100, you can purchase the needed reference books (see references on p. 77). The only other requirements are a $10 hand lens and a well-honed pocketknife. Although many woods are deceptively similar in outward appearance, under magnification, each species' anatomical structure, especially on the endgrain, will reveal the wood's unique signature or "fingerprint."

This system is not foolproof: Sometimes microscopic examination of individual cells, chemical analysis, ultraviolet tests and years of training are needed to identify a species. In some cases, not even the most advanced technology can prevail. For example, several species are sold as "white oak," and science, as of yet, has no foolproof way of distinguishing these by examining the wood alone. Nonetheless, it's surprising how far a woodworker can get with just a hand lens and some reference material.

Any lens with a reasonably broad field of view and at least 10x power will do. I prefer a jeweler's loupe with a wide-angle 10x lens at one end and a higher-power 15x lens at the other. The 10x lens will bring into focus the full width of at least one annual growth increment (the wood between two annual rings), which allows for a quick appraisal of the pore patterns. The 15x lens can then be used to study finer details.

It's necessary to have an absolutely smooth-cut surface on the endgrain of the sample or the features will be blurred. The cut should span at least one annual growth increment. For cutting, some specialists rely on disposable blades, such as scalpels or heavy-duty razor blades, but a well-honed pocketknife will suffice.

The following tips will help: Once the surface is cut, touch it to your tongue or otherwise dampen it. This brings up the contrast and makes details easier to spot. Next, position the sample so it receives maximum light. Now, bring the hand lens up as close to the eye as possible so the field of view will be as wide as the lens can provide. Finally, move either the sample or your head until the scene is brought into focus.

You will see the wood's cellular structure in about the same way it appears in the photographs here. Let's start by distinguishing between softwoods and hardwoods, then we'll examine some of the more important cabinetwoods. Here are things to look for:

Balsam fir   A   B   C   Basswood   D

Softwoods and hardwoods are normally easy to separate. While some hardwoods are softer and lighter than most softwoods, their anatomical structure is quite different. The endgrain of a typical softwood, such as balsam fir (*Abies balsamea*), reveals a simple structure made up of very small fluid-conducting cells called tracheids (A), annual rings (B) and cells that grow horizontally out from the center of the tree, which form the rays (C). Basswood (*Tilia americana*) is actually lighter in weight than balsam fir. However, being a hardwood, its endgrain reveals a more complex structure including pores (D), which are the cross sections of specialized fluid-conducting structures called vessels.

From *Fine Woodworking* (November 1988) 73:76-79

Some softwoods, such as pine (*Pinus strobus*), have resin canals (A), which under low magnification look much like the pores in hardwoods. But pores in hardwoods are many times more plentiful than are the resin canals in even the most resinous softwoods. Compare pine to walnut (*Juglans nigra*): The greater anatomical complexity of a hardwood is readily apparent.

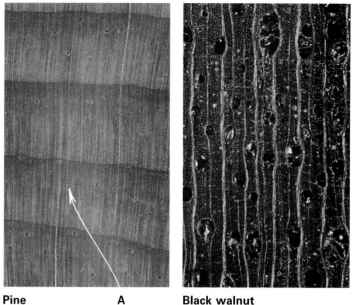

Pine   **A**   **Black walnut**

Hardwoods may be generally divided into ring-porous species, such as ash (*Fraxinus americana*), and diffuse-porous species, such as yellow poplar (*Liriodendron tulipifera*). However, many species are neither truly ring-porous nor diffuse-porous. To varying degrees, in most woods the pores are spread throughout the annual growth increment but tend to become smaller in the latewood, which is growth produced toward the end of the season. Moreover, in tropical regions, where growth occurs all year long, large and small pores may be spread throughout the wood in almost every pattern imaginable.

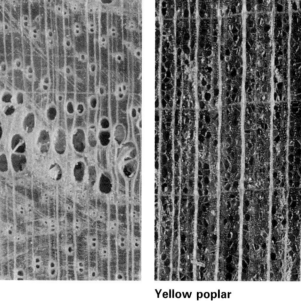

Ash   **Yellow poplar**

In most cases, an accurate identification is based on correctly appraising a combination of features. You must learn to read the entire signature. Take for instance elm (*Ulmus americana*) and hickory (*Carya ovata*): Both are more or less ring-porous (A), and both have light-color wavy bands in the latewood (B). Hickory is about half again as dense and heavy as elm, but a sample of hickory sapwood compared to elm heartwood could lead to confusion. Upon close examination, however, you can see that the light, wavy bands in hickory are formed by faint concentric rings of specialized storage cells called parenchyma, which are not associated with the latewood pores. In elm, these bands contain the latewood pores, making them bold enough to be easily seen with the naked eye. This feature, in combination with the fact that elm normally forms a single row of large, earlywood pores, helps to confirm the diagnosis. Furthermore, if the samples are fresh, elm will have a distinct, unpleasant odor, doubtless the genesis of the term "piss elm."

(continued on next page)

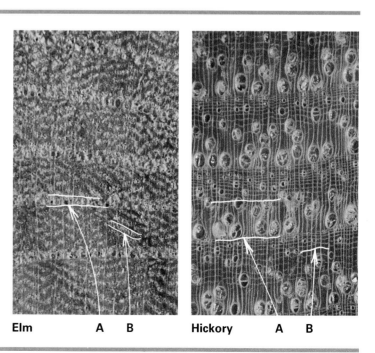

Elm   **A**   **B**   **Hickory**   **A**   **B**

Photos: John P. Limbach, Ripon Microslides; all photos have been enlarged about 2.75 times

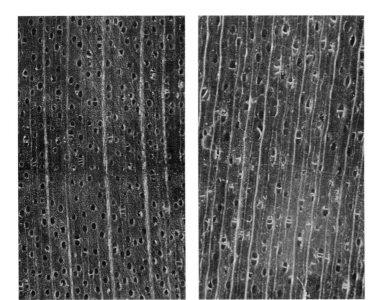

Sugar maple   **Black birch**

Sugar maple (*Acer saccharum*) and black birch (*Betula nigra*) are two diffuse-porous, fine-textured woods with comparable color and density. Under hand-lens magnification, however, the rays on the endgrain of birch are narrower than the diameter of the largest pores; in maple, there are two sizes of rays and the wider ones are as wide as or wider than the largest pores. With a hand lens, separating birch from maple is easy, but distinguishing between the many species within a genus can be tricky, especially among the maples (*Acer*) and the birch (*Betula*).

Honduras mahogany   **A**   **Lauan**

Because of the sheer number of species involved and the often confusing trade names being employed today, identifying imported woods is a special challenge. Perhaps the area of greatest confusion lies with the many woods that are marketed as "mahogany." The true mahoganies come from the genus *Swietenia*, of which Honduras mahogany (*S. macrophylla*) is the most common. Lauan (*Shorea spp.*), however, is often marketed as mahogany. These lauans are extremely variable in color and density, and there are some 70 species in the *Shorea, Parashorea* and *Pentacme* genera whose woods are intermingled in the lumber trade. Note that under the lens, the growth rings in true mahogany are highlighted by a thin band of light-color cells (A). This is usually visible on the tangential surface of the board as well, without magnification.

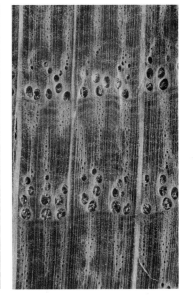

Red oak   **White oak**

Both red oak (*Quercus rubra*) and white oak (*Quercus alba*) are ring-porous woods with prominent rays. White oak, however, normally has lighter-color rays, and the latewood is denser, with many small pores. Red oak has fewer, but larger pores in the latewood. The pores of white oak are clogged with a foam-like substance called tyloses (A), while those of red oak are normally open. White oak can therefore be used to make watertight barrels, whereas red oak cannot.

Summing up—At first, resorting to a hand lens and studying reference books may seem complicated and downright academic, but it isn't that difficult. In much the same way that old-time woodworkers memorized the general characteristics of the woods they used, the hand-lens user begins to memorize the end-grain signatures of the more popular cabinetwoods. You'll find the whole process is actually fun. And, it's always pleasant to avoid the problems of mistaken identity that haunt all aspects of woodworking. For example, to edge-glue ash and elm together is one of the best ways to invite a warped tabletop or panel. Also, mixing spruce and pine can be a finisher's nightmare. These two soft, creamy white woods look very much alike in the raw state, but they don't stain the same.

As you develop your hand-lens skills, it's a good idea to develop your senses as well. Each time I work with an unfamiliar species, I study it thoroughly. I visually examine it's color, texture and figure. I heft it and jam my fingernail into it to get a sense of its density. I even smell the fresh-cut sawdust to become familiar with its scent, which is often an important key to identification. Walnut, sassafras, catalpa, elm, cedar and many others have distinct odors that are hard to mistake. These odors are the product of complex and subtly unique volatile substances, which can be identified more exactly through chemical analysis, but your nose is often the only equipment you need.

I've had some old guys tell me that almost all woods have a scent, even those that we normally think of as being odorless. When the wood is moist or freshly cut, they can separate maple from birch or basswood and pine from spruce or fir on the basis of scent alone. Personally, my nose isn't that good, and while I do not challenge their honesty (they can in fact correctly separate samples of these species), I suspect their great skill is the product of other senses working in tandem. Through their eyes and hands, they are picking up other attributes, such as color, density, figure and texture, then instantaneously processing this input through a brain-based experience/memory program that would put a computer mainframe to shame.

The scientific community doesn't scoff at these skills; they are real and documentable. But this undisciplined approach has its limitations. Perhaps the most significant limitation is that you can never identify a wood you haven't studied or worked with before. While it might once have been possible for a woodworker to amass enough experience to recognize any wood he might encounter, there are so many species available in today's world market that learning them all would be virtually impossible.

As you gain more experience with wood identification, you'll find that the need to consult reference books and guides becomes less frequent and often is used only to make a final, confirming choice between two or three possible species. These "close calls" usually require an accurate and balanced appraisal of several features, including those not easily described in a book, such as color and odor. Because of this, I think it's essential to develop a collection of known wood samples. This starts by simply saving samples of each new wood you use, but it inevitably graduates to foraging through scrap piles at the local lumberyard and ultimately to joining organizations such as the International Wood Collectors Society (see references at right). The membership of the IWCS is worldwide, and the exchanging of wood samples is one of its founding purposes.

If the wood samples still can't help you decide the wood's identify, you can take the material to a wood technologist for microscopic examination. Most species can be identified by minute differences in the tissue, such as the surface texture of the cells or the way the cells connect to one another through valve-like structures called pits. This method's degree of certainty begins to approach what you would call "beyond a reasonable doubt."

As you pursue the more technical methods of wood identification, the process begins to circle back on itself. By exploring wood's anatomical structure, you'll develop a far greater understanding of how the cellular arrangement affects the general appearance—texture and figure—of a species. This allows you to become conscious of which features are distinctive and which irrelevant. In like respect, a little book learning on organic chemistry strengthens the awareness of why woods have unique color and odor.

It would be irrational to suggest it is time for the typical woodworker to clear off a place on the workbench for beakers, vials, Bunsen burners and a microscope. After all, your basic senses can still get the job done with reasonable certainty. It's just that nowadays, in the species-glutted lumber trade, it takes a few reference books, a drawer or two of samples and a hand lens to give yourself a fighting chance. □

Jon Arno is an amateur woodworker and wood technologist in Schaumburg, Ill.

References

The books I use most often are:

Understanding Wood by R. Bruce Hoadley. The Taunton Press, Box 355, Newtown, CT 06470; 1980. Hoadley's book is an excellent place to start, presenting the basics of wood anatomy in an easily understood fashion. Fifty-four macrophotographs for major domestic species and a few imports are accompanied by clear, descriptive copy.

Wood Identification Handbook by Marshall S. White. Charles Scribner's Sons, 115 Fifth Ave., New York, NY 10003; 1982. This manual outlines the terminology of wood anatomy. It provides a fairly effective system for categorizing structural patterns and recognizing key details. The woods covered are limited to commercial woods of the eastern United States.

The Wood Handbook for Craftsmen by David Johnston. Prentice Hall Press, 200 Old Tappan Road, Old Tappan, NJ 07675; 1983. This book is currently out of print, but it may be available from libraries and used-book dealers. More international in scope, the book provides macrophotographs of approximately 100 species, including most major cabinetwoods imported into Europe and North America.

Textbook of Wood Technology by A.J. Panshin & Carl de Zeeuw. McGraw-Hill Book Co., 1221 Ave. of the Americas, New York, NY 10020; 1980. This text deals strictly with domestic species but covers the subject in complete detail. Macrophotographs are provided for virtually all native woods. This is one of the best references on the subject, but it is also very technical.

International Wood Collectors Society (IWCS), c/o Robert M. Bartlett, secretary/treasurer, 2913 3rd St., Trenton, Mich. 48183. The membership of IWCS is worldwide, and the exchanging of samples is one of its founding purposes.

A word about keys—Some reference books offer keys to guide the user through a series of "yes/no" choices until an identification is made. The keys create a trail configured something like a branching tree. You start at the bottom of the trunk, then when the tree first branches, you determine which branch to take by answering a relatively simple question, such as whether the sample is a hardwood or a softwood. From there you proceed to the next branching and the next question. The process eventually takes you to the tip of a twig and, hopefully, to the sample's identity.

In theory, this is fine, but judgement and experience are needed to answer many of the key questions. Just one wrong choice, especially early on, and you can find yourself trying to decide whether your sample is a date palm or a bullrush, when plainly it's neither.

Keys can be helpful if used with caution, but for my money, a hand lens is more accurate and easier. For positive results, either method should be confirmed by comparing the wood to a known sample. —*J.A.*

Working Highly Figured Wood

Mix hand-tool and machine methods for tearout-free surfaces

by Peter Tischler

Figured wood makes beautiful furniture but can be tough to work. *Peter Tischler's two-section ash chest with its vertical cabinet and holly inlay (left) has curly oak drawers, while his low cherry bureau with its black horizontal base (right) has flame birch drawers. In both pieces, Tischler relied on hand-tool and machine methods to surface the figured wood.*

Working difficult wood by hand—*With three favorite hand tools, the author smooths this plank of walnut. First he skews a #4½ smoothing plane (with paraffin-waxed sole) to flatten the board. Next he'll use the cabinet scraper at various angles to work the knot area. Last he'll smooth out tool marks with the scraper blade.*

Photos except where noted: Alec Waters

Cabinetmakers usually save woods with high figure and bold grain to showcase the prominent features of their work, such as tabletops, door panels or drawer fronts (see the top photo on the facing page). But until I became familiar with the underlying structure and reasons behind beautiful grain and figure, I had difficulties working the surfaces of such solid woods.

I've since built many furniture pieces using wood with pronounced grain and figure. Along the way, I developed some unusual methods to cope with these showy woods. I've found a combination of hand-tool and machine techniques can overcome tearout and make surfacing go more smoothly. I'll share these tips as well as what I've learned about what causes some common figures and grain patterns and offer suggestions for working them (see the descriptions on pp. 82-83).

Understanding grain and figure

Because descriptions can be ambiguous, it's helpful to first define a few terms that describe wood's characteristics. Consider grain as the cell arrangement and direction of the fibers in the wood. (For more on this, see *FWW* #95, p. 58.) Texture is the differences in cell size and density between early (spring) wood growth and late (summer) wood growth. Early and late wood account for contrasts in color, as shown in the chair-seat photo on p. 80. Color differences can also occur as you move outward in a log. The heartwood (center) of a tree is usually darker than the sapwood nearer the bark. Figure is a little harder to define. It refers to the patterns that appear on the radial and tangential faces of a board. Figure actually has to do with the light-reflecting properties of the wood. A further explanation of this is given in R. Bruce Hoadley's book, *Understanding Wood* (The Taunton Press).

Highly figured woods are also highly prized, so the best quality logs usually go to the veneer mills. This allows more of us to see and work the woods that have distinct signatures of nature. (For a gallery of figured veneers, see *FWW* #89, pp. 44-45.) For many furniture applications, however, veneers limit a piece's design and durability. Working figured wood in its solid form lets me reveal

Tearout-free block-planing

by John Henry Harper

Block planes offer many advantages for smoothing figured hardwoods. Because a block plane's iron is bevel side up, it requires no chipbreaker. The blade's bevel itself rolls the shaving over. Having the flat side down allows the iron to be supported from underneath, close to the cutting edge (see the drawing below), which dampens most of the tool's chatter. In addition, the ability to close the throat enables you to produce ultra-fine shavings, even in the most difficult woods. This is because the plane can be set to support the wood close to the cutter, which prevents the shaving from lifting and tearing out.

Standard vs. low angle: I prefer the higher quality block planes that have adjustable mouths. There are two basic models available: The low-angle (12 or 12½°) block plane, which is intended for end grain, but also works well at paring softwood, and the standard-angle (20°) block plane. The angle designation refers to the slope between the plane's iron and its sole. I've found that a well-tuned standard-angle block plane with a sharp, lightly set iron is the most suitable for surfacing figured woods. I actually modify the tool's edge somewhat to produce a steeper cut, which causes less tearout.

The cutting angle is the angle between a plane's sole and the direction that the shaving is diverted by the blade. On bench planes, this angle is fixed by the angle of the frog. By contrast, with a block plane you can change the cutting angle simply by grinding the bevel at the angle you want.

For general planing work, a bevel ground at 25° offers the best compromise between sharpness and edge durability. This gives a cutting angle of 45° for a standard-angle block plane. However, for smoothing figured wood, I like a 55° cutting angle. Once called the "middle" pitch, this is the angle found on many old molding planes specifically meant for hardwoods. To get this pitch, I grind the iron at a 35° bevel (a low-angle plane iron would have to be ground too bluntly). A 55° cutting angle shears off wood without causing tearout, and it works for the same reason that a cabinet scraper does—the edge is less likely to pry up the wood fibers.

Honing the iron at the same angle that I ground its bevel produces a nice edge. In other words, I don't add any secondary bevel. I begin with a 1,200-grit waterstone and then move to a 6,000-grit stone. If I'm using oilstones, I start with a soft Arkansas and then proceed to a hard Arkansas stone. As I'm honing, I ease the corners of the iron. The slightly crowned edge helps prevent the corners from digging in. I always sharpen several blades at the same time to keep handy.

Because highly figured woods exhibit frequent changes in grain direction, it's helpful to skew the plane, which reduces the shaving width. (For more on this, see *Fine Woodworking* #99, p. 67.) Even more important, though, is to vary the approach angle. I get the best results on figured woods by planing in several directions. □

John Henry Harper attended North Bennet Street School and now works wood in Bowie, Md.

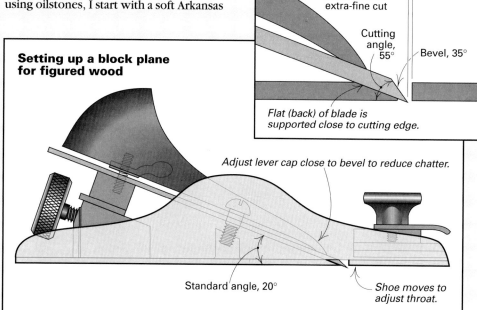

Detail of edge

Throat set for extra-fine cut

Cutting angle, 55°

Bevel, 35°

Flat (back) of blade is supported close to cutting edge.

Setting up a block plane for figured wood

Adjust lever cap close to bevel to reduce chatter.

Standard angle, 20°

Shoe moves to adjust throat.

Avoiding tearout in shaping—*The contrast of early and late wood (light and dark bands) form pleasing patterns in this walnut seat. Tischler glued up an odd number of boards, centering one for the pommel. To avoid tearout when shaping the seat, he used a power carving wheel followed by an auto grinder equipped with a coarse sanding disc. Next he removed high spots and tool scratches with a random-orbit sander. After he smoothed the contour with gouges and curved scrapers, he wet the wood for final hand-sanding.*

Jointing—*To minimize tearout, Tischler skewed the board on the left. For the board on the right, he honed a secondary bevel on his jointer knives to handle reversing grain. The tearout above the pencil point occurred before the knives were dressed.*

patterns on the face, edge and ends of a piece. I can also cut shapes into the wood and scrape and sand without fear of going through the veneer. And when I want thick veneer, I just resaw it from stock I have. I rely on several sawyers to get figured wood. Having flitch-cut stock gives me more options because I can select boards that are wider or have a natural edge. I've also learned to pay closer attention to lumber that the sawmills reject. To learn how to "read" the figure of a rough-sawn board, see pp. 86-87.

Hand-tool methods

It's not uncommon to encounter highly figured lumber that won't machine well. I often turn to hand tools for flattening and final smoothing. Getting consistent results can simply mean becoming proficient with a tool you're already familiar with. For example, one cabinetmaker friend smooths figured wood using only a block plane (see the box on p. 79). I prefer hand tools when I'm smoothing a knot region (see the box on the facing page). Worked carefully, knot wood can yield highly figured, spectacular wood.

Planing and scraping—Sharp hand tools are essential for working high-figure and changing grain. When I'm preparing a surface for a finish, I smooth in several stages, using three of my favorite tools (see the bottom photo on p. 78). First I flatten the board with a Stanley #4½ smoothing plane. To ease my effort, I keep the sole waxed, and I skew the plane. Next I take an old Stanley cabinet scraper (#80) and work in different directions, according to which way the grain runs. Because the face of a figured board can contain substantial end grain, heavy scraping may be needed, especially if the handplane didn't work well. The steep angle of the cabinet scraper blade almost always leaves a silky finish. Finally, I use a Sandvik card scraper to remove tool marks and scratches. I scrape at different approach angles, and I take both short and long strokes. Unlike working veneers where a light burr on the scraper is needed, scraping solid wood calls for a heavy burr. To get this, I use extra pressure when I'm turning the scraper's burr.

Sanding and hardening the wood—On hard, finely textured woods, scraping leaves the wood smooth—with maybe only light sanding required. However, a few figured woods will be fuzzy af-

ter scraping, particularly those with wood in tension like curly birch or quilted maple or those with high moisture content. I try aggressive sanding with the grain. I start with coarse paper and work my way up to fine to minimize the scratches.

Another way to deal with surface fuzziness is to chemically harden the problem area ahead of time. I've used everything from shellac and sanding sealers to cyanoacrylates and wood hardeners. Each time I was able to control fuzzy or otherwise difficult grain before scraping. If you use a hardener, first apply some on scrap, so you can check the substance for compatibility with the stain and finish you'll be applying to your project.

Machine methods

Much of the difficulty in machining highly figured wood comes from changes in grain directions. The amount of grain slope greatly affects how a figured board will machine. I always feed stock with the grain running "downhill" (see *FWW* #102, p. 48). But reading the edge grain can be confusing. Many boards want to be fed in two directions. Other boards that should plane well according to the edge grain will chip out severely. And when fed in what should be the wrong direction, the boards plane smoothly. This can happen when the pores of the wood are oriented opposite to the apparent grain.

Safety precautions are important when machining figured woods. Internal stresses in the wood can cause a board to plane roughly, or worse, bind and kick back at the saw or during shaping. Crotch wood will often machine surprisingly easily considering its degree of figure. This is because the grain slopes noticeably. Conversely, straight-grain quartersawn wood that has prominent fleck patterns (oak or sycamore, for example) can be difficult to machine. In this case, the rays are not parallel to the surface, which causes them to chip out easily. I've found it helpful to follow a few basic, but fundamental machining methods.

Use sharp, balanced knives, and take slow, light cuts—According to Ryszard Szymani, director of the Wood Machining Institute, there are several ways to minimize tearout while jointing and planing figured stock: First, make sure the knives are sharp. Sharpness is especially important because part of the cells may be

From *Fine Woodworking* (March 1994) 105:44-49

cut against the grain. Second, keep knives properly set and the cutterhead balanced. (For more about this, see *FWW #103*, p. 86). Third, adjust the depth of cut and feed rate according to the wood you're working. In general, take light (not over 1/32 in. deep) passes, and move the stock slowly. A slow, light pass will keep up the cutterhead speed and lessen the chance of the fibers lifting.

Adding a secondary bevel and skewing the work—Another way to reduce jointer tearout is to increase the sharpness angle of the knives by grinding a secondary bevel on them (see *FWW #102*, p. 52). This will give the knives more of a scraping action and lessen their lifting tendency. The board in the photo at right on the facing page shows the improved edge that results. If you add a secondary bevel, remember that this will increase the jointer's feed resistance, and the knives may dull more quickly.

In woods with interlocked grain (elm is a prime example), skewing the work can reduce tearout by increasing the slicing action of the cut. Skewing can be done on both the planer and the jointer. This is effective on curly maple. But with woods whose curl runs diagonally to the edge of the board (curly birch and cherry come to mind), a skewed cut can actually be detrimental. You'll just have to try it on some scrapwood to see what will happen.

Wetting the wood and power-sanding—Another aid to machining difficult stock is wetting the surface between passes. This helps control tearout in bird's-eye figure. The moisture seems to hold the fibers and flecks in place better. This technique sometimes helps when I'm running a board against the direction its grain wants to be fed. I also dampen the wood to raise the grain between sanding stages (see the photo at left on the facing page). Wetting is time-consuming; I only do it when all else fails.

If, after trying all my machining tricks, I'm still getting excessive tearout, I turn to power-sanding—but only as a last resort. Even tiny sanding scratches reduce the wood's reflective properties and thus hide the figure. A belt sander can flatten a board, remove mill marks or do heavy surfacing when the wood doesn't handplane. Power sanding also works in certain shaping operations. If I'm contouring stock with difficult grain, I rely on an auto-body grinder fitted with a coarse (down to 36-grit) disc. I used this technique on the chair seat in the photo at left on the facing page. After working my way up through the grades of sanding grit, I finished with a sequence of random-orbit sanding, scraping and hand-sanding. □

Peter Tischler is a North Bennet Street School graduate who runs a chairmaking and cabinetmaking shop in Caldwell, N.J.

Smoothing knots and filling gaps

Defects in wood can add visual interest to furniture. The best examples I've seen are from the late George Nakashima, who liked to highlight the natural forms in wood by using wavy edges, checks and knots. A while back, I was fortunate to refinish a few of his pieces. Inspired by how he handled defects, particularly knots, I now use some special methods to make a seemingly worthless piece of wood usable.

One problem with knots and their associated reaction wood is the gaps or pithy areas that surround the center (see the bottom photo on p. 78). To stabilize these regions, I first clean out any loose material. Then I fill in the voids and scrape the surface smooth. If the process is done carefully, the repaired area will gain strength, contrast and workability.

Stabilizing gaps and pithy areas: I use the sequence of steps shown in the photos below to repair loose knots. The method also works on cracks and small (vacant) knot holes. First I pound in and glue custom shaped end-grain plugs and wedges into the voids. The wedges match the surrounding wood well because most reaction wood around knots has a high percentage of end grain showing. Next I mix up some sanding dust with five-minute epoxy, and I spread it into remaining gaps.

Once the glue and epoxy are hard, I saw off the wedges. To smooth the repair, I scrape in almost every direction, which addresses the changes in grain. As I'm scraping, I try to repeat the motions that produce the least amount of scratches.

Occasionally, I'll sand difficult spots with medium-grit paper, though this won't leave as nice a feel as scraping. Next I sand with fine paper and burnish with 0000 steel wool. I dust off the surface to see how I've done. Then using alcohol-soluble aniline dye, I touch up the blemishes in the filled areas until I'm happy with the color match. Once the project is completed, I wipe on some finish, usually Danish oil, which brings out the full colors.

I try to keep an open mind when I'm handling defects because I want them to retain an organic look. When I'm willing to put in the effort, I'm rewarded with a surface that shows enhanced figure. *—P.T.*

Step A: Filling the knot *involves spreading a mix of epoxy and sawdust into the cracks and then driving and gluing in shaped wedges into the gaps.*

Step B: Smoothing the surface *with a scraper blade at various angles all around the knot and its reaction wood shows that the surface is now solid.*

Step C: Oiling the wood *reveals the colors of the repaired areas. Darkening the fillers with dye will finish them to a near perfect match of the knot.*

Approaches for different figures

Wood is not homogeneous. Similarly, every board is unique. Surfaces with high figure and striking grain can be attributed to many factors, the most likely being growth and development of the tree, cellular orientation, color variation and external influences, such as fungi, insect or mechanical damage.

The descriptions here offer at least a partial explanation of how the colors and patterns got there. I've also offered suggestions for working surfaces, though they are not foolproof because each wood can have its own peculiarities. In fact, I'm always refining my approach to working high figure because even the most unusual methods are worth it when I can fully bring out a wood's potential. —P.T.

Samples are from the following sawmills: Rob Roth, Verona, N.J.; The Burl Tree, Eureka, Calif.; Randle Woods, Randle, Wash.

Burl (maple) is an irregular growth on a tree caused by mechanical or insect damage. Burls appear as bulges on the trunk. This example shows a burl's cross section. Burl grain is tightly compacted and resembles small bud-like knots. In lumber form, burls are difficult to work and are traditionally cut into veneers or saved for carvers, turners and instrumentmakers. When preparing a burl surface for a finish, use a razor-sharp scraper in many directions.

Quilted (bigleaf maple) figure is formed by crowded, elongated bulges of growth layers. Due to its varying reflectivity, I consider quilted figure to be the most three dimensional. Quilted is mostly found in bigleaf maple native to the Pacific Northwest and in tropical species like mahogany. It often machines poorly, leaving a fuzzy feel. The fuzziness usually does not scrape well. Wetting the wood and reducing the cutting angle are helpful, but sanding through finer levels of grit is generally the most effective. Blister figure, which appears as small, uneven bulges (mostly in maple), works similarly.

Worm wood (silver maple), caused by insect damage, produces striking markings. Species that are prone to burrowing insects, such as silver and red maple and paper and gray birch, exhibit dark streaks (insect tunnels) along the surface. Because the bore holes are usually small, the wood is still usable as long as the insects are exterminated early enough. Beetles, particularly the powder post variety that attack drying lumber, form maze-like patterns in the wood. Careful scraping, sanding and filling should give an acceptably stable and smooth surface.

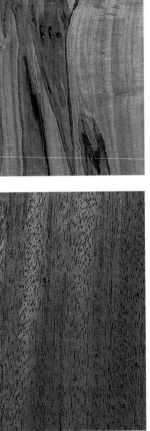

Ribbon stripe (African mahogany) figure has alternating bands of light and dark fibers caused by spiral growth. Quartersawing is needed to fully bring out the figure. Mahogany, bubinga, sapele and zebrawood are common tropical species with ribbon stripe. Elm is a common domestic hardwood with this figure. Ribbon stripe is difficult to machine cleanly. But taking slow, light passes, reducing the cutting angle and skewing the work can all be beneficial. I often harden the wood with cyanoacrylate and then scrape in both directions. When ribbon stripe is combined with a wavy grain, a mottled figure occurs.

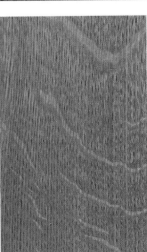

Ray flecks (quartersawn white oak) are caused by long tissue plates (called rays) oriented horizontally in a tree. Quartersawn, species with large rays, such as oak, sycamore, and beech, display highly decorative patterns. Because the ray cells are made up of weaker tissue and because they aren't always in the same plane as the surface, they tend to chip out. Keeping cutting edges, both for machines and hand tools, extra sharp is the best way to minimize chipping.

Photos these two pages: Robert Marsala

Knot and reaction wood (American elm) are caused by growth layers forming over the stem of a branch where it joins the trunk. The resulting changing grain can cause tearout on one side and not the other. But more importantly, there are hazards involved. Because reaction wood is unpredictable and because encased knots can dislodge, machining should only be done with sharp cutters and slow, light passes. This is why I prefer to work knot wood by hand. The knots tend to be hard and brittle, so I try scraping followed by sanding.

Curly (hard maple) figure is caused by the grain undulating at right angles to the length of a board. When light reflects off the surface, the wood appears wavy. Maple is the best known species to have curl, although pockets of curl, especially around knots, can be found in almost any hardwood. Common maple curl varieties include tiger stripe and fiddleback (shown here). Cherry and birch can exhibit broad diagonal curls, which are called flame. I smooth curl with coarse paper on a random-orbit sander or belt sander. I follow this with a scraper that has a heavy burr. If needed, I lightly sand with fine paper.

Spalted (beech) wood has a bold appearance, and it occurs in species that are prone to fungi attack, such as birch, maple, beech, poplar and red oak. In the initial stage of decay (before the wood becomes punky), dark stain lines form. Spalted wood works according to how much decay has taken place, and it must be surfaced before too much rot occurs. Areas surrounding the spalted area can be spongy, and they won't machine or finish evenly. Expect a large amount of waste to get enough usable, attractive wood. I work spalted wood much the same way I do worm wood.

Bird's eye (hard maple) figure is caused by localized indentations of the annual growth rings. I've seen bird's-eye figure in cherry, poplar, walnut and pecan, but the figure is most common in maple. Because the bird's eyes' dense, distorted fibers intersect perpendicularly to the boards face, they are prone to tearout. Wetting the wood between light, slow passes helps, as does reducing the cutting angle of the knives. Bird's eye usually scrapes well. To improve finishing, I use grain fillers or seal with shellac or lacquer. Applying several coats of finish and rubbing between coats is also helpful.

Crotch wood (black walnut)—Crotch wood occurs where two major branches of a tree meet and cause the cells to crowd and twist. The figure ranges from dramatic swirling patterns when sawn near the outside of the tree, as this V-shaped piece shows, to feather-shaped markings when cut through the center. Stump wood, sawn from the butt of a tree, will have figure similar to crotch when the outside of the stump is irregularly shaped due to the roots. Surprisingly, stump and crotch wood usually machine cleanly. Avoid using coarse sandpaper because the resulting scratches are difficult to remove.

Curly figure is most evident—and dramatic—in traditionally stained pieces like this reproduction of a William and Mary lowboy. Different types of figure were used skillfully to distinguish different parts of the piece (drawer front figure differs from the molding surrounding the drawers, which differs from the top).

Finding Figured Woods
Desirable defects and irregularities

by Lane DeCamp

I build mostly Colonial and Federal style American furniture in my shop, most of it in figured woods, with maple predominating. On my first projects, I'm sure I was paying well north of $20 per board foot for this lumber, even though the price sheets at the mills said $2.50 or less. Yield was awful. I was picky, and I couldn't reliably get the quality and type of figure I wanted. In those days, I ended up burning a lot of poor curly maple in my woodstove as I balanced my checkbook in disgust.

Since then, I've been fortunate enough to become acquainted with several mill owners who showed me their side of the game, and I've talked with a number of professional cabinetmakers about how they built their own woodpiles.

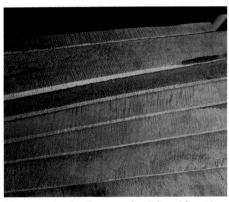

Texture is the key to the identification of curl, both on the faces and edges of rough boards. Curly figure results from wavy grain which—because it's not all in the same plane—appears as alternating bands of smooth and fuzzy wood when it's in the rough, and reflects light unevenly when it's planed.

Figured woods, regardless of the species, share a family resemblance. What is true for identifying a spectacular board of curly maple in the rough will generally hold true for identifying curly cherry, fiddleback walnut, quilted mahogany or any other figured wood. This being the case, I've chosen to discuss maple because that's the wood I use the most.

Regardless of wood technologists' or furnituremakers' distinctions, most mills distinguish only between hard maple and soft maple and then get pretty fuzzy about what is curly, fiddleback or even quilted. Nature didn't draw clear distinctions, so the mills don't either. Still, by learning what to look for, you can end up with the kind of figure you want.

Most figure only occurs in wood close to

the bark (bird's eyes are an exception). Thus, a wide board whose center comes from deep inside the tree will have curl on the sides but not in the middle. A tree will only yield a few wide boards with superb, consistent figure across their width, and the mill usually collects a dollar or two more per board foot for those boards. They're worth the extra cost, provided you can use the width to full advantage. If you're going to end up trimming the edges and cutting off the best figure, you're better off buying narrower boards or boards in which the figure is interrupted. You'll enjoy considerable savings without compromising your design in the least.

Sometimes figure jumps right out at you. Other times it's much more subtle. The physical cause of curl, the most common type of figure, is wavy-grained wood. When a log is cut into boards, the surface plane of each board becomes a section through the wavy grain. The waves present facets of different angles at the board's surface, causing light to reflect in such a way as to create the familiar rolling washboard effect (see the bottom photo on p. 86). In the rough, all you'll see are raised ridges of fuzzy grain in roughly parallel rows. Be careful, however, not to confuse sawmarks for grain. Sawmarks show up as fuzzy, raised ridges, either in arcs from a mill's circular saw or as striations from a band mill.

You should also be aware of whether there's any heartwood in a board. Unlike cherry or walnut, the desirable part of a maple tree is its sapwood. In maple, the heartwood is a small core of darker, gray-brown color. Some modern furnituremakers like boards with heartwood, but the old masters never used it, so contemporary furnituremakers who specialize in traditional furniture don't either. Often you'll find heartwood showing on one face of a board but not the other. That wood should be cheaper than boards that are heart-free on both sides. If you buy wood that's got heart on one side and you're planning to use the other face, you should anticipate losing a board every now and again as you hit heartwood while planing the sapwood side.

Where to go
I buy most of my figured lumber in eastern Pennsylvania because the selection is reliable, the kiln drying is of consistently high quality, and the prices aren't bad. If I lived in Ohio, I'd buy in Ohio or western New York. If I lived in Massachusetts, I'd go to northeastern Connecticut, Maine or New Hampshire. The point is to go to where the trees are, but not to go too far.

Many of the better mills advertise in the back of *Fine Woodworking*. I've never had a bad experience with any of them, but I always call ahead to confirm what they have in stock. These mills vary tremendously in size and character, from backyard operations to extensive warehouses. If you know what you're looking for and are courteous, you're likely to end up with some beautiful lumber.

Looking at a stack
Expect to see lumber in three states: loose in bins, in bundles on pallets and in stickered stacks. Only the endgrain is visible when lumber is stacked in bins, so you will have to remove and examine each board. It's a lot of work because the best and widest boards are usually at the bottom.

Bundles are convenient to sort through, but if you're going to have a bundle opened, plan to buy enough to make it worth the mill's time. Always check the edge-grain on a bundle you think you might be interested in—figure is usually obvious as vertical stripes on the edges. The mill will usually move a bundle into the light and provide a pallet (or a couple of logs) onto which you can transfer boards. Build a new bundle as you flip through, stacking boards flat with the ends and sides evened up. This way the mill workers can easily strap and stack it with other bundles again.

When boards are stickered, it's more work pulling, inspecting and returning them to where they belong. That's because stickering usually indicates that the lumber in question has been stacked in the order it was sawn from the log. Figure and grain will match from flitch (a horizontal section through the log) to flitch, and that commands a premium price—as long as boards are kept in order. If you mix up the boards, you destroy part of the lumber's value. If you're interested in some boards in a stickered stack, you should plan to buy several flitches at least, if not the whole stack.

Carting it away
After you've measured your purchases and paid up, it's time to pack the wood. I used to eye longingly each flatbed trailer I passed on my way to and from the mills, but no longer. For Colonial and Federal furniture construction (and for most non-architectural cabinetmaking), you'll find you can cut your rough stock down to 24-in. and 36-in. lengths without much waste. Look at cut lists or drawings for most pieces of furniture, and you'll find lengths one, two or three inches shorter than each of these nominal lengths. Because I have a pickup truck, I'll often cut 6-ft. sections (which translates to three 24-in. or two 36-in. lengths), but as my back gets worse, shorter pieces become more attractive.

If you have to transport longer lengths, be sure to bring a red flag. I use an oversized piece of fluorescent red nylon (available at most fabric stores) attached with a couple of roofing nails and some duct tape. Hardwood mills don't usually stock disposable flags, and even if they do, the plastic film they're made from won't last the drive home.

Soft curly maple

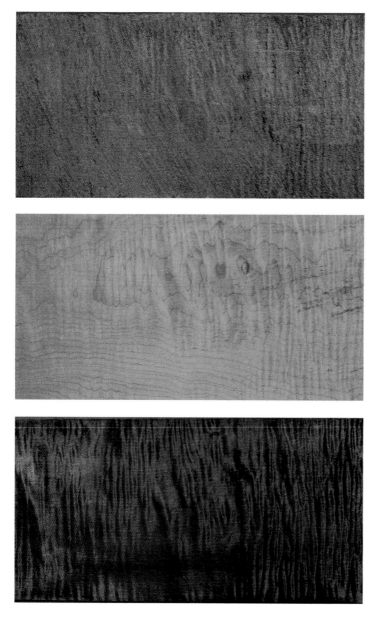

Curly maple is a staple of most specialty mills, and most of it is soft maple. Soft maple is lighter in weight than hard maple and dents with your fingernail but is, nonetheless, a good furniture wood. It doesn't warp badly, it works well with both power and hand tools and it finishes evenly. Also, it's available in wide boards (15 in. isn't unusual) and in all lengths (see the photos at left).

Soft maple curl varies widely. The boards in highest demand have tight, parallel figure of consistent intensity across the board. Depending on the tree and the way the wood was cut, the curl may travel diagonally, interlock or create many different kinds of patterns. There's no one right figure for all furniture. Instead, pick a figure compatible with your design, and pick boards with a consistent figure. Designs with mixed types of curl rarely work.

Finding good boards for the carcase seems easy after I've looked for decent legs on which to set the box. I *always* buy good curly maple in any thickness over 8/4. It's just too rare to pass up.

Good curly leg stock—if you can find it—has to meet several criteria. First it has to be free of any cracks or other kiln defects. These problems occur in plain (unfigured) maple as well, but they always seem to be worse in figured stock. I use 8/4 curly leg stock for most turned cabriole legs and usually buy this stock kiln dried. For 10/4 and thicker, I look for air-dried stock instead.

For carved cabriole legs, I usually use plain rock maple. Curly maple is harder to turn and carve anyway, and with unfigured legs, mediocre figure won't interfere with the appearance of the casework. You'll see this solution on many historic pieces.

It's a myth that Colonial and Federal cabinetmakers always had wide boards available. They too either glued up boards or settled for mediocre figure. Those old cabinetmakers also understood that wood figure doesn't have to be spectacular for a piece of furniture to be successful. There are many elements to a design, all of which contribute to its success or failure. Relying on the character of the wood to offset weaknesses in basic design is a greater mistake than using bland wood in an otherwise well-conceived design.

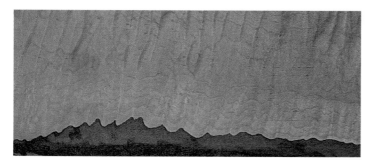

Soft curly maple boards *run much wider than hard curly maple. The board in these three photos (the same board, rough, planed and stained) is about ten inches wide, but the quality of curl is excellent. Even in the rough, beneath the arcs of the sawmarks, the curl is evident in the dirty, parallel bands of raised grain running across the board.*

Hard curly maple

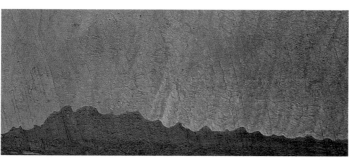

Picking hard curly maple is about the same as picking soft, but takes less effort. That's because the boards are thinner (hard maple leg stock is all but unheard of), narrower (4 in. to 6 in. is typical) and usually shorter as well. Curly hard maple has a beautiful creamy iridescence that soft maple can't offer, and the tightest curl of all (⅛ in. to ¼ in. apart or less) comes only in hard maple (see the photos at left). The wood burnishes somewhat when it's planed, so I hand scrape it just before staining to prevent an uneven finish. Otherwise, it's a beautiful, stable wood that's limited only in the dimensions available. Expect it to run a little higher in price than soft maple.

In the same way that mixed types of curl in soft maple seldom seem to work, hard and soft maples don't mix well either. Both the figures and the way they stain and finish are noticeably different. Unless you're trying to achieve a particular effect, don't use them in the same piece of furniture.

Hard curly maple *differs little from soft curly maple other than that it's slightly creamier in color and available in comparatively narrower widths. Curl occurs near the outside of the tree, hence the bark on this board. The tightest curl occurs in hard maple, but there's some variation. As with soft maple, the parallel bands of fuzzy grain are the key to recognizing hard maple in the rough.*

Blistered and quilted maple

Blistered and quilted maple are particularly common in the Northeast. Blister is my favorite type of figure, bar none. At the mills, both blister and quilted figure go for the same price as curl and sometimes for less. I've often found the best blister in the leftovers from a curly maple bin. In the rough, blister looks like very irregular curl. As long as it covers a good part of the board, you'll probably have some interesting figure. I recently picked up two 16-in.-wide boards of gorgeous quilted maple that had been part of a pallet (see the photos at left). When you find them, boards with unusual figures will surprise you, but they are worth throwing in the truck for that job you haven't planned yet.

Blister (above) and quilted figure (below) *aren't usually distinguished as such at the mills. Often you can find some outstanding examples of these figured woods in the dregs pile because in the rough, they look like extremely irregular curl—something for which the furniture industry has no use. The quilted boards were wetted with alcohol to show the figure more dramatically.*

Bird's-eye maple

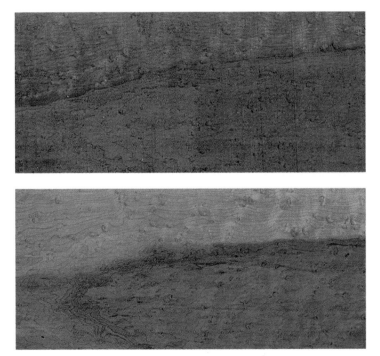

Bird, or bird's-eye maple, is the wood that cabinetmakers hate. It warps badly in the kiln, wide or long boards are rare, the figure is inconsistent and it's difficult to machine and finish. If only it wasn't so beautiful.

When you look at bird's-eye maple at a mill, look for straight lumber above all. Because of its tendency to warp, I always look for extra thickness when I buy bird. Straight boards are a blessing when you find them, but you should always try to give yourself a margin.

Consistency is the other thing to look for in bird. The eyes can vary in density, pattern and size. Everyone seems to like boards densely peppered with little eyes. In terms of workability, small eyes tend to plane and finish easily. The bigger the eyes get, the more they pull out, chip and interfere with practically any finish. Like curl, bird commands a premium price when it doesn't include any heartwood. Unfortunately, the best bird these days always seems to have some heart (see the photos at left). Japanese builders and furnituremakers discovered American maples in the last decade or so and are buying much of the best stock today.

A good example both of bird's eye and of heartwood, *this board may be representative of the future of bird. Because of its relative scarcity and of increasing demand for it, both here and abroad, good heart-free bird's eye is commanding a steep price and is becoming much more difficult to find.*

Worm scars

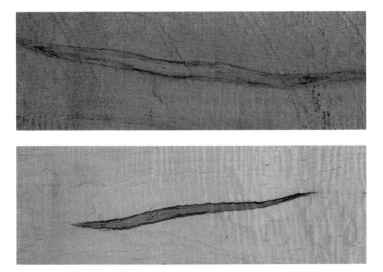

Another "defect" (depending on how you view these things) common to maple is worm scars, especially in soft curly maple. Gray-brown like the heartwood, but more concentrated, these consist of the scar tissue with which the tree has filled old worm holes (see the photos at left). They take a finish with no problem, but the long dark streak is always very evident. I happen to like worm scars, but some people don't. Boards with worm scars generally cost the same as those without. □

*Lane DeCamp injured his back moving curly maple into his workshop in Westport, Conn., so he is temporarily confined to word*working*.*

An oddity that hasn't yet become fashionable, *worm-scarred maple still has an interesting look and a certain exotic appeal. Some boards have only one or two scars (rough and finish are opposite sides of the same board here), but other boards are covered with the scars, creating interesting patterns.*

Wood Against Weather

The right product and good techniques will keep your outdoor projects from falling apart

by Jim Tolpin

With the time and effort required to construct a piece of outdoor furniture, an obvious question is what finish will protect it from the sun, rain and cold. The answers range from doing nothing to spraying on a coat of catalyzed linear polyurethane, the same stuff used to paint 747 jumbo jets. The choice of whether to finish or not to finish is not just a question of protecting the wood. You must decide how you want your outdoor furniture to look over its lifespan and how much time you're willing to invest to maintain this appearance year after year.

No finish: carefully choose the wood

Deciding not to finish means choosing a wood that is stable and rot resistant. It also means being willing to accept a coarse-textured piece of furniture that can vary in color from silver gray to dark gray or brown. The advantage of not finishing is the minimal maintenance required to keep the surface clean.

Some good woods for outdoor use are redwood, cypress and cedars. I especially like Port Orford cedar for its workability and light color. These species contain natural pesticides in their chemical makeup, and all are incredibly resistant to rot. However, these relatively soft woods offer little impact resistance, and they have been extensively over-harvested. But in recent years, several companies have formed to recycle old timbers.

For a harder wood that will stand up to bumps, choose white oak or black locust. These woods build up *tyloses*, a bubble-like formation that blocks the penetration of water into the cell structure, making them particularly well-suited for outdoor use. Two other woods usually associated with indoor furniture, black cherry and walnut, surprisingly rate with the cedars in decay resistance because of their closed-cell structure. Also, Pacific yew is a beautiful wood that outperforms even redwood in rot resistance. But these species move quite a bit with changes in moisture content,

Choose wood carefully for unfinished exterior furniture. Plantation teak, used in this bench, is a good choice because it's naturally rot-resistant and turns a beautiful silver gray. Some oth-er durable woods are white oak, cypress and cedar. These woods are easily maintained by occasionally scrubbing away dirt and mildew. Bronze caps protect the bench's feet from standing water.

Building to last

The type and quality of the finish and the material from which outdoor furniture is made contribute immensely to its beauty and to its durability. But the best of coatings and materials can be destroyed by construction techniques that trap water within the furniture. Trapped water nourishes voracious parasites that can reduce wood to a sponge cake of half-digested cellulose.

With this happy thought in mind, I'm inspired to find ways to build outdoor furniture with a second line of defense. I've learned that a structure exposed to the elements needs to be built with waterproof glues, joints that shed water without sacrificing strength and with fasteners that won't rust away.

Fasteners and adhesives

When you must attach components to one another, use a fastener made from (or coated with) a non-ferrous metal. Not only does iron rust, eventually crumbling to dust, but also it causes corrosive damage to the wood, especially to acidic woods like oak. If I don't care about appearance, I'll use a hot-dipped galvanized fastener. If appearance is important, I'll choose either stainless steel or bronze. In some applications, such as attaching thin slats to a framework, I'll use the boatbuilding technique of riveting with copper tacks and roves, a dished washer over which the end of the tack is peened (see the sources of supply box on p. 90).

Woodworkers can choose from three types of outdoor adhesives: a water-mixed plastic-resin glue, a two-part epoxy resin and Titebond II, a new one-part adhesive that the manufacturer claims will stand up to most outdoor applications except submersion. Although I've yet to try it, the convenience of an adhesive that you don't have to mix is mighty appealing. I've used Weldwood's plastic-resin glue for years. Unlike epoxy, the plastic-resin glue is not strong across gaps. But I'm allergic to epoxy, and I don't like its sensitivity to temperature during setup. For oily woods such as teak, however, epoxy remains the best choice.

Water-shedding construction

Whenever possible, I design joints so water can drain out. The canted base of the half-lap joint, as shown in the drawing at right, prevents water from accumulating under the overlapping tongue. A slot mortise-and-tenon joint, as shown in the drawing, is easy to cut, and its angled shoulders drain water from the joint. This joint exposes the tenon's end grain on a horizontal surface and should be capped, or the tenon should be stopped short, as shown in the drawing. Note that the cap has a convex top surface to shed water and a groove along its bottom edge. The groove acts as a water dam, encouraging the water to drip at this point, rather than continuing to the joint area.

Other defenses

As added insurance against water finding a home between two non-glued wood surfaces, I coat the joint's mating surfaces with a luting compound before fastening them together. Traditionally, pine tar was used for this purpose, though modern adhesive caulking compounds and specialized marine bedding compounds, such as Dolfinite by Woolsey/Z-Spar, have largely replaced pine tar (see the sources of supply box).

My last defense is common sense. Leaving unprotected legs of outdoor furniture sitting in moist soil is asking for trouble. I seal the end grain of legs with paint and set them on bricks or gravel for good drainage. I also avoid leaving my furniture sitting unprotected under blistering summer sun or under a winter's worth of snow. A tarp can protect your furniture year round when not in use, but in the winter, it's best to bring it indoors. This is why I've designed many of my chairs and tables to fold for storage. Finally, if I do decide to put a finish on the structure, I am then committed to keeping that finish intact. —*J.T.*

Drawing: Maria Meleschnig

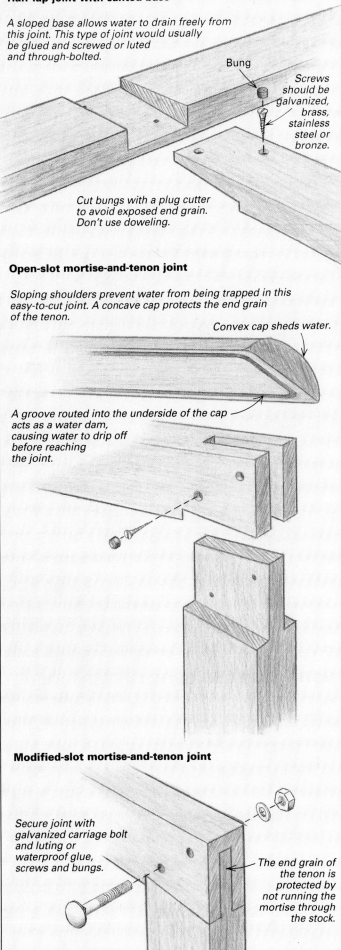

Joinery to cope with water

Half-lap joint with canted base

A sloped base allows water to drain freely from this joint. This type of joint would usually be glued and screwed or luted and through-bolted.

Bung

Screws should be galvanized, brass, stainless steel or bronze.

Cut bungs with a plug cutter to avoid exposed end grain. Don't use doweling.

Open-slot mortise-and-tenon joint

Sloping shoulders prevent water from being trapped in this easy-to-cut joint. A concave cap protects the end grain of the tenon.

Convex cap sheds water.

A groove routed into the underside of the cap acts as a water dam, causing water to drip off before reaching the joint.

Modified-slot mortise-and-tenon joint

Secure joint with galvanized carriage bolt and luting or waterproof glue, screws and bungs.

The end grain of the tenon is protected by not running the mortise through the stock.

making them prone to surface checking and warping if left unfinished.

For outstanding beauty with exceptional stability and rot resistance, nothing can beat Honduras mahogany or teak. These woods age to a gorgeous silver gray after only six months of exposure. But quotas and over-harvesting have driven prices up and availability down. The good news is that plantation teak and other lesser-known species are now being harvested, often from sustainable-yield forestry operations in tropical countries.

Inherent rot resistance is not the only criterion to consider when choosing wood to be used outside. The wood should be air-dried to a maximum 20% moisture content to provide stability and enduring, tight-fitting joints. In addition, select the stock from the heart of the tree, avoiding the sapwood. The sapwood contains—you guessed it—sap. And sap is full of sugar, a wood bug's breakfast of champions.

Selecting the right finish

To get a color other than gray and to minimize the inevitable surface checking of exposed wood, you can coat the wood with penetrating oils, varnishes, paints or epoxies. Clear penetrating oils and water sealers designed for exterior use contain ultraviolet (UV) filters and bring out the natural color of the wood. The UV filters help shield the wood from solar radiation, which destroys the lignin in the wood and reduces the wood's ability to hang on to the finish. Transparent stains and washes enhance the natural color or impart their own tint.

Finally, you can seal the wood entirely under a pigmented gloss topcoat—I call this *paint* around my shop. Paint is the right finish if you want to shield the wood from sunlight completely.

To test the longevity of the commonly available oils, stains and water seals, outdoor furnituremaker Mark Singer of Santa Barbara, Calif., subjected dozens of coated wood samples to grueling tests in an accelerated environmental chamber. After the equivalent of one year in a harsh environment, not a single sample was free from significant deterioration. Singer's suspicions were confirmed.

***Paint can't overcome poor design.** This unlined, wood planter box is destined to fail because the moist soil holds water against the wood, allowing it to seep into the joints, and these joints aren't designed to drain water. The unprotected end grain of the feet also wicks up water from the puddles in which the planter stands.*

Unless these types of finishes are constantly renewed, they loose both their protective functions and their decorative effects, and the surface of the wood eventually turns blotchy.

Gloss topcoats deliver the maximum durability in a clear finish, especially in harsh sun-drenched environments. The additives that turn a gloss finish to semi-gloss or satin soften the finish coat, reduce UV reflection and decrease longevity. Traditional spar varnish has no peer in bringing out the beauty of wood. It's durable, long lasting in a harsh marine environment and is easily renewable. As long as a varnished surface is regularly maintained (at least once a year), the color of the wood will last indefinitely. Regular maintenance includes touching up nicks and worn spots, and sanding and reapplying two new topcoats before signs of graying show up.

Modern urethane varnishes can last at least twice as long as spar varnishes, though their intrinsic hardness makes them significantly more difficult to repair. The new water-based urethane exterior varnishes are as hard and durable as their petroleum-based brethren. In addition, water-based products are less toxic during application, they recoat within hours and they are non-yellowing. None of the urethanes, however, can equal the distinctive rich glow of spar varnish.

The ultimate in long-lasting protection and gloss retention are the aerospace industry's catalyzed, two-part, linear polyurethane finishes (see the sources box). This amazing stuff, when properly applied over an epoxy undercoating, dries 50% harder than spar varnish and reportedly lasts up to five years in marine conditions. But the price is high. To coat 100 sq. ft. costs about $150.

Paint is, by far, the most protective and longest-lasting coating you can put on a piece of wood destined to live outside. The higher the gloss and the lighter the color, the better the protection. The gloss reflects the suns harmful rays, and the light colors absorb less of the heat that can break down the paint film. □

Jim Tolpin is a woodworker in Port Townsend, Wash.

Sources of supply

The following companies manufacture or supply products that can be used for building and finishing outdoor furniture:

Exterior finishes and supplies:

Detco Marine (also carries linear polyurethanes), PO Box 1246, Newport Beach, CA 92663; 800-845-0023 or 714-631-8480

Hydrocote Co. Inc., PO Box 160, Tennent, NJ; 908-257-4344

Interlux Co., 2270 Morris Ave., Union, NJ 07083; 908-686-1300

Woolsey/Z-Spar Marine Paints, 36 Pine St., Rockaway, NJ 07866; 800-221-4466

X-I-M Products, Inc., Westlake, OH 44145; 800-262-8469

Brushes and painting tools:

The Wooden Boat Store, PO Box 78, Brooklin, ME 04616; 800-225-5205

The Wooden Boat Shop, 1007 N.E. Boat St., Seattle, WA 98105; 800-933-3600

Exterior fasteners:

Doc Freeman's, 999 N. Northlake Way, Seattle, WA 98103; 800-423-8641

Jamestown Distributors, PO Box 348, Jamestown, RI 02835; 800-423-0030

Copper nails and roves:

Ray Speck Boatbuilding, 228 37th. St., Port Townsend, WA 98368; 206-385-4519

Waterproof adhesives:

DAP Inc., PO Box 277, Dayton, OH 45401; 800-543-3840

Franklin International, 2020 Bruck St., Columbus, OH 43207; 614-443-0241

Gougeon Brothers Inc., PO Box 908, Bay City, MI 48707; 517-684-7286

Information on tropical woods:

Woodworkers Alliance for Rainforest Protection (WARP), PO Box 133, Coos Bay, OR 97420; 503-269-6907

Rainforest Alliance, 65 Bleecker St., 6th Floor, New York, NY 10012; 212-941-1900

Photos except where noted: Jim Tolpin

Applying exterior finishes

Pros use certain tricks to get outstanding results every time. While these tricks may not make you a pro overnight, they are sure to improve your results. But first, you might as well get used to hearing this timeless platitude: A finish is only as good as its preparation. This is as true for simple wipe-on stains as for the most expensive catalyzed urethane paint.

Preparing the surface

Preparation means well-sanded surfaces, including sanding after raising the grain with a damp rag. Hardwoods need only be sanded to 120-grit, as long as all sanding scratches from the previous grit have been removed. Softwoods should be sanded to 220-grit. Never use steel wool to smooth wood destined for the outdoors. The remnants of steel in the pores of the wood will rust and ruin the finish.

Preparation also means well-cleaned surfaces. Wash off oily handprints with a rag dampened with thinner and follow with a light sanding. Before applying the first coat of a primer or a sealer, thoroughly vacuum the wood, and then use a tack rag to wipe away any remaining particles.

Most finishes can be put on directly from the can by brushing, wiping or spraying. The only trick is to not recoat too quickly. Follow the manufacturer's directions. Some finishes, especially the penetrating oils, should never be applied in direct sunlight. Bill Kennedy of Specialty Furniture Co., a manufacturer of outdoor furniture in Mt. Pleasant, Mich., says that sun-heated wood can bleed out the finish, which then glazes on the surface. Because oil finishes are not designed to stand on the surface like a varnish, they quickly crack and craze, and eventually peel off, requiring stripping and sanding to a clean, solid surface before refinishing.

Applying varnish

For a clear, smooth and uniform coating of varnish, follow these basic practices:
● Mix varnish by gently stirring with a paddle, never by shaking it. The resultant bubbles end up as holes and bumps in the surface film.
● Never use the finish straight from the can. Instead, strain it through a paper cone filter into a clean bucket.
● Use professional varnish brushes made from fine China bristle or badger hair grouped into an oval cross section. These brushes cost a small fortune, but they contribute immensely to the illusion that your varnish job had a pro behind the brush. Never use your varnish brushes for paint.
● Avoid varnishing in cool, damp conditions, or in direct sunlight. Cold prevents the film

from hardening properly, and the sun's heat hardens the outer surface of the film too quickly, resulting in wrinkles and sags. Also, gases in the warmed wood bubble up through the finish, leaving pock marks.

I'm pretty good at applying varnish, but Julia Maynard, a full-time, freelance painter and varnisher in Port Townsend, Wash., is the best I've seen. Here are her recommendations for a durable professional-looking varnish finish:
● Use a marine-grade spar varnish with ultraviolet (UV) filters. Beginners would do well with a less dense, less expensive variety such as Interlux's Schooner Varnish (see the sources of supply box). It flows easily and sets up quickly to reduce wrinkling and sagging problems, and it holds up nearly as well as the most expensive varieties.
● To extend the life of the varnish coating, especially when applied to oily woods such as teak, use a volatile and highly penetrative undercoat. The best is Flashbond 300, made by X-I-M Products (see the sources box).
● To build up enough UV filtration to really protect the wood, especially in sunny climates, apply at least five coats of varnish.

No finish lasts forever. This white oak door, built for a client seven years ago by the author and finished with six coats of spar varnish, shows the effects of exposure and neglect. The finish at the top of the door, protected by the overhanging wall, is still in good shape, but at the fully exposed bottom, the finish is completely gone.

Apply each coat carefully—think of each layer as the final coat. To avoid lap marks, apply the varnish from the dry area back to the wet area.
● Use a hand block, never a power sander, to sand to 280-grit between coats, removing all brush marks and other imperfections.
● Never use thinner to clean off the dust between coats (it reduces adhesion). Instead, vacuum and wipe with a tack rag.
● For a super final finish, go to a sixth coat. But first, sand the gloss off the last coat with 320-grit wet-or-dry paper, being careful not to cut through the topcoat. Clean away the dust, and apply the last coat with all the skill you've acquired over the first five coatings.

Applying paint

As with varnish, there are similar precautions to take for a durable, first-class paint job. Don't shake—stir the paint. Don't use it straight from the can; filter it into a clean bucket. Apply paint at room temperature and out of the direct sun. And finally, use a good China bristle brush to apply paint.

Follow these steps to achieve a top-notch paint finish:
● Fill countersunk screw holes with wood plugs (bungs), fixing them in place with shellac or varnish. Don't glue the bungs if you might want to get to the screws again.
● Sand the surfaces to 120-grit for hardwoods, or 220-grit for softwoods. Raise the grain with a damp rag at the 100-grit stage, and then sand off the protruding fibers.
● Fill small defects with a glazing compound (be sure it is compatible with your paint) or a specialized surfacing compound such as Interlux's #257 (see the sources box).
● Vacuum and tack the surfaces thoroughly. Julia Maynard then wipes the surfaces with a rag dampened with isopropyl alcohol to pick up fine dust and draw any surface moisture out of the wood.
● Apply the primer coats. Yes, that's plural. Build up the paint thickness with three coats of primer. Maynard, and many other professional exterior painters, do not, however, recommend using standard primers. They think the surface left by primers is too chalky for the best topcoat adhesion. They prefer a thinned-down semigloss topcoat paint. White is okay for most colors, but gray is best for low-hide colors like red and yellow. Sand between primer coats with 150-grit paper to remove all brush streaks, runs and drips.
● Sand the last coat of primer to 400-grit, clean up, and apply the gloss topcoat, always brushing from the dry area back to the wet area to avoid lap marks.

To make all this worthwhile, buy the most expensive enamel. It will only be a few bucks more per gallon. Oil or latex-based enamels are about equal in durability. But don't bust the bank on marine oil-based enamels unless you know the furniture will be exposed to salt air, intense sunshine and an occasional splash of gasoline. —*J.T.*

From *Fine Woodworking* (May 1993) 100:88-91

Buying and Drying
How to find and season your own lumber

by Todd Scholl

Fig. 1: Log yield

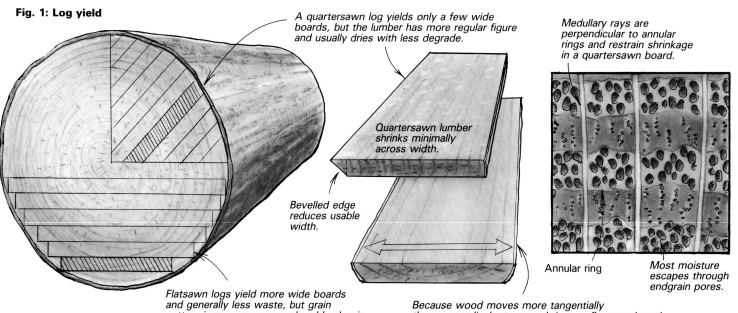

A quartersawn log yields only a few wide boards, but the lumber has more regular figure and usually dries with less degrade.

Medullary rays are perpendicular to annular rings and restrain shrinkage in a quartersawn board.

Quartersawn lumber shrinks minimally across width.

Bevelled edge reduces usable width.

Annular ring

Most moisture escapes through endgrain pores.

Flatsawn logs yield more wide boards and generally less waste, but grain pattern is more pronounced and lumber is more susceptible to warp.

Because wood moves more tangentially than perpendicular to annual rings, a flatsawn board shrinks and swells considerably in width.

Getting lumber from the sawmill to the tablesaw yourself can be a long and difficult process, but it is a worthwhile one. Professionals and amateurs alike can realize hefty savings by buying lumber right at the mill and drying it themselves. You can save 50% or more by dealing directly with a sawmill instead of with a lumber retailer.

Economics aside, there are other less-tangible benefits. Having operated my own small sawmill at one time, I enjoy talking to sawyers and rummaging around sawmills. I've developed a greater understanding of wood and have learned that handling it carefully early on produces better material and ultimately benefits the furniture I build. I find great satisfaction in buying green lumber, drying it and turning it into a fine piece of woodwork.

Before you set out to hunt lumber at the source, you need to decide what species, size and quality wood you want. If you're building furniture, you'll probably be most interested in hardwoods, but you'll need to get straight on the thickness (4/4, 6/4, 8/4, and so on); the width (typically most mills saw boards in random widths up to 16 in.); and the lengths (which are also most often random). For the best furniture work, the highest hardwood grade, firsts and seconds (FAS), is appropriate. But good bargains can be had in the lesser grades that most sawmills are likely to deal in. For more on grading, consult the reading list at the end of this article.

The entire business of grading is a tricky matter. Often sawyers' interpretations of grading will vary so greatly from the official rules that it renders the issue moot. In fact, "run-of-the-mill" is the most common grade I've found used by backwoods sawyers. Any board that comes off the mill is given this general designation, good or bad. Some mills are only slightly more sophisticated, separating lumber into vague categories like "good" or "bad." Good is anything that's No. 2 common or better; bad is anything worse. This is further confused by regional terminology: In central Kentucky, where I ran my mill, what a lot of sawyers called "barn lumber" would be called utility, pallet or secondary lumber in other parts of the country. Disregard this hazy grading and learn the official rules. That way, you'll be less likely to be duped by a fast-talking sawyer and better able to compare prices quoted by various mills.

The output of small sawmills varies widely. At my mill, we sawed lumber for a variety of purposes, including furniture, but many of the neighboring mills sawed only for barn wood or pallets—a grade that's of little use to woodworkers because it has too many defects and is often too thin after drying to produce a board usable for furniture work. If possible, you should locate a mill that saws for grade rather than for yield. Grade sawmills treat logs more carefully and they're equipped and willing to saw logs that will produce furniture-grade lumber. Those that saw for

From *Fine Woodworking* (January 1988) 68:58-61

yield are more interested in large volumes of lower-quality lumber. I know many sawyers who don't know (or care) about sawing for grade and are more interested in production; the more board feet the better. Having been in the business, I can sympathize. Frankly, it often doesn't pay for a sawyer to sort out and market the few furniture-grade boards a marginal log yields. Often high-quality logs never make it to the sawyer anyway, having been skimmed off and sent directly to a veneer plant.

Finding a mill—One of the best ways to find a sawmill is by talking with other woodworkers. If you can find a woodworker who deals directly with a mill, you've eliminated 80% of your worries. First off, you'll be talking with another woodworker—someone who speaks your language. You'll also be dealing with a mill that has worked with a woodworker and thus should have a better idea of what you'll need.

There are other ways to find green lumber. Try the Yellow Pages for sawmills or lumber dealers. Local lumberyard workers may have knowledge of local mills, or you can consider contacting the local forest or agricultural extension agent, because many mills get their logs from government land. If all this fails, a drive in the hills might turn up a shed or barn built of freshly sawn lumber. You might stop and ask where the lumber was purchased and go from there.

I have lived in many parts of the country and have always found a suitable mill within 50 miles of my home. Once I have a lead on a mill, I usually call (if there's a phone) to find out what wood species the mill saws, what they charge per board foot, green, and whether their lumber is graded. I also ask if the lumber is stacked and stickered, if it's covered, and if I can pick through the pile. If the answers sound promising, I'll check out the mill in person.

It's useful to walk around the mill before you buy to see what kinds of logs are being sawn, how they're sawed and what kind of job the mill is doing. If you don't know what you're looking for, you're in a less-desirable bargaining position and missing a good opportunity to learn more about lumber buying. Check to see if the lumber is sawn heavy, which means it is ⅛ in. oversize in thickness. If you're buying green 4/4 lumber, it should be at least a full inch thick and, ideally, ⅛ in. thicker. If it's not the full 4/4, you'll be lucky to get a ¾-in.-thick finished board when it shrinks and dries. Consistency is the measure of a well-run mill, too. A worn-out head rig, sloppily operated, might saw a 4/4 board that's a full inch thick at one end, but 1½ in. thick at the other end. Such boards are trouble. When you feed the thin end into the planer, it jams when the feed rollers encounter the greater thickness.

Ideally, the lumber stacks should be level, stickered properly, covered against the weather and sorted by grade and species. Steer clear of lumber from crooked stacks sitting in a muddy yard or bleaching in the sun, no matter how inexpensive the lumber is. Such stacks are likely to contain lots of warped, bowed and crowned lumber, which only causes grief later. If the mill checks out, ask the sawyer specifically what he charges. As in any purchase, quality costs money and you'll probably pay more at a well-run mill where the sawyer takes time to stack his wood. At our mill, we charged 25 cents per bd. ft. for run-of-the-mill oak—stacked, but not graded—and 30 cents for No. 2 or better. Some mills won't dicker with you on price, some will. We were always willing to discount the price if the buyer helped out by stacking lumber. But be clear on what you are getting into before you offer to trade labor for lumber. Find out too if the sawyer

Dick Pawloski, a sawmill operator in Bethel, Conn., hefts a flat-sawn FAS 4/4 oak plank fresh from the mill. The board has been edged, trimmed to length and graded, and is ready for drying.

Sawyers can get so busy that they often don't have time to properly stack the lumber they've sawn. The back stack is good, but steer clear of lumber piled like that in the foreground. Lumber from such piles often contains a high percentage of cracked, cupped, bowed and twisted boards.

will let you pick through the stacks if you promise to restack and resticker it. We found, however, that most people didn't know how or didn't care to restack our lumber. Assure the sawyer you'll be different from the rest.

Custom sawing—An interesting way to work with sawyers is to bring your log to the mill and have it sawn to your specifications. You'll need a basic knowledge of sawing and a good rapport with the sawyer before you try this. My experience with custom sawing has been good and I've enjoyed sawing other people's logs for them. If you have your logs sawn, make sure they are clean and free of rocks, nails, and especially barbed wire. If we hit wire, nails or any foreign object, it was our policy to charge the customer for a new set of sawteeth. Before having your log sawn, find out what the sawyer will charge for a damaged blade. It can cost anywhere from $200 to sharpen teeth to $1,000 or more to replace a blade. A sawyer will want to know whether a tree came from the forest or from someone's yard where it could have acquired any number of metal objects, such as fence wire, pocket knives, nails or screws. Forest trees will likely be cleaner, but avoid trees along boundary lines. Look for deformities on the bark that indicate metal lurking within.

If it's your log being sawn or the sawing is being done to your

Rhode Island woodworker Geoff Warner's drying shed has a large overhang to protect lumber against rain. Although not critical, lumber sheds should be oriented to be open to the north, with the southern exposure covered to prevent losses from rapid drying.

specifications, consider having the lumber quartersawn. Left to their own, most mills don't like to quartersaw because it's slow and somewhat wasteful. As is shown in figure 1, a quartersawn log produces more narrow boards, many of which will have beveled edges that reduce their usable width. But in exchange for narrower boards, quartersawing in species like oak and ash yields delightful grain patterns. In addition, quartersawn lumber is more stable than plainsawn, because its annual rings are perpendicular to the face of each board rather than tangential; as a result, most shrinkage occurs in the board's thickness rather than its width. Even a log that is plainsawn, however, will produce a few quartersawn boards at its center.

Drying your find—Once you've bought a load of lumber, you need to dry it. This process begins with air drying, progresses to indoor drying, or to custom drying done at a commercial kiln. The lowest moisture content you can air dry wood to in most climates, except for the desert, is about 12%, but ranges from 15% to 20% are more likely. Kiln drying will further reduce moisture content to the 6% to 8% suitable for furniture.

Air drying lumber is not particularly difficult, but because you're at the mercy of the weather, it's not a controlled procedure like kiln drying, so some precautions are necessary. Long before I consider stacking the lumber, I take steps to reduce rapid moisture loss, which will cause end checking. Immediately after bucking logs to length, or taking possession of them, I coat their ends with glue, polyurethane varnish or paraffin to reduce moisture loss through endgrain. I see to it that the logs are sawed into boards as soon as possible and then preferably stacked immediately after sawing, because this is when the most rapid drying takes place. If I've bought already-sawn lumber, I end coat the boards as soon as I pick them up at the mill or immediately after stacking. This is critical during the summer: A board left in the hot summer sun for an hour could split disastrously, and end coating helps to reduce radical moisture loss.

Some sawmills dry lumber in the open without cover, some stack it vertically on racks, and some just dead stack it (without stickers between the layers). I strongly recommend against all these methods, because they are likely to produce a high degree of degrade lumber, ranging from cupped or bowed boards to fungi stains that form when damp boards lie together. I have been most successful in drying lumber in a well-ventilated shed built for that purpose or in a drafty barn. Such a structure protects wood from too-rapid drying from direct sunlight, while shielding

it from rain and snow. A reasonable size for a drying shed is about 20 ft. long, perhaps 10 ft. wide, with an open-facing long wall on one side and a louvered, or burlap-draped wall on the other. Its siding boards should have no more than 2 in. and no less than ½ in. between them to allow for air circulation. Variations on this design are endless, but the point remains: The lumber needs to be protected from rain without being sealed off from breezes that will carry away the moisture.

I stack the thinnest boards at the bottom so wood stacked on top will weigh them down against bowing. Where possible, wider boards should go inside the pile rather than near the edges where too-fast drying might cause them to split. Boards that are very long should be stacked on the bottom of the pile as well—an unsupported end from a long board sticking out from the center of a stack may sag as it dries, crooking the board. To separate each layer from the next, place ¾-in.-square stickers about 24 in. apart along the length of the pile. As you build the stack, keep the stickers vertically aligned to keep uneven weight distribution from kinking your boards. For stability, the stacks should be neatly piled and level. This could require that you keep a few extra stickers on hand that are a little thinner or thicker than ¾ in. to make up for inconsistencies in the thickness of the lumber. Leave a foot or two between each stack to ensure adequate air movement. If your shed has a dirt floor or you are just drying wood outside with a sheet of plywood over it, support the stack at least a foot off the ground. A foundation of timbers supported on concrete blocks spaced about 16 in. on center, front of the stack to back, works well.

The old-timer's rule of a year of air drying per inch of thickness is, at best, a speculative way to determine when your lumber is dry enough. The only sure-fire way to track all of the variables at work in air drying is to use a moisture meter to periodically test a sample board. You can buy a moisture meter for about $100 or make your own (see the reading list). In any case, select a board from *inside* the stack for testing and measure the moisture every few weeks until it gets down to 20% or lower. This could take anywhere from a few months to a year or more, depending on the species, its thickness, the location of the stack and the climate where you live. Far and away, temperature and humidity most affect how fast wood dries. Generally, the best drying period runs from July to September, but the farther north you go, the shorter the season. Thus, a stack of 4/4 oak that dries in a single season in Alabama might require two years or more to dry in northern Minnesota.

If you intend to make a habit of air drying, keep records of how long it takes to dry the various species you are working with. Also, date each stack of lumber; it's easy to loose track of how long a stack has been drying, especially when you have several going at once.

Finish drying—Once your wood has dried to the 20% range, you're ready to finish dry it. If you've paid 30 cents per foot for 100 bd. ft. of FAS oak, you now have an investment of $30 plus your time. You must now decide whether you want to hold your costs to the bare minimum by drying the wood in a heated room, or spring for the additional cost of drying in a commerical kiln. Commercial drying is affordable, provided you have enough lumber to make it worth transporting to the kiln. Typically, expect to pay 15 cents to 20 cents per bd. ft. for kiln drying.

In the East and Midwest, hardwood kilns are quite numerous; the sawyer you buy from is likely to know where one is located or you can check the phone book for leads. If the kiln does custom drying, the operator will want to know what species and how much lumber you have, its thickness and length, the current moisture content and what you want the finished moisture content to be. In most cases, this will be 6% to 10%. Plan as far ahead as you can. Every species requires a different drying schedule, and where one kiln might mix species in a drying run, another will not.

Final inspection—Kiln operators don't generally guarantee results, so inspect your lumber carefully before and after it comes from the kiln. The boards should emerge bright, free of stains, cracks and cup, and they should machine normally. Lumber that's been pushed too fast through the drying schedule might become casehardened. This occurs because the board's outside shell dries too fast, causing it to shrink around the wet core. This puts the shell in tension and causes it to set oversize. When the core eventually shrinks, the shell is pulled into compression. (Or, the wood itself may give during improper drying, which can cause deep surface checking or internal failures such as collapse and honeycombing.) Kilns usually try to ensure against casehardening by conditioning the wood, slowly raising the humidity at the end of the drying cycle. Figure 2, right, shows how to test for casehardening and reverse casehardening, which occurs when the conditioning is carried too far, causing the core to be in compression and the shell in tension. For more information on kiln degrade, I suggest reading the *Dry Kiln Operator's Manual* (see reading list). The good news is that if you find the lumber has been casehardened, you can take it back to the kiln and ask the operator to condition the lumber again. If the lumber is reverse casehardened, however, it's ruined.

If you plan to dry several hundred board feet yearly, heated-room drying is the most economical way to go. Of course, you can't do thousands of feet of lumber (unless you have a very large house), but it is feasible to dry up to 800 bd. ft. a year. And, I find it satisfying to see wood that will later become furniture drying in my living room. You can also use your attic, but be careful here: During the summer, an attic will get too hot, accelerating drying and causing horrible checking. Be sure the attic is well ventilated, preferably with a fan, so the moisture released from the wood can escape.

Before bringing it indoors, inspect your lumber for pests such as spiders, ants and more-destructive boring critters like powderpost beetles or termites. If you find suspicious-looking holes in the wood or tiny frass hills, leave it outside. Strip off any bark or decayed areas on the boards that might conceal insects. And though you may be tempted to hasten the drying process, leave adequate space between a stack and radiators, electric baseboard heaters or hot-air ducts. Similarly, stacking wood near a wood stove or fireplace is inviting splits and cracks, not to mention the danger of fire. Stack the lumber as you would outside, with evenly spaced stickers.

With your moisture meter, continue to monitor your lumber. As soon as its moisture content nears 10% or less, remove the stickers and dead stack the lumber. Leaving the stickers in place will encourage air flow between the boards and they'll actually begin to pick up moisture rather than lose more. Store your lumber in a rack or blocked up off the floor in the shop or the place where you intend to use it. That way, the wood will arrive at an equilibrium moisture content with the environment, reducing the chances of unexpected twists, warps and bows. Once machined, it's important to stack boards on a flat surface and weigh them down to reduce bowing or cupping. By the way, the same holds true for glued-up panels—they only look stable, and if left on their own, they can bow or cup. Wood will always move, so cover

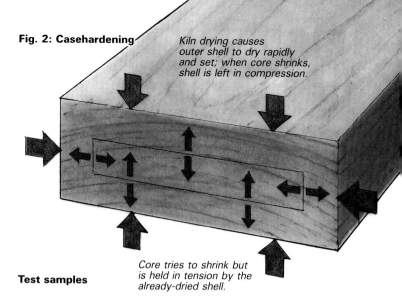

Fig. 2: Casehardening

Kiln drying causes outer shell to dry rapidly and set; when core shrinks, shell is left in compression.

Core tries to shrink but is held in tension by the already-dried shell.

Test samples

Saw core from sample piece

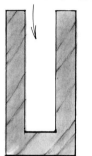  

In correctly conditioned sample, prongs remain parallel.

Prongs turn inward if the board is casehardened.

A reverse casehardened sample shows results of overconditioning. Core is in compression and shell in tension, turning prongs outward.

the panels to prevent marring and then weigh them down.

How much can you save by drying your own wood? I can buy run-of-the-mill green walnut at 80 cents per bd. ft. From a lumber dealer, kiln-dried FAS walnut would cost $3 or more per bd. ft. Even after driving to the sawmill, picking through the stack, stacking, air drying and moving it indoors, I will not have significantly added to my cost. If I decide to pay an extra 20 cents to have 1,000 ft. kiln dried, I'd still save about $2,000 that I can invest in more machinery or, better yet, more wood. □

Todd Scholl is a woodworker and teacher. He lives in Wray, Colo. Barbara Rowley, a freelance editor, contributed to this article. She lives in Florissant, Colo.

Further reading

Rules for the Measurement and Inspection of Hardwood and Cypress, $5.00 ppd.; *Introduction to the Grading and Measurement of Hardwood and Cypress*, $1.25 ppd. National Hardwood Lumber Association, P.O. Box 34518, Memphis, TN 38184-0518.
Drying Eastern Hardwood Lumber, $5.50 ppd.; *Dry Kiln Operator's Manual*, $7.00 ppd.; *Air Drying of Lumber, A Guide to Industry Practices*, $4.75 ppd. Superintendent of Documents, U.S. Government Printing Office, Washington, DC 20402-9325.
Understanding Wood, A craftsman's guide to wood technology by R. Bruce Hoadley, 1980, $17.95; *FWW On Wood and How to Dry It*, $7.95; containing articles on wood species, how to air dry wood, how to build a kiln, how to build a moisture meter and related topics such as sawmills and basic woodlot management, 1986. The Taunton Press, Box 355, Newtown, CT 06470.

Taking the Measure of Moisture Meters

A neglected tool becomes more versatile

by John Sillick

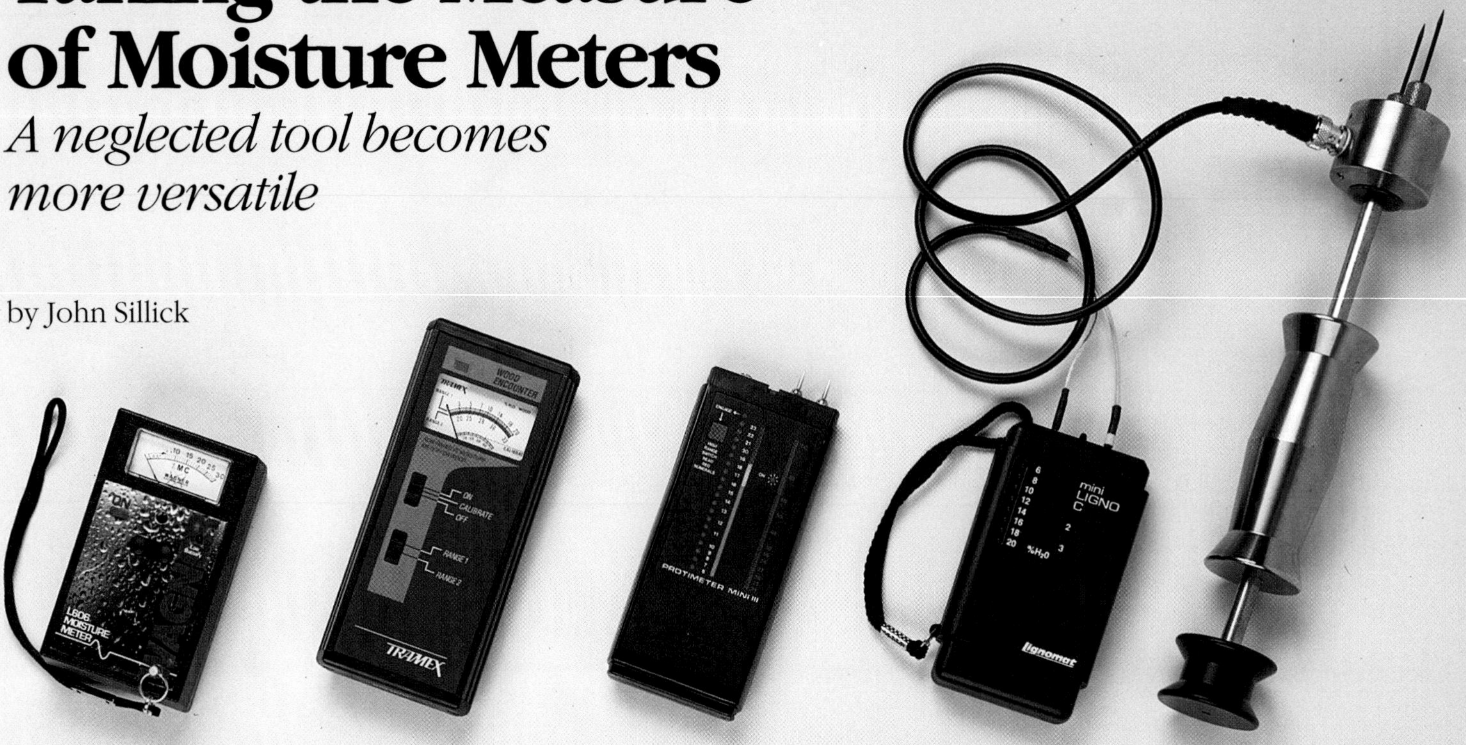

Meter types vary—*The author measured moisture with 18 meters from nine manufacturers for this article. Shown here from left are the Wagner L606 and the Tramex Wood Encounter, both pin-less units that use an electromagnetic field to detect moisture; the Protimeter Mini III and the Lignomat Mini Ligno C, with an optional remote probe for deep measurements.*

I suffered my greatest woodworking embarrassment some 20 years ago. Friends of ours with a large family needed a big kitchen table that wouldn't cost too much. I decided I could oblige. I trucked over to the lumberyard and bought a half dozen spruce 2x8's, reassured by the "kiln dried" stamped all over them. The finished table looked all right, in a clunky, overbuilt way. That is, it did until two months later when each board in the top had shrunk away from its neighbor, and it compared unfavorably to a picnic table. In the years since, through making and restoring furniture and drying my own lumber, I've come to understand that learning to deal with moisture and shrinkage is the most important lesson a worker in solid wood has to learn.

Moisture leads to most of the failures in things made of wood. (The other cause, wild teenage parties, is a distant second.) Tenons on chair stretchers that have higher moisture content (MC) than the legs they join can shrink and sabotage the joint. Parts cut from thick sticks of wood that aren't thoroughly dried will stress anything they're built into because they'll shrink unevenly. A beautifully planed and sanded panel can wind up uneven if it's glued up with adjacent boards at different moisture contents: When the boards reach equilibrium in their new environment, some will have shrunk or expanded more than others. Drawers and doors that swell too much for their openings and stick can cause frustration, abuse and breakage. In many cases, you have to be able to anticipate not only that the wood is going to move with the exchange of moisture but also how much it's going to move.

Luckily, predicting wood movement has gotten a lot easier for the small-shop and the part-time woodworker in recent years. A moisture meter small enough to slip into your pocket can tell you what you need to know to anticipate what any given board will do in the future. With the profusion of moisture meters in the marketplace now at prices as low as $29, there's no excuse for overlooking moisture-content problems any longer.

To sort through the field of available moisture meters, I recently gathered 18 of them, from the most basic to the more sophisticated, and put them to work measuring the moisture content in some boards I'd been air-drying. I've put together a chart (see pp. 98-99) with the specifications of all the meters, the features I think are most important to weigh in deciding between them, and the results of my evaluation of the meters. To put the chart in context, I'll describe the different types of meters and how they work, the range of features and accessories available, and the time-honored oven-drying method I used for comparing their readings.

Two types of meters

All moisture meters function by measuring the way moisture affects the electrical properties of wood, but different meters measure different properties. There are two main types of meters, probed and probeless, as shown in the drawing on the facing page. The great majority are probed. They have two or more pins that are pushed into the wood, and they operate as sensitive ohm-meters. Direct current travels out one pin into the moist wood and is picked up by another pin. Dry wood allows little current to pass, damper wood permits more. The meter reads how much resistance there is to the current and correlates the resistance to moisture content.

A second group of meters can measure moisture content without piercing the wood with probes. These meters emit electrical waves through a sensor that is pressed against the wood. The waves create an electromagnetic field (EMF) the size of the sensor to a depth of up to ¾ in. The field behaves differently depending on how much moisture is in the wood. EMF meters can measure the capacity of the wood to store energy (capacitance), the amount of power the wood absorbs from the field (power loss), or the wood's resistance to the field (impedance). Some meters use one of these means; others use several in combination. Like their

Photos except where noted: Sloan Howard

Low tech and high-tech meters—Prices and features ranged widely among the meters, from $29 for the Sonin Rapitest pictured here at center, to $750 for the Delmhorst RDM 2S at right, which stores 3,000 readings and can be linked to a computer. The other meters in the photo are, from left, the Electrophysics MT 270, the Timber Check and the Moisture Register DC 2000.

probed cousins, these meters then translate this electrical information to determine what percentage moisture is present.

Probing questions—Most probed meters have a pair of pins on one end of the unit. The consensus among manufacturers is that the pins should penetrate one-fifth to one-quarter of the thickness of the stock to get a legitimate reading of a board's moisture content. On a 4/4 board, the probes can read true if pushed in only ¼ in. On an 8/4 board, the probes should penetrate ½ in. Under the pounding they take, pins will sometimes bend or break, but most are easily and cheaply replaced.

To take readings on thick or dense stock, it's best to hook up your meter to an external probe. These come in several types. One style has a heavy weight that you slide along a steel shaft to help drive and extract the pins, as shown in the photo above. Another type can be hand-driven or tapped in with a mallet. Many meters have jacks for the leads to external probes. Others have caps that link the external probe leads to the pins on the case. A low-tech alternative for meters without an external probe is to drive a pair of nails into the board and connect them to the pins on the meter itself with wires and alligator clips (see the photo on p. 98). External probes and the depth of penetration they provide constitute one of the strongest advantages of probed meters. The major drawback of probed meters, of course, is that you have to pierce the stock to take a reading.

Look Ma, no pins—Electromagnetic-field meters don't require a lot of finesse to use. You press the meter's sensor against the surface of the board, and take a reading. The wood can be in the rough, milled flat or part of a finished piece of work. The meters do like to have complete contact between the sensor and the wood, so it's best to push firmly when checking rough-milled stock. To get a fair reading, the wood must be at least as wide as the sensor, which in most EMF units is 2 in. to 3 in. And when using EMF meters, you must remember they are capable of reading right through thin lumber and factoring in the moisture content of your benchtop.

Unlike probed meters, which read the wettest gradient their pins pass through, EMF meters average the moisture content in the area of their magnetic field. With an EMF meter, you can quickly get a picture of the moisture content of a board all

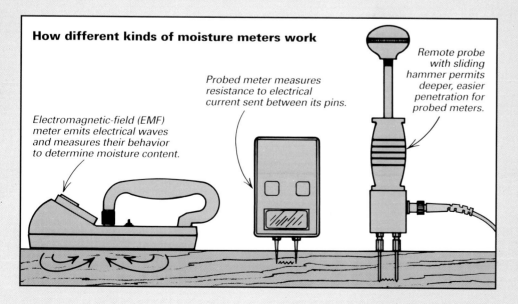

How different kinds of moisture meters work

Electromagnetic-field (EMF) meter emits electrical waves and measures their behavior to determine moisture content.

Probed meter measures resistance to electrical current sent between its pins.

Remote probe with sliding hammer permits deeper, easier penetration for probed meters.

Drawing: Maria Meleschnig

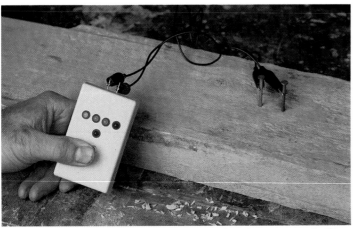

Probing deep in the wood—*A couple of nails, wires and alligator clips let you take deep readings with an ordinary meter. Electrophysics supplies this kit with its inexpensive meters.*

Moisture meter review Model	Country of origin	Type of sensor	Reading range (% moisture content)
Delmhorst J-88 (800) 222-0638	USA	Probe, ½ in.	6-20%
Delmhorst J-3	USA	Probe, 5⁄16 in.	6-30%
Delmhorst RDM-2S	USA	External probe	4.5-60%
Electrophysics MT-80 (519) 668-2871	Canada	Probe, ½ in.	6-15%
Electrophysics MT-270	Canada	Probe, ½ in.	4-30%
Electrophysics CT-1000	Canada	EMF+	0-40%
Lignomat Mini Ligno C (800) 227-2105	USA	Probe, 3⁄16 in., 7⁄16 in.	6-20%
Lignomat Mini Master H	Germany	External probe	6-75%
Moisture Register DC 2000 (909) 392-5833	USA	Probe, 7⁄16 in.	5-62%
Moisture Register Model L	USA	EMF	0-25%
Protimeter Mini III (800) 321-4878	England	Probe, ½ in.	6-100%
Sonin Rapitest (800) 225-1153	Taiwan	External probe, 9⁄16 in.	10-28%
Timber Check B350 (800) 667-2986	Canada	Probe, ¾ in.	6-25%
Tramex Compact (303) 582-3538	Ireland	Probe, 3⁄8 in.	7-42%
Tramex Wood Encounter	Ireland	EMF	3-33%
Tramex Moisture Encounter	Ireland	EMF	10-20%
Wagner L606 (503) 582-0541	USA	EMF	5-30%
Wagner L601 DF	USA	EMF	5-30%

+ EMF = Electromagnetic field

along its length, without marring it in the slightest. But with thick stock, core readings will be out of reach, as the electromagnetic field's depth of penetration is fixed, usually at ¾ in. or less.

Features

Deciding which moisture meter to buy is largely a matter of sorting through the features: how they account for different species of wood and metering conditions, the range of moisture they're equipped to detect, how those readings are displayed and how well the manufacturer explains the product and its uses.

Species correction—Just as different species of wood have different working properties, their characteristic structural and chemical qualities cause them to have different electrical properties. In dry wood (say, 7% MC), the difference between species is negligible. But for moister wood, in the 12% to 15% range that's normal for air-dried lumber, different species will display significant differences. The readings of both probed and EMF meters are affected by these differences. A piece of white pine may read as much as 4% different from a piece of white oak at the same moisture content. Each meter is equipped in some way to deal with these disparities. Most meters come with a table of corrections that lists common species of wood and gives you a number to add to or subtract from the meter reading to calculate the correct moisture content. Tables can be fairly cursory, with few species and simplistic corrections or extremely detailed, with a broad range of species and corrections tagged to specific readings. Some meters replace such tables with internal corrections for a wide range of species: You punch in the species and the microprocessor does the rest. Others have more general internal corrections, with a dial that is flipped between two or three classes of species.

Whichever way it is done, species correction adds accuracy. You'll have to decide whether you want to pay for the convenience of electronic corrections and whether the meter you want has corrections for the species you normally work with. Because the tables will be used for years, it behooves manufacturers to provide printed corrections in a conveniently portable format and with a durable cover and paper. As it is, many meters come with the corrections printed on stapled sheets of copier paper.

Temperature correction—The temperature of the wood significantly affects moisture readings in probed meters. For every 10° above or below 70°, the reading on a probed meter can be off by 1%. If you check a stack of lumber outside on a 0° day, for example, you may wonder how your air-dried stock that read 13% last summer now reads 20% despite the dry winter air. The same boards at 200° in a kiln could read 6%. Correction figures for temperature are provided either internally or on paper with most of the probed meters. EMF meters are not affected by temperature changes.

Zeroing and calibration—Some units, especially those with analog readouts, require a simple procedure to "zero" the meter. Others have indicators to show that the meter is in proper calibration. Some units come with resistor caps that, when in contact with the pins, tell you if the unit is in a truthful mood. If it isn't, there are often easily accessible adjustment screws. If you zero your meter and continue to get peculiar readings, you might check your batteries. As the batteries lose power, the readings will wander. Most

Type of readout or display	Size (in.) and weight (oz.)	Compatible external probes	Species correction	Type of carrying case	List price	Averaged deviation from oven test MC %	Comments
Lights	4¾ x 2¾ x 1¾ 10 oz.	Yes	Extensive chart w/ variable corrections	Stiff leather pouch	$110	1.1%	Display is easy to read in low light
Analog	4¾ x 2¾ x 1¾ 12 oz.	Yes	Extensive chart w/ variable corrections	Stiff leather pouch	$165	1.5%	Built-in calibration check
Digital	7½ x 4 x 2¼ 3 lbs, 8 oz.*	External only	Inboard, 33 species	Hard shell attaché case	$750	1.0%	Interfaces with computer; temperature compensation; stores 3,000 readings
Lights	3½ x 2 x 1½ 5 oz.	Yes Alligator clips	Chart; divides wood in 7 groups	None	$49	0.8%	Informative owner's guide
Analog	4½ x 3 x 1½ 8 oz.	Yes	Chart; divides wood in 7 groups	None	$95	1.6%	Dial easy to read; informative owner's guide.
Analog	6 x 3 x 1 14 oz.	N/A	Chart; divides wood in 7 groups	None	$215	0.5%	Easily calibrated; excellent owner's guide
Lights	5 x 2½ x 1 5 oz.	Yes	2-position range selector	Vinyl pouch	$122	1.4%	Compensates for weakening battery
Digital	5 x 2½ x 1 14 oz.*	External only	Inboard, 20 species	Hard-shell case	$280	1.0%	Temperature-stable circuitry
Digital	6½ x 3 x 1 7 oz.	No△	3-position range selector; extensive chart	Nylon pouch	$168	1.2%	No battery-saving feature
Analog	8 x 4 x 3½ 2½ lbs.	N/A	Very extensive chart	Aluminum attaché case	$665	2.0%	Easy calibration and zeroing; heavy-duty construction; built-in battery charger
Lights	6½ x 2½ x 1 7 oz.	Yes	Very extensive chart	Nylon pouch	$211	0.7%	Auto-off; surface moisture accessory
Analog	4½ x 3 x 1½ 6 oz.*	Lightweight External only	None	None	$29	1.5%	Dial difficult to read; no battery-saving switch
Lights	5 x 1½ dia. 6 oz.	No	Limited chart	None	$80	2.2%	Cylindrical shape is easy to grip and push; useful owner's manual
Analog	6 x 3 x 1 10 oz.	Yes	Limited, general chart; Eurocentric	Vinyl cover	$159	1.6%	Sturdy aluminum casing
Analog	6 x 3 x 1 10 oz	N/A	Limited, general chart; Eurocentric	Vinyl cover	$295	2.1%	Easy calibration check; sturdy aluminum casing; no battery-saving switch
Analog	6 x 3 x 1 9 oz.	N/A	Limited, general chart; Eurocentric	Vinyl cover	$295	1.2%	Also tests plaster, masonry and roofing; no battery-saving switch
Analog	4½ x 2½ x 1½ 6 oz.	N/A	Very extensive chart w/ variable corrections	None	$197	1.0%	Easy calibration and zeroing. Excellent owner's manual. No corrections for imported species
Analog	7½ x 4 x 3 1 lb., 3 oz.	N/A	Extensive chart w/ variable corrections	None	$499	1.8%	Easy calibration and zeroing; easy-to-read dial

* Includes external probe   △ Version available with external probe only ($188 plus $105 for probe)

units have low-battery signals, and some can automatically compensate for a weakening battery.

Instruction manuals—When you buy a moisture meter, read the owner's manual. The manuals often invite meter owners to call with questions and comments, and when you do, instead of being stuck on hold, you talk immediately to someone knowledgeable, perhaps even the person who designed your meter.

Reading range—Is a moisture meter more useful if it has an expanded range of readings? Not necessarily. Wood above fiber saturation point (about 30% MC) is notoriously difficult to read for moisture content because it has water everywhere. And in any

case, shrinkage does not really start until the water leaves the cells and starts to vacate the cell walls at approximately 27% MC (fiber saturation point). For someone who dries wood by kiln, though, the higher range of readings could be useful in a relative way to track and control the loss of moisture.

Readout on moisture meters is indicated via digital and analog displays, by computer printout or by a pattern of LED lights. What's the best? Personally, I appreciate my old LED meter: It is easily read in the half-darkness of my lumber sheds.

The case for a case—Most manufacturers make a strong plea for sensible care of their units. Unlike most woodworking tools, moisture meters have delicate components, which are sensitive to impact, extremes of temperature, dampness and dust. Probes have to be be kept clean. Oils and grime can have an insulating effect and distort readings. Left uncovered, the pins could take an inadvertent reading of your personal moisture content. All these factors make a protective case particularly valuable with these tools.

Oven-dry evaluation

To compare the accuracy of the meters I'd collected, I took readings on three samples of wood—hard maple, black walnut and white oak. I cut the samples from the middle of air-dried boards that had been kept under cover for at least three years. I took multiple readings with each meter and averaged them.

When I had used all the meters and recorded their readings, I determined the actual moisture content of the samples with the standard oven test: I cut two pieces from each sample (1 in. thick by about 3 in. by 4 in.) and put them in the oven at 200°. With a sensitive electronic scale, I measured the starting weight and kept checking and logging my findings until the samples quit losing weight. (It's helpful to marry someone who doesn't mind you tying up the oven for a few days.) I calculated the moisture content of the original sample by dividing the weight lost by the final dry weight. A piece of wood that weighed 6 oz. wet and 5 oz. oven dry is considered to have had a 20% moisture content when wet: (6-5) ÷ 5 = .2

Then I compared the meter readings (after the required species corrections) to the oven-derived moisture content. For each unit, I determined the variance from the oven-dried figures, and that's the figure I used in the chart. As a group, the meters did well, staying within 1.45% of the oven-dry result.

It would be a mistake to consider the figures I arrived at to be an absolute measure of the accuracy of the meters. What the process told me was that most of the meters are in the same ballpark; therefore, the features and accessories each one has to offer are the most important factors in choosing between them. I must say, though, I was pleased to discover that the Lignomat Mini-Ligno I have been using for the last 10 years has been accurate within 1.5%. I am not sure I have told the truth that much myself.

I found I liked something about nearly all the meters I surveyed. But if I were to go out and buy a meter right now, I'm pretty sure I'd go for the Wagner L 606. It has EMF technology at a reasonable price and wonderfully extensive correction tables. It's easy to use, and it's lightweight and compact. A real winner. If I were choosing at the low end of the price spectrum, I'd probably get the Electrophysics MT 80. You get good species corrections, good accuracy, and with their alligator clip setup, you can get deep readings when you need them. □

John Sillick is a teacher and woodworker in Lyndonville, N.Y.

Calculating wood movement

by Christian Becksvoort

My moisture meter is one of the most important tools I own. Whenever I fit a door, drawer or back, I have to know the moisture content (MC) of the wood. If I know the wood's moisture content and the total anticipated change in moisture content, from the driest January to the most humid August, I can accurately project the gap required above drawers of any given size.

I keep two cards (see the chart at right) with my moisture meter, which tell me the total wood movement for quartersawn and flatsawn cherry for an 8% change in moisture content, as well as a worst-case scenario (e.g., someone moving from Phoenix to Seattle) of 10% change in moisture content.

How did I come up with these magic figures? I sat down with my calculator and a simple formula and figured each change in dimension. The formula listed below can be found in *Understanding Wood* by R. Bruce Hoadley (The Taunton Press, 1980):

$\Delta D = D \times S (\Delta MC \div FSP)$ where:

ΔD = Change in dimension
D = Initial dimension
S = Total shrinkage percentage (from *Understanding Wood*, p. 74; use tangential shrinkage for flatsawn and radial shrinkage for quartersawn.)

ΔMC = Change in moisture content expressed as a decimal; must be less than the fiber saturation point (FSP) of 28%
FSP = Fiber saturation point, use 28%

Some examples: How much movement can be expected for a flatsawn cherry board 10 in. wide if the MC is expected to fluctuate from 14% to 4%?

$\Delta D = 10(.071) (.14-.04 \div .28)$
$\Delta D = (.71) (.36) = .2556$ in.

The dimension change will be just over ¼ in.

The same board exposed to an MC change from 12% to 6%:

$\Delta D = 10 (.071) (.12-.06 \div .28)$
$\Delta D = (.71) (.21) = .1491$ or between %4 in. and ⁵⁄₃₂ in.

For each species, S remains constant for flatsawn and constant for quartersawn. S is the percent of shrinkage from the green state (considered to be 28% MC) to oven dry (0% MC). These values (for domestic as well as imported species) can be found in *Understanding Wood* or in *The Wood Handbook: Wood as an Engineering Material*; Agricultural, Handbook #72, Forest Products Lab, 1976. This handbook is available from the Superintendent of Documents, United States Government Printing Office (Washington, D.C. 20402) or your local library. □

Christian Becksvoort is a contributing editor to FWW and a furnituremaker in Gloucester, Maine.

Width of board (in.)	Movement of cherry			
	8% change in MC* (from 6% to 14 %)		10% change in MC (from 4% to 14%)	
	Change in width of flatsawn board (.071)	Change in width of quartersawn board (.037)	Change in width of flatsawn board (.071)	Change in width of quartersawn board (.037)
1	.0203	.0106	.0253	.0132
2	.0406	.0211	.0507	.0264
3	.0608 ¹⁄₁₆**	.0317 ¹⁄₃₂	.0761 ⁵⁄₆₄	.0396 ¹⁄₃₂
4	.0811	.0423	.1014	.0528
5	.1014	.0528	.1268	.0661
6	.1217 ⅛	.0634 ¹⁄₁₆	.1521 ⁵⁄₃₂	.0793 ⁵⁄₆₄
7	.1420	.0740	.1775	.0925
8	.1623	.0846	.2028	.1057
9	.1826 ³⁄₁₆	.0951 ³⁄₃₂	.2282 ¹⁵⁄₆₄	.1189 ⁷⁄₆₄
10	.2028	.1057	.2536	.1321
11	.2231	.1163	.2789	.1454
12	.2434 ¼	.1268 ⅛	.3043 ⁵⁄₁₆	.1586 ⁵⁄₃₂
Notes: * MC = moisture content		** Approximate fractional equivalent		

The author loads his kiln before shutting its airtight door and turning on the automatic dehumidifier and low-temperature heater. His kiln runs automatically, but shuts off and rings a bell if the air in the chamber gets too hot.

A Dehumidification Kiln

A compact system for drying your own wood

by William Bolf

I collect Appalachian hardwoods that I buy at bargain prices from local sawmills and estate auctions. Until recently I could only air dry the lumber to about 14% equilibrium moisture content (EMC) by stacking it in my unheated barn for a few years. Then I became interested in dehumidification lumber-drying kilns and set out to see if I could build an inexpensive kiln suitable for a hobby woodworker like myself. The result is the kiln shown in the photo above, in which I can dry up to 250 bd. ft. of 8-ft.-long ¾ hardwood boards to 7° EMC in about 60 days. This is ideal for my needs. As a spare-time cabinetmaker working in a basement shop, the features I required for my kiln are as follows:

• Since I am a hobby woodworker, my kiln should be as inexpensive and as small as possible.
• The kiln should be solidly constructed so that repairs and maintenance are minimal.
• The kiln should have an automatic control system so that it can operate for days without attention.
• It should be absolutely safe and free of any potential fire hazard.
• It should have a humidification capability for lumber conditioning after the drying cycle (see the sidebar on p. 103).

My kiln can be built for less than $600, and I can dry a stack of lumber at about 10 cents per board foot. The whole setup fits in the corner of my basement, as shown in the photo on the previous page, where the temperature remains near 60° year-round. This means that the kiln's equipment doesn't freeze during the winter, and less energy is needed to maintain the kiln's operating temperature at 110°. Its temperature and humidity are controlled automatically, and the kiln shuts off and an alarm sounds if the internal temperature rises above 125°, which might damage some parts of the equipment.

The kiln's control system will work in any type or size kiln, but the capacity of the heaters, dehumidifier, fans and humidifier may need to be altered for smaller or larger kilns. If you modify my kiln's design, the electrical current capacity of the switches and relays should be checked against requirements of larger equipment.

My kiln's low operating temperature deprives me of two advantages of a high-temperature commercial kiln: It cannot kill lycus powder post beetles or their larva, and it cannot dry out (set) the resin (pitch) in pines and firs. To kill powder post beetles, the kiln temperature must be higher than 125° for 48 hours. An adjustable temperature control, instead of my fixed one, would be necessary, and the dehumidifier would need to be removed to avoid being damaged at that temperature. To dry resin pockets, the kiln would need to be run at 170°, which is not possible with my kiln. So I dry pine first and then cut out and discard wood with resin pockets.

Building the kiln

My kiln isn't as complicated to build as you may think, and you don't have to be an electrician to wire it (see the photo on p. 104). I built the kiln with solid-wood framing, plywood and foam insulation. You can increase the size of the chamber, but if you do, you may need larger mechanical equipment and your control system may need to be upgraded to handle it.

I stack lumber on top of my kiln, so I load wood to be dried through its front door, which is hinged on the top of the kiln. A door on the left accesses the equipment in the chamber. Before building the doors and the chamber, I primed and painted both sides of the plywood with oil-base enamel. Then, as I screwed the plywood and the frames together, I caulked all the joints with silicon rubber, which doesn't degrade in the damp heat. I insulated the top, bottom and back of the kiln with 1½-in.-thick styrofoam, and I used ½-in.-thick foil-faced polyurethane insulation on the

front doors and the right end (both types of insulation were available at my local lumberyard). The left end, which contains the kiln's control system, isn't insulated, and the insulation on the front doors and top is removable to cool the kiln if, under some condition, the internal heat rises to more than 110° without the heaters on. I made the doors airtight with ¼-in.-thick by ¾-in.-wide self-sticking foam rubber weather stripping. For safety reasons, I didn't use self-locking latches that might entrap a child.

To create uniform air flow through the kiln, I installed a ¼-in.-thick chipboard baffle in the back of the kiln (see figure 1 below). The baffle creates a plenum, like on a forced-air furnace, and an aluminum deflector at the right end spreads the air evenly through the lumber pile. Two fans pull dried air from the dehumidifier and blow it past the three-light-bulb heater in the plenum. The air passes through the lumber on its way back to the dehumidifier.

Installing the mechanical equipment and controls

I spent a good bit of time shopping for safe, inexpensive equipment and a control system that could maintain the kiln's temperature at +/- 2° and the humidity at +/- 10%. (The equipment and sources for it are given in the kiln parts list on p. 105.) Although some of the components were available at local hardware stores and home centers, I had to turn to the mail-order sources listed on p. 105 for the control sensors.

My kiln's dehumidifier is an old 18-pint Sears machine, which stands on the floor at the left end of the kiln chamber. The two "muffin"-type circulation fans are mounted in cutouts in a transverse baffle on the left end of the plenum behind the dehumidifier. The fans, specified in the parts list, are rated for 149°, which means their bearings can withstand the kiln's normal operating temperature. As shown in figure 2 on p. 105, the ultrasonic humidifier (from a home center), which is used during the conditioning cycle, vents through a flexible automotive defroster hose and then into a duct, which I made from plastic pipe. Air, which is under pressure, enters the duct at the front of the chamber, and the humidified air is drawn into the duct and plenum by the vacuum created by the fans. Three 100-w. light bulbs in ceramic fixtures maintain the kiln's air temperature at 110°, even when the humidifier cools the air during the conditioning cycle. A kiln that is larger than mine may need the higher heating capacity of a household

(continued on p. 104)

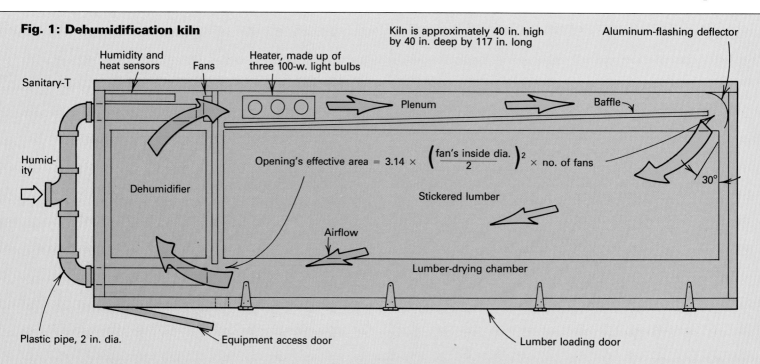

Fig. 1: Dehumidification kiln

Kiln is approximately 40 in. high by 40 in. deep by 117 in. long

Aluminum-flashing deflector

Humidity and heat sensors

Fans

Heater, made up of three 100-w. light bulbs

Sanitary-T

Plenum

Baffle

Humidity

Dehumidifier

Opening's effective area = $3.14 \times \left(\dfrac{\text{fan's inside dia.}}{2}\right)^2 \times$ no. of fans

30°

Stickered lumber

Airflow

Lumber-drying chamber

Plastic pipe, 2 in. dia.

Equipment access door

Lumber loading door

How a kiln dries wood

Moisture content in a piece of wood is related to the air's relative humidity. We raise or lower the relative humidity so the board will absorb or release moisture until it's in equilibrium with the air. We dry wood by gradually reducing the kiln air's relative humidity until the wood reaches a desired equilibrium moisture content. Kilns do this in one of two ways. The first is the oven-drying method, which dries the chamber air by heating it. The second is the dehumidification method, which removes water from the air without heating it. My kiln, shown in the photo on p. 101, uses both methods. It has an auxiliary heater (three 100-w. light bulbs) that warms the air and an inexpensive household dehumidifier that removes the moisture.

Here's how my kiln works. Two fans circulate air through the stickered wood pile and then through the dehumidifier. The dehumidifier's chilled evaporator coils cool the air below its dew point, and condensation forms on the coils where it's collected and removed from the kiln to a storage bottle. Unlike an air conditioner, the dehumidifier increases the kiln's air temperature slightly, so additional heat is not always needed to maintain the 110° operating temperature. My kiln's thermostat setting is fixed at 110°F, and I lower the humidistat setting to control the rate of drying.

The key to successful lumber drying is close control of the rate of moisture removal. I monitor the rate daily by weighing the water collected in the bottle outside the kiln (1 gal. of fresh water weighs 8.32 lbs.). I then adjust the humidistat to extract water at the prescribed rate, which is listed in the lumber-drying schedule above right.

Reading a lumber-drying schedule: Kiln schedules are determined by years of trial and error. My schedule, which has proven safe for all domestic woods I've dried, is based on the size of the load, its equilibrium moisture content and the kiln's 110° operating temperature. As you read across a row in the kiln schedule, the number in the first column is the kiln air's relative humidity, expressed as a percent; the second column is the wood's equilibrium moisture content, also a percent; the third column is the maximum extraction rate, expressed in pounds of water per day per 100 sq. ft. of lumber surface (figured on one side of each piece). If the extraction rate is less than the level prescribed by the schedule, I lower the humidistat setting; if the rate is higher, I raise the setting.

My drying cycle takes about two weeks for thoroughly air-dried lumber and two months for nearly dry green lumber. Although a schedule with a faster drying rate may be possible for softwoods, I've never been in a hurry. To set up your own schedule, consult the Agriculture Department's *Handbook #188 Dry Kiln Operator's Man-*

ual, available for $12 plus postage from Hardwood Research Council, PO Box 34518, Memphis, Tenn. 38184-0518.

Drying a load of lumber: After loading the kiln, I calculate the size of the load and conservatively estimate the moisture content of the wood. Since my wood is thoroughly air dried (some for years), I "guess" that it's at about 14% equilibrium moisture content (EMC). (You can measure moisture content using the method described in the sidebar below.) Then I close the kiln and set its humidistat at 80% relative humidity (RH). If, after a day or so, the kiln isn't extracting water at the prescribed rate, I lower the humidistat 5% RH per day until the extraction rate is on schedule. On the other hand, if the initial rate of extraction exceeds the 8-lbs.-per-day rate prescribed for 80% RH—an indication that my wood is wetter than I guessed—I slow the rate by raising the humidistat setting to 85% RH. I then reduce the humidistat in 5% RH increments while maintaining the prescribed maximum rate of extraction; each step takes from one day to five or six days. When the rate of extraction is less than 1 lb. per day, indicating about 5% EMC, I stop the drying cycle.

Conditioning the dried wood: After drying the wood as much as possible, I humidify (add moisture to) the chamber's atmosphere to equalize the moisture content throughout each board. For drying to take place, there must be a sufficient difference between a board's surface, or outer shell, and its core so moisture can move from the wet area to the dry area. If at the end of the drying cycle the unconditioned board's shell is still drier than its core, then there are internal stresses within the board and it is said to be casehardened. If you rip a straight casehardened board, the result may be two bent pieces.

To condition the lumber, I set the humidistat at 42% RH—the average humidity in Maryland, which is where the furniture I make will be used. The kiln schedule tells me that I want my wood to be at 7% EMC. The ultrasonic humidifier automatically comes on, and I let the kiln run at 110° until 42% RH is maintained for several days.

Testing for casehardening: Before removing the lumber from the kiln, I test for casehardening by crosscutting a ½-in.-thick section from the middle of a test piece at the front of the kiln. I bandsaw the piece into a tuning fork shape like the samples shown above. If the fork's tines remain straight, the sample isn't casehardened. If the tines turn inward, casehardening is still present, indicating the need for longer conditioning. If the tines turn outward, reverse casehardening is present, so I set the humidistat 5% RH lower and run the drying cycle for a few days.
—W.B.

Lumber-Drying Schedule

Relative Humidity (%)	Equilibrium Moisture Content	Maximum Extraction Rate*
90	21.0	11
85	16.0	10
80	15.0	8
75	13.3	7
70	12.0	6
65	11.0	5
60	9.9	4
55	9.2	3
50	8.4	2
45	7.5	2
40	6.7	1
35	6.0	1
30	5.2	1

* Pounds per day per 100 sq. ft. of lumber surface
(100 sq. ft. = 200 bd. ft. of 2-in.-thick lumber)

Testing for casehardening

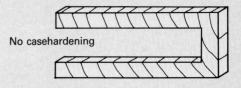

No casehardening

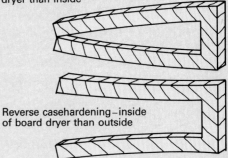

Casehardening–outside of board dryer than inside

Reverse casehardening–inside of board dryer than outside

Measuring wood's moisture content

You can measure a sample's moisture content without an expensive meter. Weigh a 1-cu.-in. sample (taken from the middle of a test piece) immediately after removing it from the kiln. Put the sample in a 225° oven for two hours and weigh the sample again immediately after removing it. Then subtract the oven dry weight from the original weight, divide the result by the oven dry weight and multiply that result by 100. The answer is the moisture content (percentage) of the board from which the sample was sawn. This test can be used to indicate the final EMC of your kiln load and to determine the humidistat setting when starting the kiln.   —W.B.

From *Fine Woodworking* (November 1991) 91:83-87

electric baseboard heater, but be sure it can be safely operated in the kiln—even though the kiln is equipped to shut off automatically if it becomes overheated.

Wiring the kiln

The wiring diagram in figure 2 on the facing page shows the arrangement of the control circuit. Below the power plug is the kiln's temperature limit switch—the fail-safe switch. When the kiln temperature exceeds the 125° limit set on the sensor, its contacts open, shutting off power to the entire kiln and sounding the alarm. To shut off the alarm, I must turn off the main power switch, which controls every system except the alarm. The heater circuit consists of an on/off switch, another temperature sensor, which controls the heater, and an indicator light. The two fans run whenever the main power switch is on. The humidity control circuit is a humidistat and a relay. When the humidity is higher than the humidistat setting, a relay switch turns on the dehumidifier; when the humidity falls below the setting, the relay turns off the dehumidifier and turns on the humidifier.

I assembled the control circuit after installing all the mechanical components. First I prepared the pull box, which is shown in the photo at right and in figure 2, by removing only the necessary knockout plugs. Before screwing the box to the drying chamber's left end wall, I installed the three indicator lights and the relay. I had to enlarge the knockout holes in the box to install the lights.

Next, I connected the humidistat and the utility boxes that contain the sensors, switches and outlets to the pull box with metal (EMT) or plastic (PVC) conduit. I ran a ground wire through the plastic conduit. (The metal conduit serves as a ground.) I wired the runs to the heaters and fans with 16-gauge service cord, terminating it with a crimp lug. I used 14-gauge solid wire to connect the outlets for the humidifier and dehumidifier, making wire-to-wire connections with wire nuts inside the junction boxes.

Before installing the Fenwall fixed-temperature sensor, I set it to operate my kiln at 110° (a higher temperature may shorten the life of the dehumidifier). I tested the sensor following its directions by immersing its probe in a pot of hot water. This unit didn't come with its own box, but its mounting screws and probe match the two small holes and center knockout hole in the bottom of a surface-mounted 4-in.-sq. by 2-in.-deep electrical box. An adjustable sensor (in the kiln parts list) can be substituted for my fixed-temperature control sensor for adjustable-temperature operation.

I set the temperature limit switch using the unit's right-hand pointer to trip at 15° above the kiln's 110° operating temperature. I also put an inexpensive combination thermometer/hygrometer behind a Plexiglas window in the equipment access door to monitor the kiln's atmosphere.

Checking out the system

After I completed the installation of equipment and wiring, I checked that everything was working properly. Before plugging in the kiln, I turned off the main power switch, the heat switch, the dehumidification switch and the humidification switch, and I set the humidity control to minimum. I also turned on the dehumidifier and set its humidity control to the lowest setting. I then turned on the humidifier and set its humidity control to maximum. Next, I plugged in the kiln and turned on its main power switch. As I anticipated, the humidifier, demumidifier and heater were off, both fans were running and air was flowing in the correct direction.

I then checked the drying circuits by turning on the heat switch and verifying that all three heater bulbs lit up. Next, I turned the humidistat dial to a level that was lower than my basement's relative humidity, shown on the access door gauge, and switched on

The kiln's controls are on its left end. The pull box, which contains the humidistat relays and indicator lights, is beneath the manual switches. The temperature sensors and humidistat, which are mounted to the left of the pull box, monitor air in the kiln chamber. A dehumidifier inside the kiln collects the water extracted from the drying lumber and deposits it in the milk bottle via a rubber tube. And the humidifier, which is outside the kiln, releases moist air into the PVC pipe's air duct to condition the wood after the drying cycle and to prevent casehardening.

the dehumidification switch—the dehumidifier began operating. I then turned the humidistat dial to a higher level than the relative humidity and checked that the dehumidifier turned off.

Next, I checked the humidification circuit by turning the dehumidification switch off and turning the humidification switch on. With the humidistat still set for a high level, the humidifier turned on. To confirm that the vacuum in the plenum was drawing in humidified air, I closed the kiln doors and held the end of the flexible hose about 2 in. away from the opening in the sanitary-T. Sure enough, vapors were drawn into the pipe duct. Finally, I rotated the humidistat to a level less than my basement's relative humidity and confirmed that the humidifier shut off. Everything checked out, and so I turned off all the switches and loaded 1-in.-thick pine into my kiln.

Kiln maintenance

The following periodic maintenance is required. The dehumidifier's evaporator coils accumulate a coating of dirt and sawdust, so I clean the coils with a stiff brush (not a wire brush) and a vacuum. I also clean the dehumidifier's catch pan and blow out its drain hose. If I don't use distilled water in the humidifier, its transducer may accumulate scale, which I scrape off. And since the heater's light bulbs have short lives, I check that they light before starting a new load. □

William Bolf is an electrical engineer and amateur woodworker in Myersville, Md.

Fig. 2: Kiln control wiring diagram

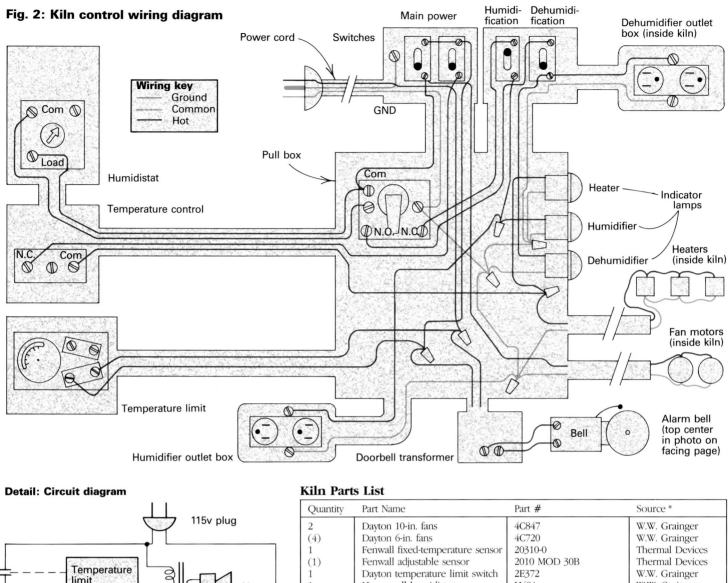

Wiring key
- Ground
- Common
- Hot

Humidistat — Com, Load

Temperature control — N.C., Com

Temperature limit

Humidifier outlet box

Doorbell transformer

Power cord — Switches — GND

Pull box — Com, N.O. N.O.

Main power | Humidi-fication | Dehumidi-fication

Dehumidifier outlet box (inside kiln)

Heater — Indicator lamps
Humidifier
Dehumidifier
Heaters (inside kiln)
Fan motors (inside kiln)
Alarm bell (top center in photo on facing page)
Bell

Detail: Circuit diagram

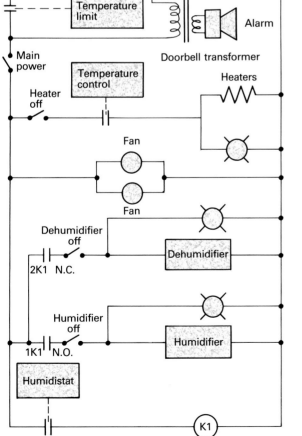

115v plug

Temperature limit

Doorbell transformer — Alarm

Main power

Heater off — Temperature control — Heaters

Fan — Fan

Dehumidifier off — 2K1 N.C. — Dehumidifier

Humidifier off — 1K1 N.O. — Humidifier

Humidistat

K1

Kiln Parts List

Quantity	Part Name	Part #	Source *
2	Dayton 10-in. fans	4C847	W.W. Grainger
(4)	Dayton 6-in. fans	4C720	W.W. Grainger
1	Fenwall fixed-temperature sensor	20310-0	Thermal Devices
(1)	Fenwall adjustable sensor	2010 MOD 30B	Thermal Devices
1	Dayton temperature limit switch	2E372	W.W. Grainger
1	Honeywell humidistat	H49A	W.W. Grainger
1	Ultrasonic humidifier		
1	18-pint dehumidifier		
1	Thermometer/hygrometer		K-Mart
1	Pull box, 8 × 8 × 4		
1	Utility box, 4 × 4 × 2		
	½-in.-dia. conduit, EMT or PVC		
	Conduit fittings		
4	Switches (15 amps)		
2	Double-switch boxes and covers		
2	Duplex outlets		
2	Single-switch boxes and covers		
1	Doorbell transformer		
1	24 VAC bell		
3	Indicator lights (red, amber, green)	2620T1, 2620T2, 2620T5	IDI
3	Porcelain lamp sockets		
	3-conductor service cord, #16		
5 ft.	2-in. PVC DWV pipe		
	Fittings for PVC pipe		
	14-gauge solid wire, 300v PVC ins		
	16-gauge stranded wire, 300v ins		
	Crimp lugs		
	Wire nuts		
1	Dayton relay, SPDT, 115 VAC coil	3X745	W.W. Grainger

( ) = Alternate parts
* = Parts without a source are available from hardware stores and/or home centers.

W.W. Grainger Co., 5959 W. Howard St., Chicago, Ill. 60648; (312) 647-8900
Thermal Devices, Inc., PO Box 560, Mt. Airy, Md. 21771; (800) 282-9100
IDI (Industrial Devices, Inc.) 260 Railroad Ave., Hackensack, N.J. 07601; (201) 224-4700

VAC = volts alternating current   EMT = electrical metallic tubing
DWV = drain waste vent   PVC = polyvinyl chloride
ins = insulation   SPDT = single pole, double throw

Fig. 1: Kiln construction

Detail A: Securing glass on top rafters

Glass

Block, 1 in. by 2 in.

2x4 rafter

Gap, ⅜ in., between glass panes

Plywood siding, ½ in., exterior grade

Additional rafters may be used for added support.

64

187

96

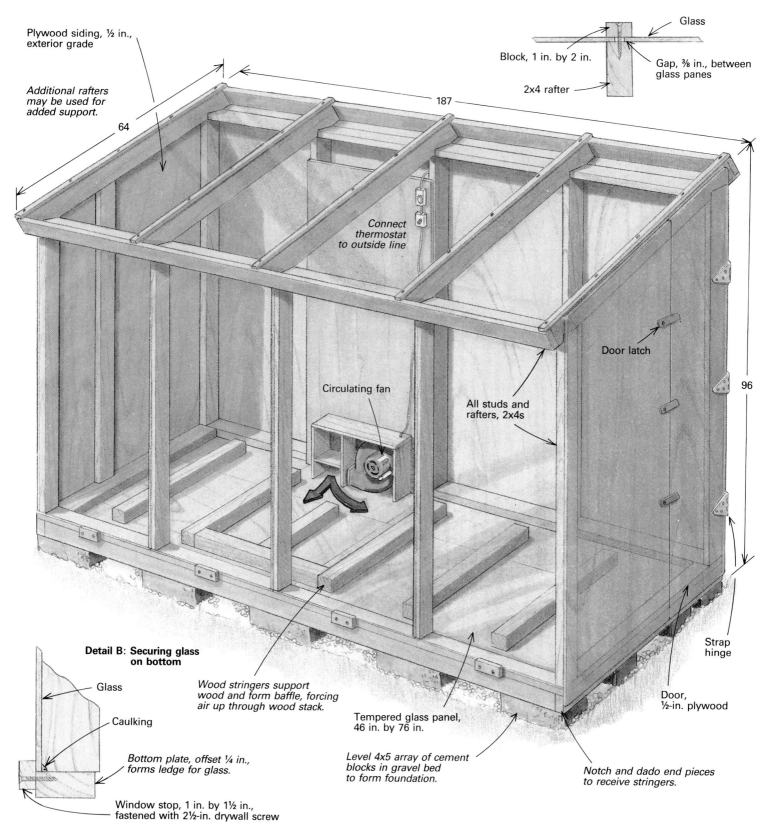

Connect thermostat to outside line

Circulating fan

Door latch

All studs and rafters, 2x4s

Strap hinge

Door, ½-in. plywood

Detail B: Securing glass on bottom

Glass

Caulking

Bottom plate, offset ¼ in., forms ledge for glass.

Window stop, 1 in. by 1½ in., fastened with 2½-in. drywall screw

Wood stringers support wood and form baffle, forcing air up through wood stack.

Tempered glass panel, 46 in. by 76 in.

Level 4x5 array of cement blocks in gravel bed to form foundation.

Notch and dado end pieces to receive stringers.

A Solar Kiln for Drying Wood

Dry, defect-free wood and a place to store it, too

by John Wilson

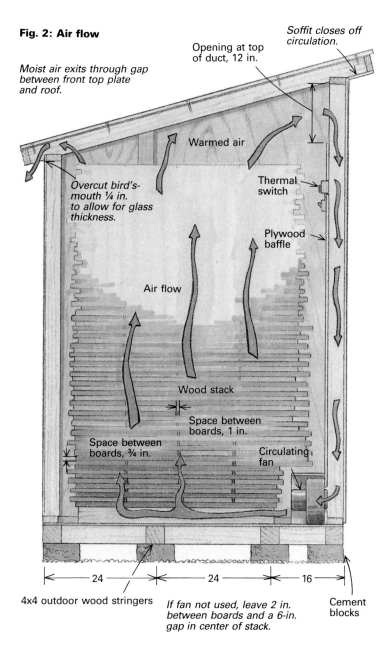

Fig. 2: Air flow

Moist air exits through gap between front top plate and roof.

Opening at top of duct, 12 in.

Soffit closes off circulation.

Warmed air

Overcut bird's-mouth ¼ in. to allow for glass thickness.

Thermal switch

Plywood baffle

Air flow

Wood stack

Space between boards, 1 in.

Space between boards, ¾ in.

Circulating fan

24 — 24 — 16

4x4 outdoor wood stringers

If fan not used, leave 2 in. between boards and a 6-in. gap in center of stack.

Cement blocks

My solar kiln holds about 1,500 bd. ft. of lumber and can produce two batches of uniformly dry, check-free wood each year. The kiln can be built as a temporary or permanent structure by two men in a single day for about $375. My only operating cost is for running a small fan to circulate air and to exhaust moisture. The kiln also doesn't require extensive monitoring or sophisticated moisture meters. Another real plus for a small shop like mine is that the kiln can be used to store the wood indefinitely; the natural day/night drying-and-relaxation cycle prevents stress damage even after the wood is dry.

The kiln will work effectively in any area of the country. I've even had good success near my home in south central Michigan, an area that holds the distinction of having the worst solar energy use-potential in the country because of its combination of cold temperatures and overcast skies.

In addition to letting me control both the supply and quality of my wood, the kiln lets me work with treasured oddities of burl, crotch and spalted wood, which commercial mills consider as defects to be graded out, left to rot or used in someone's fireplace. Also, several wood species that do not grow in sufficient amounts for commercial operations are available from time to time in my locality. Finally, there is an abundance of green lumber available at attractive prices to the person with the capacity to dry it.

Solar-kiln anatomy—My solar kiln is 16 ft. long by 5½ ft. deep and 8 ft. high. The photo on p. 108 shows the completed structure. Its foundation is concrete blocks laid on a level bed of gravel. These blocks support 4x4 pressure-treated stringers under a plywood floor. Exterior-grade plywood and standard framing lumber are used to form the back and sides. Tempered glass panels salvaged from scrapped sliding patio doors make up the roof and front. Because the tempered glass can't be cut, you may have to change the dimensions of the kiln shown here to accept your glass panels. Therefore, you should get the glass before you start construction. The roof slopes down from the back toward the south-facing front. You could experiment with various slope angles in your area of the country to maximize the solar-collection efficiency, but it isn't critical for drying wood. I've used 3½:12 pitch here, which works well and arises conveniently as a result of using standard-size glass panels for the front wall and 4x8 plywood sheets for the back wall. The slope is also adequate for keeping the glass clear of snow during the winter.

Simplicity of solar wood drying—I've long enjoyed the advantage of direct-gain (passive) solar design in my home and shop. Direct entry of sunlight through windows provides warmth and gives needed light on the darkest of overcast days. A complex, intermediary heat-transfer system is not required as in the more elaborate (active) solar systems. On the debit side, a passive system requires balancing day and night levels of energy and avoiding summer overheating through the architectual coordination of blinds, ventilation and thermal mass.

Passive solar heating adapted for drying wood is equally effective, but simpler than for a home or shop application, because there is no need to be concerned about the extreme high summer and low winter temperatures. It is a system best suited for drying small batches of wood, but it can be scaled to handle larger quantities.

The solar kiln's limitation is that it takes three or four months to dry a batch of wood; a commercial kiln can do the job in a month. But, I consider the kiln's long drying time a small inconvenience for the individual woodworker or the small woodshop in light of the solar kiln's low capital investment, minimal operating cost and self-regulating operation. To the individual woodworker or small woodshop, these advantages, plus the defect-free lumber the solar kiln produces, are much more important considerations.

The kiln's size is limited only by the amount of space available and the quantities of wood you want to dry; it can range from a small coop to a large garage. It must, however, be located and constructed to maximize sun entry to heat the air inside. A kiln facing between southeast and southwest, unobstructed by trees or buildings, works best. A modest fan system working in conjunction with a baffle helps circulate and funnel the warm air effectively throughout the stickered pile of boards. Vents to release warm, moist air and provisions for loading and unloading the wood are also necessary.

Little else is required. This may be surprising if you've heard stories about wood ruined by poor drying practices. Many woodworkers recall the experience of cutting into honeycombed or case-hardened boards from commercial kilns. What protects solar-dried wood from a similar fate is nature's daily cycle: The sun provides the drying warmth during the daylight hours, and the dark night hours provide a "rest" period—every 24 hours. This rest period allows the wood to normalize, permitting higher moisture levels at the core of the wood to migrate to the surface before the next drying period begins. Because the sun dries in short, daily bursts, the drying time is extended from four weeks to four months, but there is

Drawings: Bob La Pointe; photo: John Wilson

The simplicity of the solar-kiln construction is evident in the above photo. The plywood panel from one end is removed to allow access for unloading a dry batch of lumber.

Recycling glass for kilns

I use tempered glass for my solar kiln. Ordinary plate glass will work, but it's not strong enough to withstand snow loads in the northern part of the United States. Plastic also lacks strength and will rapidly succumb to strong winds and deterioration from ultraviolet radiation. Fortunately, the wide use of tempered glass panels in sliding patio doors makes them readily available at a reasonable cost. New ones cost about $80; used ones are a real steal (about $10) if purchased as scrap.

Finding old patio doors may require a little effort, because most glass companies usually dump the old ones. Try talking to these companies about saving the next ones they replace. Glass thermo panes are frequently replaced because of failed (or damaged) seals, which allow moisture to enter the airspace between the two panels. The resulting condensation etches the glass, forming a milky, translucent precipitate that fogs the panel. Usually only the outside glass pane, the one on which condensation occurs, will be affected; the other pane remains clear. I haven't discovered a way to completely remove the surface coloration, but it's not a problem for solar-kiln application. Energy transmission through the glass is virtually unaffected.

When you get the salvaged patio doors home, remove the panels from the frame. A thin strip of aluminum between the glass panels forms an airspace. This in turn is sealed by a rubber gasket between the aluminum strip and each glass panel. A sharp utility knife works well to slice through the rubber seal. Cut around both sides of the aluminum strip to fully separate the panels. You don't have to clean off the seal material that remains stuck to the glass, because it will be helpful in holding the glass in place when you install the panels in your kiln.

My kiln has single-thickness tempered panels that are 46 in. by 76 in. These panels are from the standard 4-ft.-wide patio sliding doors, but you might also find 3-ft.-wide doors with 34-in. by 76-in. glass. The law now requires that glass be tempered for strength and safety reasons, so check to make sure older panels are tempered as well. If they are tempered, the words "safety glass" will be etched in one of the corners.

Two further words of caution: The process of tempering creates large internal stress within the glass. As a result, the glass is very sensitive to pressure or shock, which causes it to shatter, just like an automobile windshield. This also is why the glass cannot be cut. So, it's important to base your detailed layout on the actual glass panel size. Also, when handling the panels, be especially careful to avoid knocking the edges. —*J.W.*

great assurance that the end product will be free of drying defects. Because a natural balance is established between the drying wood and its environment within the kiln, "overdrying" isn't a problem.

Kiln design—My experience with solar kilns includes the construction and operation of five units in as many years. I also learned from previous experimenters. The Forest Products Laboratory has published a report on a small solar-heated dryer (Report FPU-7, available from Information Services, U.S. Forest Laboratory, 1 Gifford Pinchot Drive, Madison, Wis. 53705-2389). That kiln, like mine, has a simple design and is easily built using readily available construction materials. With a south-facing flat plate attached, it uses an overhead fan to drive the heated air down through the stack of lumber.

I also read about other designs using condenser curtains to remove moisture, but I've concentrated on simplifying kiln design. My structure costs about one-tenth that of a similar-size commercial unit, is built from readily available materials and works as effectively as the more complex Forest Products Laboratory model. In addition, my design is virtually maintenance free.

Construction—Building the kiln is straightforward, and you'll find the necessary dimensions and details in the drawings on p. 106 and p. 107. Here I'll tell you the procedure I used to build my kiln, as well as offer some hints to make the job easier for you. Begin construction by selecting a location that affords a good southern exposure, unshaded by trees or buildings. Cover the area with gravel and level a 6-ft. by 16-ft. section for the concrete block foundation. Now, cut and assemble the floor frame using the 4x4 stringers. Cut dadoes in the end pieces to terminate the stringers. Next, nail the plywood floor in place.

When building a kiln in a temporary location, I sometimes replace the concrete blocks with sturdy hardwood pallets and fasten the floor directly (no stringers) to them using drywall screws. In fact, I use these screws, up to 3 in. in length, to put together the entire kiln. They install easily, hold well and enable me to quickly and conveniently disassemble the structure to relocate it later on.

The kiln is framed with standard 2x4 studs covered with plywood. The south wall and roof support the recycled patio glass panels you've scroungd up (see the sidebar at left). The kiln shown here uses the most commonly available 46-in. by 76-in. glass panels. Four panels are used for the south wall and another four make up the roof. Allow for a ⅜-in. gap between panels. You'll need the spaces later for installing the window stops.

Fabricate the back, side and front walls separately, then attach the plywood siding. Incidentally, don't worry too much about getting the joints and seams tight. Air will infiltrate into the kiln through cracks in the same way air in your home is replaced periodically. A "leaky" kiln is desirable, because it improves the air circulation through the wood stack and results in more efficient moisture removal.

Access to the kiln for loading and unloading wood is accomplished by simply removing one of the end walls, so for convenience, use a minimum number of screws to secure this wall in place. For the infrequent visits to the kiln to monitor drying progress, I've installed a simple, strap-hinged door in one of the end walls. Lastly, note the plate detail at the bottom of the front-wall frame (see figure 1, detail B on p. 106). The plate extends out ¼ in. to serve as a sill for the glass panels to rest on. Because the plate is exposed, it's a good idea to make it out of pressure-treated wood.

Next, you'll need to create a baffle by nailing a partial sheet of plywood to two of the back-wall studs. The bottom opening of the baffle will have to be custom-fit to work effectively with your circu-

From *Fine Woodworking* (January 1989) 74:74-77

lating fan. The idea here is to install the fan so it can draw warmed air from the top of the kiln down through the baffle and then direct it up through the bottom of the stacked lumber. I used a 150cfm squirrel-cage fan with an integral $1/10$-HP motor, which costs about $50. It's similar to the exhaust fans commonly used in bathrooms or kitchens, and it is sold by building-supply stores. Install a line-voltage thermostat that's adjustable in the range of 35°F to 90°F. I used a Dayton #2E158A, which can be purchased from heating- and cooling-equipment suppliers for about $24. The thermoswitch is wired in the same way as a commonly used single-pole switch. You'll need to adjust the switch seasonally so the blower turns off when temperatures drop below 55°F in the winter and 80°F in the summer. You may also want to install a power on/off switch so you can control the system manually. If your site is remote and electrical power is unavailable, you can do without the fan and baffle, but you'll need to provide more space between pieces of lumber in the stack to improve the air circulation. Leaving a 6-in.-wide chaseway up through the center of the stack will help considerably. The kiln will work this way; drying just takes longer and takes place less uniformly within the stack. Lumber located in the "dead" areas, away from the freely circulating air, will dry more slowly. For example, I've found that after four months of drying, the top one-third of the stack has reached 6%MC to 8%MC, but the remainder of the stack is still a "wet" 10%MC to 12%MC.

If you already have your wood, load it into the kiln now; you can use the stack as a platform while building the roof. Notch the rafters as shown in figure 2, p. 107. The notch, or bird's-mouth, which joins the top plate of the front wall, holds the front glass panels in place. So, it needs to be cut large enough to accommodate the thickness of the glass. Take care to maintain this space for the glass when you install the rafters. The rafters support the glass roof panels along the edges and centerline of each panel. If you have smaller panels than those used here, the center rafter can be eliminated. Tempered glass is strong—it's used for skylights—and the rafter layout used here provides ample support.

When you install the glass panels, be especially careful to avoid knocking the edges: They shatter easily. It's a good idea to use stop blocks or a toeplate at the lower end of the rafters to hold the roof panels in position. Cover the edges of the glass panels with 1-in. by 1½-in. wood strips, which can be screwed to the rafters or studs through the ⅜-in. space between adjacent panels. For a more permanent setup, apply a silicone caulk bedding for the strips and cover them with an aluminum cap. One final comment: A 2-in. gap is intentionally left under the roof panels at the top of the front wall so moist air can escape from the kiln.

Using the kiln—My experience with this kiln isn't much different than the results reported for the more complex Forest Products Laboratory design. The time required for drying depends on your particular location, the time of year and amount of available sunshine. The species of wood also affects the drying time: High-density woods like oak dry slowly; low-density woods like pine dry more rapidly. In southern Michigan, a batch of 1-in.-thick hardwoods can be dried to about 8%MC in four to five months if started in March; a second batch can be dried by November. The winter months are marginal because there are too few sunny days.

I'm continuing to experiment with the kiln to reduce the drying time. I've found that the air circulation can be improved by positioning the 4-in. stringers (which support the wood stack), as shown in figure 1, to form a baffle, which helps force the air through the stack. I've also tried reducing the air gap at the top of the front wall during the final stage of drying to reduce air flow and increase temperature. The effectiveness of this fine-

tuning remains an open question.

If you decide to experiment with your kiln, you'll find a moisture meter to be a good investment. Moisture meters are available from woodworker supply houses for as little as $30 (see the article on pp. 96-100). The article on pp. 110-112 describes a shop-built model. Moisture content can also be determined using a simple weight-loss method described in *FWW* #73, p. 20. □

John Wilson teaches woodworking part-time at Lansing Community College in Lansing, Mich. He specializes in making and selling Shaker oval boxes, and he depends on his solar kiln for his wood supply.

Wood-drying basics

You can dry wood simply by passing air over its surface. Left outdoors and protected from the elements, a stack of 4/4 hardwood with freely circulating air will dry to about 15%MC in about a year in the northeast United States. Further reduction isn't possible, because the moisture in the air, normally about 75% to 80% relative humidity (RH), is in equilibrium with that of the wood. (Relative humidity is a measure of the air's capacity to hold moisture and is defined as the ratio of the amount of moisture contained in the air at a given temperature to the maximum amount of moisture the air can hold at that same temperature.) Our home environments are much drier, however, typically about 40%RH to 50%RH and often as low as 20%RH in the winter. This difference causes problems for woodworkers. Furniture, to remain stable, must be constructed from woods with a moisture content no greater than 6% to 8% to be in equilibrium with the drier indoor air. In the very dry Southwest, the moisture content will be lower; in the more humid South, it will be higher. So the problem of drying wood comes down to circulating dry-enough air to produce these lower moisture levels within a reasonable amount of time.

One way to dry the air is to dehumidify it using a compressor. This is exactly what many of us do to prevent our basements from becoming too damp. Some wood kilns operate on the same principal, but of course on a larger scale: They use large compressors to remove moisture from the air inside the kiln; heat produced as a byproduct of the compressor operation keeps the temperature in the 120° range. This option is usually too expensive for the home woodworker.

Most often, dry air is obtained by heating it. More precisely, moisture is not removed from the air but rather the air's capacity to absorb and retain water is increased as a result of increasing its temperature. Saturated air (100%RH) at one temperature is something less than 100%RH at a higher temperature. This difference, by the way, accounts for our homes feeling drier in the winter: The cold infiltrating air is heated, making it relatively dry.

When air is heated, its ability to absorb moisture is increased dramatically. For example, air saturated at 30°F can hold three times as much moisture when heated to 70°F. Heating the air an additional 40°, to 120°F, increases its capacity to hold moisture by tenfold. This is the practical working range for solar kilns. A kiln can start the day with the ambient air at 70°F and 100%RH, but after being warmed by the sun for an hour or so, the temperature will be close to 120°F. The air will be very dry at this temperature—about 10%RH—and able to absorb a large amount of moisture from the wood.

For more information on the relationship between wood and air-moisture levels, see *FWW on Wood and How to Dry It* or Bruce Hoadley's book *Understanding Wood*, The Taunton Press, Box 355, Newtown, Conn. 06470.   *—J.W.*

Shop-Built Moisture Meter

Printed circuit guides you through electronic maze

by Rick Liftig

Even though I've occasionally had problems with wood warping and cracking or joints coming loose because of moisture-related wood movement, I never could justify spending $100 or so to buy a moisture meter to check my stock before I used it. I've always been interested in electronics, so I decided to build my own meter. My home-built version, shown in the photo on the next page, cost $30. I've relied on fairly simple electronic procedures, so even if talk about soldering and circuits makes you uncomfortable, you should be able to build the meter.

The moisture content of wood can range from 0% for oven-dried samples to more than 100% for soaking-wet green wood, where the water in the wood weighs more than the wood tissue itself. Traditionally, technologists determined the moisture content by weighing a wood sample, oven-drying it until it was bone-dry, then weighing it again. The weight difference divided by the oven-dry weight, multiplied by 100, gives you the percentage of moisture content. This time-consuming method requires such an extremely accurate scale that it's impractical in most shops.

My meter, and many commercial models, bypasses drying and weighing by taking advantage of the fact that wet wood conducts electricity, while dry wood, a good insulator, resists

the flow of electricity. By measuring this electrical resistance (expressed in units called ohms) and comparing your reading with standards developed by the U.S. Forest Products Laboratory and other agencies, you can determine wood's moisture content. The system works fine if the wood moisture content is in the 6% to 30% range, which is fairly common. Depending on the season and locale, most air-dried wood has 12% to 15% moisture content. Properly kiln-dried wood should be 6% to 10%. The electrical resistance in very wet or very dry samples is too erratic to give accurate readings.

Since we are measuring ohms, you might think that any off-the-shelf ohmmeter could measure resistance in wood. Wood is such a good insulator, however, that only a high-range ohmmeter capable of measuring in megohms (one million ohms) can be used. Early instruments used vacuum tubes and expensive high-voltage circuits, but my unit uses a modern, integrated circuit called an operational amplifier which can be wired to compare the wood's resistance to known resistances in the meter circuit. The details aren't too important; what's important is that the meter is sensitive enough to measure the moisture in a wood sample. Once I worked the bugs out of the system, I modified my meter dial to

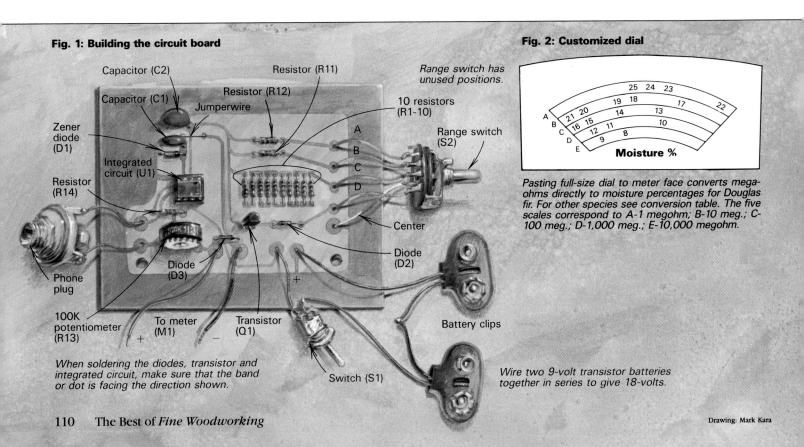

Fig. 1: Building the circuit board

Capacitor (C2)
Capacitor (C1)
Jumperwire
Resistor (R12)
Resistor (R11)
Zener diode (D1)
Integrated circuit (U1)
Resistor (R14)
10 resistors (R1-10)
A
B
C
D
Center
Range switch (S2)
Range switch has unused positions.
Phone plug
Diode (D3)
Diode (D2)
100K potentiometer (R13)
To meter (M1)
Transistor (Q1)
Switch (S1)
Battery clips

When soldering the diodes, transistor and integrated circuit, make sure that the band or dot is facing the direction shown.

Wire two 9-volt transistor batteries together in series to give 18-volts.

Fig. 2: Customized dial

25 24 23
19 18 17 22
A 21 20 14 13
B 16 15 10
C 12 11
D 9 8
E
Moisture %

Pasting full-size dial to meter face converts megaohms directly to moisture percentages for Douglas fir. For other species see conversion table. The five scales correspond to A-1 megohm; B-10 meg.; C-100 meg.; D-1,000 meg.; E-10,000 megohm.

Drawing: Mark Kara

show percentage directly, as shown in figure 2 on the facing page, so I wouldn't have to keep checking resistance charts. Just glue figure 2 to your dial face with rubber cement and you're ready to go. I find my readings, based on Douglas fir standards, are accurate enough for most uses, but if you want more accurate readings that account for the physical differences of each species, use figure 5. If the species you are testing isn't listed, you can assume its readings would be much the same as one of the listed species from the same geographic area and with similar density and structure. The values are probably within 2% of each other. Even within one board, you may find that much of a variation because of wood structure, uneven drying and contamination.

Construction—The simplest way to build the meter is to make a printed-circuit board from the pattern shown, drill holes to accept components, then solder the components on. The completed board, along with its gauge and switches, can be housed in any type of box—I used a cherry case fitted with a ¼-in. walnut deck. The printed circuit is not as mysterious as it looks—it's just a way of replacing wiring with thin copper lines drawn and etched on a board. All you have to do is buy a printed circuit kit from Radio Shack, or some other supplier, and follow the instructions in the package to the letter.

The probe is a 1¼ in. dia. piece of Plexiglas rod drilled to accept the probe leads, which are soldered to the steel points (taken from a cheap drawing compass) epoxied into the rod. I spaced the electrodes about ¾ in. apart, but the spacing isn't critical. Make the probes long enough to penetrate one-fifth to one-quarter the thickness of the boards you want to test. If you don't want to bother with a probe, drive a pair of nails into the wood and connect them to the meter with alligator clips.

Calibration and use of the meter—The meter must be calibrated before use. Solder four 10-megohm resistors together in a four-unit "daisy chain" series. Touching the ends of the chain to the probe tips, adjust R13 (the 100-K potentiometer) to read 14% moisture content, with the meter set to scale C. Do not touch the

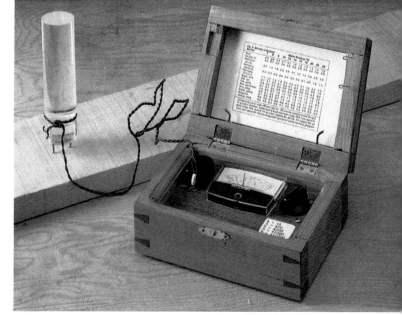

A few common electronic components, a plastic probe and species chart let you gauge moisture levels and anticipate wood movement for about $30. Jazz the unit up with a custom made box.

Fig. 5: Species corrections				Meter Readings (%)							
Species	**7**	**8**	**9**	**10**	**12**	**14**	**16**	**18**	**20**	**22**	**24**
Birch	0.9	1.0	0.8	0.7	0.7	1.0	1.0	1.3	1.4	1.6	1.6
Douglas Fir	0.0	0.0	0.0	0.0	0.0	0.0	0.0	0.0	0.0	0.0	0.0
Mahogany, African	0.7	1.4	1.6	2.0	2.8	3.2	3.6	3.8	3.8	3.8	3.8
Mahogany, Honduras	0.3	0.3	0.3	0.4	0.6	0.5	0.2	0.0	-0.5	-1.0	1.5
Mahogany, Philippine	-1.2	-1.2	-1.5	-1.9	-2.4	-2.8	-3.3	-3.7	-4.5	-5.2	-5.8
Maple, hard	0.7	0.7	0.4	0.1	-0.2	-0.1	-0.2	0.0	0.2	0.5	1.0
Oak, red	-0.4	0.0	0.0	0.0	0.0	0.0	0.0	0.0	0.0	-0.2	0.0
Oak, white	-0.1	-0.2	-0.4	-0.5	-0.5	-0.6	-0.8	-1.1	-1.5	-1.8	-2.0
Pine, ponderosa	0.4	0.6	0.7	1.0	1.4	1.6	1.6	1.4	1.2	1.2	1.6
Pine, white	0.0	0.1	0.2	0.3	0.7	1.1	1.3	1.3	1.2	1.1	0.4
Poplar, yellow	0.1	0.6	0.7	0.7	1.2	1.6	1.6	1.6	1.7	2.0	1.7
Redwood	0.0	0.0	0.0	0.0	-0.2	-0.5	-0.8	-1.0	-1.0	-0.2	0.0
Walnut, black	0.5	0.6	0.4	0.4	0.4	0.5	0.3	0.2	0.0	-0.2	-0.4

Conductivity varies with different species. All species compared with Douglas fir standard. Example: When testing birch and meter reads 10%, look opposite Birch under 10%. Add 0.7% to meter reading for 10.7%. For woods not on chart, use figures for species of similar hardness and grain configurations.

Adapted from *Furniture and Cabinet Making* by John L. Feirer ©1983, Bennett & McKnight, Peoria, Ill.

Fig. 3: Printed circuit

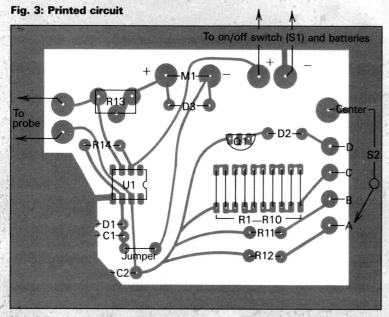

Use diagram to layout printed circuit and add components. Black lines are connections on the top of the board. Grey patterns are circuits printed on underside of board. Underside of board is shown here. The parts are coded and refer to the parts list at right.

Fig. 4: Parts list

Qty.	Radio Shack Part Number	Diagram Code	Description
1	270-1752	M1	0-1 milliamp DC meter
1	276-561	D1	6.2 volt, 1 watt zener diode
1	None	U1	LM308 N Op Amp
1	276-2009	Q1	MPS2222 Transistor
	276-1576		Printed circuit fabrication kit
	276-1577		Direct etching dry transfers
2	276-1620	D2 & D3	1N914 Silicon diode
1	271-220	R13	Printed circuit potentiometer 100K
15	271-1365	R1 - R11	10 Megohm resistors ¼ watt
1	271-1325	R14	2200 ohm resistor ¼ watt
1	271-1356	R12	1 Megohm resistor ¼ watt
1	275-625	S1	On-off switch (SPST)
1	275-1385	S2	One pole 12 position rotary switch
2	270-325		9-volt transistor-battery clips
1	274-252		Phone Plus
1	274-256		Phone jack
1	274-414		Knob for switch
2	272-134	C1 & C2	0.05 UF disk capacitors

Misc: 5 in. section of 1¼-in. diameter Plexiglas rod, 22-gauge wire, solder for electronics.

Parts available from Radio Shack; Jameco Electronics, 1355 Shoreway Road, Belmont, Calif. 94002; or Digi-Key Corp., P.O. Box 677, Thief River Falls, Minn. 56701. Unless you're very familiar with electronics, don't try to substitute electronic components.

Gauging wood movement

by Tom Liebl

Many people will tell you woodworking is a simple enough craft—the right tools (with plenty of horsepower), the right glue, no problems. Then, when your beautiful table-top cracks even though you glued and screwed hefty cleats across its underside, you wonder if maybe there's more to it.

"That's wood movement for you," the pros say as they scan your cracked top, but what does that mean? With a careful reading of Hoadley's *Understanding Wood*, the fundamental characteristics of wood will become clear, but in the workshop we are more often interested in how much movement than why. Few of us can get too excited about searching out just the right book, wading through a bewildering mass of data aimed at scientists, not craftsmen, then tracking down a pocket calculator just to figure out how much slack to build into a set of drawerfronts.

You could wing it, but cutting it too close could bring a summertime house call and a tarnished reputation. Leaving a ¼-in. gap would be playing it safe, but doesn't do much for looks. To solve this dilemma, I developed this chart on the movement and tendency to cup of most commonly used wood species.

I use the wood movement chart most, and when I combine potential movement with the cupping tendency of flatsawn lumber, I get a good idea of a species' dimensional stability. If I had a choice between red or white oak for a tabletop, I'd lean toward the white.

To use my chart, you must know three factors: the width of the piece, its annual ring orientation and the moisture content (MC) range where you live. The table is based on 12-in. wide boards, a convenient size for measuring expansion and contraction. Ring orientation may be either tangential (flatsawn) or radial (quartersawn). When in doubt, assume tangential since they move more than quartersawn.

After wood has been kiln- or air-dried

Dimensional changes			
Species	Movement of 12 in. wide board over 7% change in moisture content		T/R[1]
Hardwoods	Radial	Tangential	
Ash, white	.14 in.	.23 in.	1.6
Basswood	.19	.28	1.4
Beech	.16	.36	2.2
Birch, yellow	.22	.28	1.3
Butternut	.10	.19	1.9
Cherry	.11	.21	1.9
Elm, American	.12	.28	2.3
Hickory	.22	.35	1.4
Locust, black	.13	.21	1.6
Maple, sugar	.14	.30	2.1
Oak, red	.13	.31	2.1
Oak, white	.15	.31	1.8
Sassafras	.12	.18	1.6
Sycamore, American	.14	.25	1.7
Walnut, black	.16	.23	1.4
Willow, black	.09	.26	2.6
Yellow, poplar	.13	.24	1.8
Softwoods			
Baldcypress	.11	.18	1.6
Cedar, Alaska	.08	.17	2.1
Douglas-fir (coastal)	.14	.22	1.6
Pine, eastern white	.06	.18	2.9
Redwood (second growth)	.08	.17	2.2
Spruce, Sitka	.12	.22	1.7
Imported Woods			
Khaya	.12	.17	1.4
Lauan, Dark red	.11	.22	2.1
Mahogany	.14	.20	1.4
Teak	.08	.16	1.8

Decimal equivalents

.03 = ¹⁄₃₂-in.   .125 = ⅛-in.   .31 = ⁵⁄₁₆-in.   .44 = ⁷⁄₁₆-in.
.06 = ¹⁄₁₆-in.   .25 = ¼-in.   .38 = ⅜-in.   .50 = ½-in.

[1] *Ratio of tangential to radial shrinkage (green to oven-dry) indicates tendency to cup in flatsawn lumber. Higher ratio means a greater chance of cupping.*

to equilibrium with its environment, it will continue to shrink and swell with any change in relative humidity. You can determine your annual moisture range by monitoring local conditions or by consulting a moisture-change map, like the one in Hoadley's book.

I feel that for my area (and much of the midwest and the northeast), a 7% change in MC (5% to 12%) is appropriate for wood that has been treated with a moderately moisture resistant finish, like polymerized oil. Wood with a highly resistant finish (lacquer, shellac or varnish) might change as little as 3%. For many coastal areas, plus much of the south, a 3.5% range would work nicely.

Think of the measurements in the table as baselines, which you can adjust for changes in width, MC, or both by simple arithmetic. For example, take an 18-in. flatsawn red oak door panel. The table gives a movement of .31 in. over a 7% MC cycle for a 12 in. width. Since movement is directly proportional to width, the calculation is simple—18 is 1.5 times 12, so the movement for an 18-in. board is 1.5 times the movement of a 12-in. board or $1.5 \times .31 = .46$ in.

The MC range is figured in the same way. If you live in a 3.5% area (half of our 7% baseline), simply halve the result of your movement calculation.

For best results, you also must determine the current moisture content of the wood, usually with a meter like the one shown on p. 111. If we want to install the 18-in. panel in a frame, our answer of .46 means that we must allow for at least a .23 in. movement in each side slot, but we must know the panel's current moisture content to decide whether to fit tight or loose.

Fitting tight in the summer and loose in the winter is a general rule. In any case, it's best to allow a little extra for movement, especially if you can't determine the current MC or face conditions that could produce extreme variations—say, furniture built in the dry southwest being shipped to the Pacific northwest. Once you understand how moisture affects wood movement, almost any situation can be anticipated. □

Tom Liebl designs and builds furniture and boats in Madison, Wisc.

---

probe tips or resistors with your hands as this will change the reading. The meter is now calibrated for all ranges, and should remain accurate as long as the batteries are good.

To use the meter, jam the probe straight into a clear area of the board's face, so that an imaginary line between the points runs parallel to the grain. For the most accurate reading, measure the wood at room temperature. Also, don't insert the probe towards the end of a sample, which will probably be drier than the rest of the board. When measuring, switch the meter ranges from lowest to highest (i.e. A to E) and stop at the position that gives a mid-range reading, usually the most accurate and easiest to read. If you can't get a reading, the sample probably has a moisture content of

6% or less. Readings may vary from one part of the board to another due to improper drying, abnormalities in grain structure, dirt and other surface contamination. If you have any doubts about a reading, probe several other areas of the sample.

I've found that having such a useful and inexpensive instrument in the shop is a real plus. If you're contemplating working with wide panels it would be wise to determine the moisture content of the stock before you begin work. The time and trouble you'll save is well worth the effort. □

Rick Liftig lives in Meriden, Ct., where he dabbles in woodworking and electronics.

Managing a Rain Forest
A *Peruvian experiment in sustained yield*

by Scott Landis

Magazines and newspapers are filled with accounts of the rain forest in retreat. The cumulative effects of cattle ranching, slash-and-burn agriculture, timber mining, hydroelectric dams and overpopulation have rolled across the tropics and the media like wildfire. Notably absent in all these pages of print are any signs of progress.

Part of the problem, I think, is that people have been looking in the wrong direction, banking on grandiose schemes. In the Amazon at least, spectacular attempts almost always end in magnificent failure. Two of these examples are Henry Ford's defunct rubber-tree plantation, "Fordlandia," and shipping magnate Daniel K. Ludwig's "Jari," a billion-dollar pulpwood farm the size of Connecticut. Ludwig's and Ford's misadventures provide extravagant lessons in the futility of applying temperate-zone silvicultural practices to the tropics.

In the Palcazú Valley of central Peru, however, a small experiment in sustainable tropical-forest management is different from previous attempts. While most timber-management operations in the Amazon rely on plantations of a few non-native species, the Palcazú project is dedicated to retaining the diverse selection of regional species. And where most commercial woodcutting operations are in the hands of large companies, this project is managed by the Yanesha Forestry Cooperative, made up of a small native group of Yanesha Indians. These people account for about half of the 6,500 residents of the Palcazú Valley. The rest are mainly expatriate European coffee farmers and cattle ranchers and their descendants, along with a small population of mestizo Peruvians. The valley's 12 Yanesha communities, which occupy only 40% of the land, control more than 60% of its best production forest. The fact that the Yanesha own the land they are harvesting and rely on it to support their traditional culture gives them a stake in its survival. What's more, tropical timber is usually cut on a one-shot basis, and initial results of the Palcazú project suggest that the co-op's methods are sustainable.

When I visited Peru in March of 1989, I found the Yanesha Forestry Cooperative tenaciously clinging to life, despite a distinctly hostile climate. Unlike Jari and Fordlandia, however, which ran afoul of the ecological realities of the tropical rain forest, the Yanesha cooperative is threatened more by Peru's economic and political crises than by the natural environment. In fact, the co-op's innovative approach to forest management sheds light on what is otherwise a very dark landscape. And it may have important implications for harvesters and users of tropical hardwoods around the world.

The strip shelterbelt system—The centerpiece of the Yanesha project is the strip shelterbelt system, which involves clear-cutting and removing all trees and woody plants within a narrow strip of forest. These strips range from 20 yds. to 50 yds. wide and are designed to simulate the natural gap created when a mature tree is

As many as 1,000 species of trees grow in central Peru's Palcazú Valley rain forest. The area's Yanesha Indians are experimenting with a forest-management system that they hope will bring a sustained yield of valuable lumber and wood by-products.

blown down. The artificial openings in the canopy are wide enough to permit sunlight to stimulate the regeneration of many fast-growing, light-loving native species, yet they are narrow enough for unassisted, natural reseeding from the surrounding forest on either side (shown in the left photo on the next page). The effects of erosion and the disruption of animal habitat are minimized by the small size of the strips, which are more efficiently harvested with teams of oxen than with heavy skidders. Oxen are less expensive and more easily maintained in the Palcazú Valley—where a gallon of gasoline costs $2, or about as much as a co-op bush worker makes in a day—and their impact on the soil is much more benign.

The strip shelterbelt system was promoted by ecologists Gary

Left: The strip shelterbelt system involves clear-cutting and removing all trees and woody plants from narrow lands of forest to simulate the clearing created when a mature tree falls. The three-month-old regrowth shown was possible because of sunlight penetration and natural reseeding from the nearby forest. Right: The small strips are efficiently harvested with teams of oxen, which are less expensive and more easily maintained than heavy skidders that may heavily damage the ecosystem.

Hartshorn and Joseph Tosi and their colleagues at the Tropical Science Center (TSC) in Costa Rica. Commissioned in 1981 by the United States Agency for International Development (USAID) to devise a management scheme for the project, the TSC was unwilling to accept conventional wisdom, which considered the tropical rain forest unmanageable.

Hartshorn discovered that the Yanesha are "superb woodsmen." They not only know the forest plants and trees, they intuitively "capture the underlying ecology" behind the strip shelterbelt system. What's more, their traditional communal society made them more receptive to the cooperative structure than their European counterparts. The result is the first indigenous forestry co-op in tropical America, and perhaps the only one in the world dedicated to natural forest management.

The Palcazú Valley is a true tropical environment. Rain falls year-round, but it is torrential in the summer (November to March), and regularly interrupts work and transportation. The valley is less than 150 miles from Lima and the arid Pacific coast, but has a median temperature of 77°F and receives nearly 20 ft. of rainfall a year. I visited the co-op near the end of the wet season, and witnessed the speed with which rains pass through the highly erodible, acid soil. After an intense predawn thunderstorm on the first morning, my party crossed the roiling, coffee-color Iscozacin River, which flows into the Palcazú River and eventually joins the Amazon. Guides maneuvered the motorized dugout canoe around standing waves several feet high and entire trees swept downstream in the maelstrom. When we crossed the river later that afternoon, it had dropped more than 6 ft. since the morning flood stage and was a relatively placid current.

At the landing on the other shore, we piled into the back of the

For more information _____

The following organizations promote sustainable development of the tropical rain forest.

Friends of the Earth, 218 D St. S.E., Washington, DC 20003; (202) 544-2600.

Fundación Peruana para la Conservación de la Naturaleza (FPCN), Chinchón 858/A, San Isidro, Aptdo. 18-1393, Lima, Peru; 422 796.

The Nature Conservancy, 1815 N. Lynn St., Arlington, VA 22209; (703) 841-5300.

Tropical Science Center, Apartado 8-3870, San Jose 1000, Costa Rica.

Woodworkers Against Rainforest Destruction (WARD), 20 Stearns Court, Northampton, MA 01060; (413) 586-6126.

Woodworkers Alliance for Rainforest Protection (WARP), c/o Scott Landis, Hundred Acres Road, Newtown, CT 06470.

World Wildlife Fund, 1250 24th St. N.W., Washington, DC 20037; (202) 293-4800.

co-op's battered, four-wheel-drive Toyota pickup for a 40-minute, bone-crunching ride to the project site. The truck forded a creek and wallowed above its axles through rocky mud holes. Along the way, we passed a number of small homesteads, where the Yanesha raise coffee, citrus and tropical sheep, perhaps a cow or some chickens, and more traditional crops like cassava, upland rice and yucca.

Preserving the diversity—The combination of perpetual rain and heat results in what one of our guides called a "pandemonium of growth." The mature rain forest I saw is crawling with highly adapted and predatory plant and insect life. Very little sunlight penetrates the canopy, so the understory remains relatively free of small trees. There are an estimated 1,000 species of trees in the Palcazú Valley, perhaps as many as 200 in a single hectare (roughly 2½ acres) of its wettest lowlands. Compare this diversity to that of a hectare of rich Appalachian forest in the U.S., which has no more than 25 different tree species. At least 10% of the Palcazú species are still unidentified and the working properties of many of their woods are unknown.

We began our tour by visiting two production strips. On the first strip, which was 30 yds. wide by 100 yds. long, cutting had begun in 1988, when the smallest trees were harvested as utility posts. The last of the large sawlogs were removed and the strip was cut clean only three months before my visit. Significant new growth already had sprouted from stumps and airborne seeds.

At a second strip, well away from the first one, only the smaller trees and lianas, the woody vines that wrap themselves around the trunks and tie the canopy together, had been cut. By cutting the lianas first and allowing them to decompose, they are less likely to interfere with felling the larger timber. A ganglion of lianas is capable of holding a mature tree upright after its trunk has been severed, making it necessary to drop several trees at once.

Hartshorn and other co-op advisers estimate a regeneration cycle of 30 to 40 years, which is one-half to one-third as long as in most managed temperate-zone forests. The project plan calls for cutting several strips per year, with new strips located at least 100 yds. from others recently cut. Limited thinning or selective planting may be used to augment the natural succession.

Although it will take at least one or two cycles to fully evaluate the strip shelterbelt system, the initial results are impressive. Two test strips were studied in April 1988, when one was 2½ years old and the other 2 years old. In the first strip, 20 yds. by 75 yds., 209 tree species were identified—almost three times the number originally harvested. In the second strip, 50 yds. by 100 yds., there were 285 different species. In both strips, the crown was completely closed by the second year, indicating successful regeneration.

Besides producing lumber in its sawmill, the Yanesha Forestry Cooperative also treats posts and railroad ties in a pressurized-post-preserving facility. Small and crooked parts end up in the co-op's charcoal kiln.

High-yielding strips—Wood is processed in the co-op's facility, shown in the photo above, which includes a sawmill, a pressurized post-preservation plant and a charcoal kiln. All logs greater than 12 in. in diameter are run through the sawmill. Smaller logs, between 2 in. and 12 in. in diameter, are diverted to post production. And anything too small or gnarled to become a post or sawlog is turned into marketable charcoal.

The variety of hardwood timber is staggering. Perhaps to the valley's benefit, it is too wet to grow mahogany, rosewood or cedar, which probably would have been extracted long ago. But there are a host of other valuable, native species (see the chart on the next pages). In a small shop adjacent to the sawmill, co-op workers have begun to test wood properties and build simple furniture, which promises to bring a greater financial return out of each board.

Although I was most interested in sawlogs, lumber represents only about 40% of the co-op's total production. According to Michel Krones, the Argentinean forester who supervised the construction of the sawmill and preservation facility, "The goose with the golden egg is in posts." Without preservatives, the densest hardwoods might last four to five years in contact with the soil; in the tropics, softer hardwoods will rot in less than a year. But Krones estimates that when those same softer hardwoods are properly treated, they will last 10 to 15 years under the most extreme conditions in the valley, and much longer in the Andes or on Peru's arid coastal plain. The more valuable hardwoods will last even longer. And there is a ready market in the developing world for well-preserved fence posts, railroad ties, mining timbers and utility poles.

The key to the success of the strip shelterbelt system is using most of the wood in each strip. If demand for valuable hardwood was to cause the co-op to cut only a few of the most marketable species, the devastating slash-and-burn cycle would be inevitable. Similarly, if the understory is cleared of small timber to meet a sudden demand for posts, the diversity and natural succession of the forest will be destroyed. Properly harvested, the potential yield of the local rain forest has been estimated at 250 cu. yds. of wood per hectare. Compared with the more typical yield of 3 cu. yds. to 5 cu. yds. per hectare of average South American rain forest, the economic and environmental benefits of the strip shelterbelt management system are manifest.

Not out of the woods—So far, the co-op's success is encouraging, but many concerns must still be addressed. What are the long-term effects of removing the biomass? How many slow-growing species will be sacrificed by the proposed 30- to 40-year production cycle? Can the co-op establish markets for unknown species of hardwood lumber and guarantee a steady supply? What are the chances of duplicating the experiment in other communities? At the time of my visit, only 5 of the 12 Yanesha communities were co-op participants, with about 150 members and 27 active employees.

The fact that research and production are taking place simultaneously at the Yanesha co-op worries Howard Clark, a USAID consultant I spoke with in Lima. "That's the scary thing," Clark said. "You're supposed to do the research one day, and use the data the next." But he also acknowledged that "there is *no* appropriate technology. Everything that's been tried in the Amazon in the last two centuries has failed—so everything is research."

The co-op also faces economic and political pressure. In the towns surrounding the valley, commercial loggers hope to gain access to the timber. Peru is one of the poorest countries in Latin America and its inflation rate, which was 3,000% in 1988, makes it hard to buy and maintain co-op equipment. And just as the project was finally getting on its feet, the reported presence of Sendero Luminoso, the Shining Path guerrilla group, caused USAID to remove its advisers from the Palcazú in the fall of 1988 and reallocate remaining funds. As of this writing, the co-op is being kept afloat by the Fundación Peruana para la Conservación de la Naturaleza (FPCN), with funding from the General Service Foundation and the World Wildlife Fund.

As one observer in Lima explained, "es un periodo bastante critico"—a critical period not only for the co-op, but for all of Peru and its rain forest. And while Hartshorn admits that more information would be useful, he warns that "we don't have the time to sit around and wait 10 to 20 years for proper research to be done." If we wait that long, there may not be any rain forest left to study. □

Scott Landis is a writer in Newtown, Conn., and a founder of Woodworkers Alliance for Rainforest Protection (WARP). Photos by author.

Efforts to revalue tropical timber

Among many woodworkers, there is a growing sense of urgency and despair at the destruction of the rain forest and the dwindling supply of precious hardwoods. Some of these craftspeople are trying to become part of the solution, with proposals that range from stock-piling endangered species to boycotting tropical rain-forest timbers. Unfortunately, neither approach is likely to have more than a short-term effect, and both may hasten the destruction they seek to forestall. In fact, a successful boycott is probably the surest way to guarantee the forest's conversion to crop or ranch land. I think that unless Third-World countries can be convinced that their rain forests are worth more alive than dead, their governments will readily trade them for immediate survival needs. And who can blame them?

These issues trouble Californian John Shipstad, chairman of the Sonoma County Woodworker's Association (SCWA), who was looking for a more satisfying outlet than just donating to environmental groups.

Shipstad found a receptive ear in John Curtis of The Luthier's Mercantile, a wood and tool retailer (Box 774, 412 Moore Lane, Healdsburg, Cal. 95448; 800-477-4437). After many negotiations and a trip by Curtis to Peru's Palcazú Valley, The Luthier's Mercantile organized the first export shipment of hardwoods from the Yanesha Forestry Cooperative. Wood samples and descriptions from this shipment are given in the chart on the next two pages.

It's a unique arrangement: Members of

SCWA and other interested organizations and individuals invested $1.50 per bd. ft. up front, against an estimated break-even cost of $1.91 per bd. ft. The Yanesha co-op is paid $1 per bd. ft. and the rest is absorbed by shipping, customs, container rental and travel costs. All participating woodworkers listed their first, second and third choice of woods, based on 19 samples they received. They'll pay the difference between their down payment and the actual cost when they pick up their order.

Approximately 7,300 bd. ft. of lumber was trucked across the Andes to Lima for transshipment by container to California. The co-op truck made three round-trips, each one a four-day ordeal over switchback, washed-out roads that puts years on any vehicle and takes them off the life expectancy of its driver. A 20-ft. container generally carries 10,000 bd. ft. of lumber, but the density and moisture content of the wood made a considerable dent in the weight of the first load. Curtis hopes that future loads will be dried in the valley before shipping.

Australian hardwoods: James Heusinger of Berea HardWoods (125 Jacqueline Drive, Berea, Ohio 44017; 216-243-4452) is working with Cockatoo Timbers of Australia to develop a line of exotic Australian hardwoods. Almost everything he gets is salvaged from other cutting operations and comes in several categories: readily available, regularly available (every eight months or so) and one-time only.

Heusinger rattled off an impressive list of write-offs, such as unworkably hard desert acacia, a batch of she oak that checked into pieces during shipment and some Tasmanian blackwood that was "so ugly and checked" he will be lucky to unload it. But there were pleasant surprises too. When slicing open an unspectacular log of blackheart dorrel, Heusinger struck a vein of multicolor heart stain that develops striking flame-shape fingers in the sides of a turned bowl.

The efforts of individuals: Not long ago, furnituremaker Silas Kopf organized a group called Woodworkers Against Rainforest Destruction (WARD) (see p. 114 for address) to deal with the economic and ecological issues of the rain forest. Kopf admits that custom woodworkers make a very small dent in the worldwide consumption of tropical hardwoods. But he hopes that their example will pressure the rest of the industry to conduct itself more responsibly. WARD proposes that a flexible surtax be levied on any piece of furniture that uses tropical hardwoods and the proceeds go to support sustainable timber-harvesting of the rain forest. As of this writing, Kopf and WARD have joined forces with a more broad-based organization, the Woodworkers Alliance for Rainforest Protection (WARP), which is planning a conference for this fall. —S.L.

Little-Known Exotics from Peru

Notes:

Wood samples provided by John Curtis, The Luthier's Mercantile.

Information compiled from data by Curtis and *Tropical Timbers of the World,* Martin Chudnoff, Forest Products Laboratory, USDA Forest Service, Box 5130, Madison, Wisc. 53705.

Description/Working Properties

Almendro, *Caryocar glabrum*: Attains height of 170 ft. with straight-bole diameters of 5 ft. to 7 ft.; free of branches for 60 ft. to 70 ft. Interlocked grain with a ribbon figure. Heartwood is honey color; sapwood is white. Resistant to rot and marine borers. Moderately abundant. Moderately difficult to saw; fair re-

Cachimbo, *Cariniana* sp.: Attains height of 150 ft. with trunk up to 30 in. in diameter; free of branches to 70 ft. Grain is roey with a fine texture. Heartwood and sapwood are indistinguishable when dry and can be yellowish-, pinkish- or reddish-brown with purple tinge and dark streaks. It is easy to saw, plane, turn

Chontaquiro Amarillo, *Diplotropis martiusii*: Attains height of 120 ft. with straight trunk of 30 in. or more in diameter; may be free of branches to 70 ft. Texture is coarse with yellowish sapwood and light- to dark-brown heartwood, which is very resistant to rot. Trees are relatively abundant. Works well with

Marupá, *Simarouba amara*: Attains height of 140 ft. with a straight trunk up to 36 in. in diameter; may be free of branches to 90 ft. Wood is straight grained and has a uniform texture. Sapwood and heartwood are indistinguishable and become yellowish-white when exposed. Somewhat susceptible to some rots

Quinilla Colorada, *Manilkara bidentata*: Reaches height of 100 ft. to 150 ft. and trunk diameters of 2 ft. to 4 ft. Boles are clear and straight to 60 ft. Wood is hard and heavy, grain is usually straight with occasional waviness; texture is fine. Heartwood is light- to dark-reddish-brown, but often not distinct from whit-

Requia, *Guarea* sp.: Suggested as a mahogany substitute. Reaches height of 150 ft. with diameters to 4 ft.; free of branches to one-third its height. Its straight, interlocked grain produces a ribbon figure with a medium texture. Sapwood is yellowish and heartwood is pinkish-, brownish- to reddish-mahogany,

Tornillo, *Cedrelinga catenaeformis*: Attains height of 150 ft. with straight, well-formed trunk over 4 ft. in diameter; free of branches for 80 ft. Wood is straight grained to roey with occasional wavy grain. Sapwood is off-white and heartwood is pink to golden brown. Texture is medium to coarse. It is fairly durable.

Turupay, *Clarisia racemosa*: Attains height of 130 ft. with well-formed trunks to 40 in. in diameter; free of branches to 60 ft. Grain is usually interlocked, producing a ribbon figure on the radial surface. It has a medium texture. Heartwood is pale to bright yellow and remains golden on exposure. Sapwood is

[1] Stability is the sum of percent radial and percent tangential dimensional changes. Small is less than 3.0%, medium is 3.0% to 4.5%, and large is over 4.5%.

[2] Compression parallel to the grain, in psi.

* No information available.

† Strength at 12% MC

Description/Working Properties (cont.)	Specific Gravity	Weight, lbs./cu. ft. at 12% MC	Tangential Shrinkage, % green to dry	Stability or Movement When in Use[1]	Bending Modulus of Rupture, psi†	Modulus of Elasticity, 1,000 psi†	Maximum Crushing Strength[2]
sults from planing; sands smoothly and turns well. Used in boatbuilding, furniture, flooring and applications requiring wear resistance.	.67 to .80	50 to 58	8.0	Small	17,060	2,160	8,410
and bore; it sands well and takes a smooth, glossy finish. Some species have a high silica content and will dull tools. Used for construction, furniture, shipbuilding, flooring, veneering and turnery.	.50 to .70	31 to 43	5.4	Small	13,800	1,410	7,100
saws and edge tools, and sands to a fine finish; only fair turning results are reported. Used in construction, furniture, parquetry, cabinetry and interior finish.	.74	46	*	Small	*	*	*
and stains. Trees are fast growing and abundant. Wood is reported to saw easily. Planing results are excellent; it turns fairly well and sands well. Wood stains and finishes easily and glues well. Uses include interior construction, boxes, furniture, veneering, patternmaking, millwork and particleboard. Reported to be excellent for carving.	.30 to .45	19 to 28	5.0	Small	8,350	1,290	4,900
ish or pale-brown sapwood. Trees are widely distributed and highly frequent. Reported to be moderately difficult to saw and sand, but all other sharp-edge tool working properties are rated excellent. Gluing requires special care. Steam-bending properties are rated excellent. Uses include construction, turnery, boat frames, bent work, violin bows and billiard cues.	.90 to 1.20	56 to 75	9.4	*	29,200	3,520	13,300
which is very resistant to rot, fungus and insects. Its frequency is reported to be medium and it's widely distributed. Easily worked with all tools. It has a tendency to tear when bored. Uses include furniture, cabinetry, turned pieces, musical instruments, boat planking, veneering and millwork.	.46 to .57	34 to 44	7.0	Small	12,750	1,400	6,950
Behind eucalyptus, it's the second most frequently sawn wood and accounts for more than 14% of woods produced by Peruvian sawmills. Easy to saw, but leaves woolly surfaces. Planing requires sharp edges to produce smooth surfaces in interlocking or cross-grain pieces. Turns and bores easily. Uses include interior carpentry, furniture, turnery, carvings and drawer sides.	.41 to .60	25 to 38	*	Small	7,568	1,280	4,026
white. Trees are widely distributed in scattered clumps. Easily worked. Rated fair to good in all machining operations. Requires sharp tools to produce a smooth surface. Sawing often produces woolly surfaces. Uses in construction, flooring, furniture and millwork.	.50 to .65	31 to 40	6.1	Small	16,700	2,340	9,620

Tacho negro, *Terminalia* sp.*

Pashaco, *Albizzia* sp.*

Roble negro*

Tropical Deforestation
Are woodworkers to blame?

by George Putz

Woodworkers who regularly build with rosewood, padauk and other exotic timbers may sometimes worry that they are encouraging the destruction of tropical forests, but the amount of wood they use is almost insignificant. While it's true that 1.7% of the world's moist tropical forests are being cleared annually, the exotics prized by woodworkers are what commercial fishermen would classify as a "bicatch," a saleable material gathered incidentally to the real business at hand—cutting trees for construction lumber and firewood, and clearing land for pulp-tree plantations, hydroelectric projects, cattle ranches, farms and roads.

The destruction of these forests would continue even if small cabinet shops and hobbyists stopped buying exotic timbers. This is not to say that woodworkers are blameless. Our contribution to the problem is smallest among the lumber consumers, but it's the most specific. We are virtually the sole users of such exotic species as cocobolo, rosewood, ebony and purpleheart. The money we pay for these timbers trickles down to loggers in Africa, South America, Asia and other countries and encourages them to continue the "harvest" of exotics. This might be acceptable if the jungle regenerated quickly and easily from this cutting, but it doesn't. It can take hundreds of years for a tropical forest to regenerate and even then, many species of plants and animals may never come back. We owe it to ourselves as craftspeople to understand the problem and wield what clout we can to encourage the preservation of these virtually irreplaceable forests.

You must realize, though, that in much of the world, tropical timbers are not prized for their beauty or considered very valuable. The wood is so cheap in Asian countries that vast quantities are used for dunnage, a trade name for pallets and ship ballasts. Hardwoods that would be a woodworker's delight in this country become paper, plywood or cheap mass-produced furniture for growing Asian markets. It may seem criminal to waste magnificent trees for such mundane products, but they are crucially important sources of hard cash in the tropical forests of developing Third World countries, where day-to-day survival is more of an issue than the environment or conservation.

Human survival versus forest conservation—Explosive population growth and unsound farming practices also promote tropical deforestation. The populations of many developing countries are growing at alarming rates. Brazil's population, for instance, is expected to double in the next 30 years. Hundreds of thousands of landless, urban poor are relocating to the Amazon basin as part of the government's land reform policy. The peasants move into the forest, cut trees for lumber and firewood, then slash and burn much of the remaining timber to create farmland.

Unfortunately, the jungle floor is not fertile enough to sustain many crops. After several meager harvests, which further deplete the soil, the peasants bring in cattle to range on any remaining scrub growth. When the land won't even support cattle, it's abandoned—a highly eroded, parched semi-desert. The peasants move on to clear-cut another jungle tract, and the cycle is repeated. There are similar jungle resettlement programs underway in Peru, Bolivia and Colombia.

It's not surprising that Third World people don't understand the problem or need for reform. Much of the rest of the world is equally unaware. Too often, vital news concerning these forests goes unreported. In 1982, a sawmill waste fire ignited a blaze that consumed 3.9 million acres of Borneo jungle. Weeks later, the fire received one paragraph on the third page of the *New York Times*. And, much of what little is reported is wrong and misleading. Several timber-exporting countries, apparently unaware of environmental-monitoring satellites, habitually lie to the international community about their forest cutting. India and Indonesia are worst in this regard, underreporting their cuts by as much as 800%.

The importance of rain forests—Like Mideast oil wells, tropical forests are far from Western woodworkers, but they are important to us. Life-saving drugs, like vincristine and vinblastine, used to treat leukemia are produced from the rosy periwinkle, a jungle plant destroyed in clear-cutting. Gums and resins produced in the rain forests are components of varnishes and inks. Oils from the tropics provide the essence for mouthwashes, perfumes and deodorants. Other oils and waxes, like carnauba, are still gathered solely from forests in northeast Brazil. The latex used in paints comes from both forests and plantations. This is to say nothing of the potential, undiscovered resources within these forests. With every tree burned, up in smoke go undiscovered organisms for genetic research, future food crops and other possible life-saving drugs.

Tropical forests can infinitely supply food, fuel and lumber, providing these products aren't taken at a rate that exceeds the forest's ability to supply them. Agro-forestry is the science of cultivating the forest so it continuously supplies more than just wood. For instance, citrus and mulberry trees have been planted successfully in the jungle throughout Polynesia. Third World countries are beginning to realize that agro-forestry can provide much of their country's needed foreign exchange while preserving their forests.

These forests have more than economic importance. Even though they comprise only 7% of the world's forest cover, scientists believe they are crucial to maintaining the carbon dioxide level in

From *Fine Woodworking* (May 1988) 70:80-85

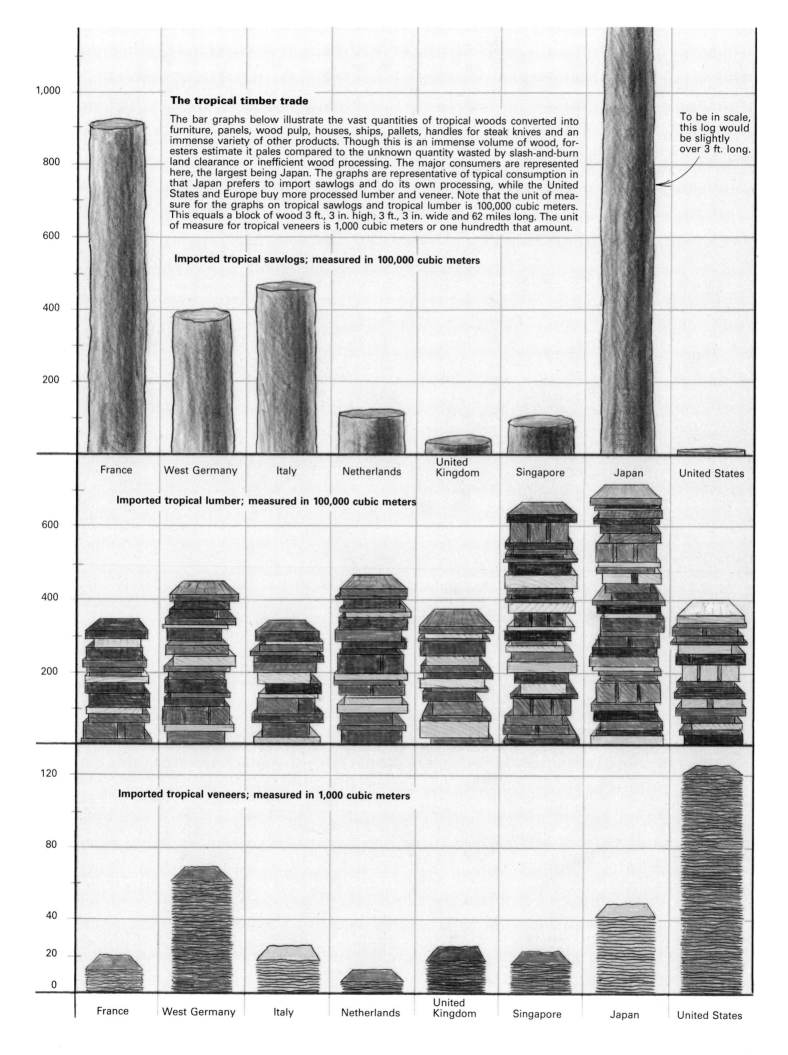

The tropical timber trade

The bar graphs below illustrate the vast quantities of tropical woods converted into furniture, panels, wood pulp, houses, ships, pallets, handles for steak knives and an immense variety of other products. Though this is an immense volume of wood, foresters estimate it pales compared to the unknown quantity wasted by slash-and-burn land clearance or inefficient wood processing. The major consumers are represented here, the largest being Japan. The graphs are representative of typical consumption in that Japan prefers to import sawlogs and do its own processing, while the United States and Europe buy more processed lumber and veneer. Note that the unit of measure for the graphs on tropical sawlogs and tropical lumber is 100,000 cubic meters. This equals a block of wood 3 ft., 3 in. high, 3 ft., 3 in. wide and 62 miles long. The unit of measure for tropical veneers is 1,000 cubic meters or one hundredth that amount.

Imported tropical sawlogs; measured in 100,000 cubic meters

To be in scale, this log would be slightly over 3 ft. long.

France · West Germany · Italy · Netherlands · United Kingdom · Singapore · Japan · United States

Imported tropical lumber; measured in 100,000 cubic meters

Imported tropical veneers; measured in 1,000 cubic meters

France · West Germany · Italy · Netherlands · United Kingdom · Singapore · Japan · United States

the Earth's atmosphere, important for plant photosynthesis and, in part, for maintaining the Earth's atmospheric temperature. The vegetation of the tropical forests soaks up rainfall and maintains proper continental drainage patterns, preventing flooding and reducing erosion.

Tropical versus temperate forests – Rain forests exist in a wide swath, extending hundreds of miles north and south of the equator. They are found in southern Central America, northern and central South America, throughout much of Southeast Asia, western, coastal and central Africa and northern Australia. Rainfall in these areas often exceeds 100 in. a year (as compared to about 44 in. to 46 in. where I live in northern New England). The diversity of plant and animal life in tropical forests is staggering. They are home to several thousand tree species (as opposed to about 700 found in the United States and Canada), millions of insect species, and at least 100,000 species of birds, fish and reptiles.

Tropical forests are a product of the basic biological axiom that organisms thrive and diversify in a nurturing environment. Forests that grow in harsh environments have large numbers of fewer species. To illustrate this, compare a one-acre plot from the three forest types that produce many of our wood stocks: a birch-beech-maple forest in northern New England, a mixed hardwood forest of West Virginia and a Brazilian rain forest.

A fully developed northeastern hardwood stand would include about two dozen species of woody plants, including shrubs. About a half dozen of these species, including ash, red oak and maple, are suitable for woodworking. The West Virginia forest contains about 70 species—two dozen of them suitable for woodworking. Added to some of the species previously mentioned would be walnut and cherry. In the Brazilian stand, more than 100 tree species grow in an acre and perhaps 75 of them would be suitable for woodworking.

If a woodcutter seeks a particular tree species, he will find as many as 30 in the Northeastern forest, perhaps eight or nine in the West Virginia forest, but only one in the Brazilian forest. Harvesting a large quantity of good clear logs of a particular species is rather simple in fully developed temperate forests—say 30 oak trees can be taken from one acre. To get just one Brazilian rosewood tree, however, entails a comparatively huge effort and yields enormous waste as surrounding trees are bulldozed away to make logging trails or damaged by the felling and skidding process—a situation only slightly improved where elephants are used in Southeast Asia. A huge area, perhaps hundreds of acres, must be cleared to take 30 rosewoods. In tropical logging, the rule of thumb is that 50% of the forest must be cleared to extract 10% of its wood.

Then there is the problem of how tropical forests grow. Consider that the hardwood stand in the northeastern United States is only about 10,000 years old and that all the vegetation you see represents about 23% of the living matter in the forest. The rest is in the soil. On the other hand, the usual tropical forest is between 40 million and 70 million years old, and as much as 93% of the forest's living matter exists above the soil. Cut all the trees in the temperate woods, and we still have a lot of resources left with which to grow a new forest. Cut down a tropical forest, and we've taken the whole biological ball of wax.

Furthermore, the thin and fragile topsoils are compacted by the bulldozers that clear logging roads and drag out felled trees. Without the shade provided by the tree canopy, the exposed soil bakes in the sun and is pummeled by rainfall that otherwise would have been deflected by the leaves. Instead of being absorbed, the water runs along the ground's surface and gains speed going down hills, washing away meager topsoil and leaching the few nutrients in the soil left behind. In Costa Rica, scientists studying soil erosion in clear-cut forests have found that suspended matter (soil and organic debris) in lakes and streams near the felled area increases by 1,600%. Nitrogen, an element vital to soil health, leaches from the soil into the water, with increases of 800% found. It's estimated that it takes 1,000 years for a badly eroded forest soil to completely regenerate, whether it be in a tropical or temperate forest.

In a northern forest, a responsibly harvested clear-cut, one in which measures have been taken to reduce erosion, has good rich soil on which to regenerate and lots of parent stock nearby to reseed the barren area. In a tropical forest, the nearest tree of the same species is acres away. Tropical forests should not be thought of so much as a stand of trees, but rather as a very complex and diverse community of organisms. Tropical tree species need more than just another tree to provide seeds for continuation of a species; they need an enormously complex and diverse system involving mammals, birds, insects, reptiles and other pollinators and seed dispersers.

This complex system is easily disturbed. Every time an exotic tree is cut, we risk throwing a wrench into the tropical forest's ecosystem. The more trees removed, the more damage done. If trees are to be harvested for lumber, they need to be taken sparingly and carefully to allow the forest enough time to regenerate.

Growing demand, shrinking supplies – The supply of exotic sawlogs exported to the United States is bound to dwindle in coming years for at least two reasons, aside from blatant deforestation. As Third World nations develop their economies, they will pocket more profit from their wood exports by turning their own timber into chipboard and finished or semi-finished wood products like desk accessories, furniture parts or finished furniture. They will saw more of their own lumber and slice more of their own veneer rather than export sawlogs. Their paper consumption will also increase, and trees that otherwise would have been sawn for furniture-grade lumber may be pulped instead. You would think that those trees worth more for lumber or veneer than for pulp would be reserved for those products, but expediency often rules the day in developing nations, and the logs may be pulped regardless. The result is that wide, solid planks of exotic timber will be more expensive and scarcer. Woodworkers will have to use more veneer and more veneered panels produced in the exporting countries.

Increasingly, exotics and other timbers are being traded as a future's commodity in the same sense that soybeans and corn are. When you buy a select piece of exotic lumber, you may be competing with traders buying vast quantities of the same wood. Lumber is not as readily available as yearly food crops, so when timber futures are traded, vast quantities are locked up in warehouses, awaiting the day when the contract comes due, perhaps 10 years hence. I've heard that vast quantities of premium softwoods have been warehoused in British Columbia. I'm not sure whether premium exotics have been warehoused as well, but it wouldn't surprise me, in light of the demand for exotics (see the bar graph located on the previous page). Too, fads can wreak havoc. In the late 1970s, the Japanese discovered bowling, and in 18 months, built 50,000 lanes, driving up the price of rock (sugar) maple from 70¢ a bd. ft. to $4 a bd. ft. Entire groves of sugar maples evaporated, and several furniture, flooring and cabinet veneer mills were driven to their knees as a result. A similar situation could occur just as easily with tropical timbers.

A call to action—Though at ever-increasing expense, there is a sufficient supply of exotics to meet the needs of industry and the small-shop woodworker for another 30 years. During the next 15 years, when traditional species give out or near depletion, new species with unfamiliar names and working qualities will appear on the market. Whether or not woodworkers use these exotics will have a negligible effect on tropical deforestation. My advice is to buy quality stocks now—store and protect them. They should appreciate at about double the general inflation rate, and you will have them regardless of fluctuations in the timber market.

As woodworkers, we should organize into acquisition cooperatives that monitor the forest policies and cutting practices of tropical-wood exporters. We can then contract with those countries to buy exotic timbers, paying the premiums and costs necessary to maintain forests on a sustainable basis. This has the effect, essentially, of buying easements on the future tranquility of these forests. This would be very expensive to do and would make for extremely expensive exotic timbers, so I'm not hopeful that this will come about.

We should exert what influence we can, because small doesn't necessarily mean insignificant. The cumulative effect of our efforts, plus those of biologists, botanists and others who care about the future health of the rain forest, can be substantial. We should take what actions we can, while there are still rain forests left to save. □

George Putz, a freelance writer, editor and naturalist in Vinalhaven, Me., is currently working on a book on global deforestation to be published by Houghton Mifflin Co. For more information on rain forest destruction, contact the Environmental Defense Fund, International Program, Suite 150, 1616 P St., N.W., Washington, D.C. 20036; Rain Forest Action Network, Suite 28, 300 Broadway, San Francisco, Calif. 94133; or Friends of the Earth, 530 7th St., S.E., Washington, D.C. 20003.

A *cabinetmaker visits the jungle*

by Lucinda Leech

Bougainville, Papua New Guinea: "Temperature in the mid-90s (Fahrenheit), ground extremely muddy. Struggling to balance on logs and clumps of palm leaves in the mud. I frequently slip or get caught and tripped up by barbed vines. Razor-edged leaves shredding my legs. I stop for a minute to catch my breath and find flies and inch-long ants crawling in the mixture of sweat and blood around my ankles. Struggle on, hot, tired, thirsty, hungry, longing to find a bulldozer and hitch a lift back. Oh, you concerned environmentalists sitting on your backsides in comfy city offices—what do you want to save this hell of a jungle for? You think it pretty, yet you don't bother to come here to see for yourself. As for me, I'm too busy trying to find a footing and keep up with my guide to stop and gaze."

This excerpt from my diary, May 16, 1987, reminds me of how intense the jungle can be to a cabinetmaker such as myself, whose only contact with the tropics was with the wood I worked. An overreaction, fortunately I felt better after lunch. Mind you, I wasn't hacking my way through the jungle, but was slogging along a bulldozed logging trail with the manager of an Australian timber company. The rain forest is a beautiful and compelling place, true to the image nurtured in glossy coffee-table books, but it's also hostile. Jungles are as impenetrable as they are said to be, but you're attacked by ticks, leeches and ants rather than exciting tigers.

My interest in rain forests began a few years ago when I started hearing more and more about tropical deforestation. I wondered what my responsibilities as a wood user were and was determined

The author visited rain forests such as this one near Aseke, P.N.G., while investigating tropical deforestation in Southeast Asia, South America and Australia.

to find out firsthand if the horror stories I had read about were true. In 1986, with the help of a travel scholarship from the Worshipful Company of Furniture Makers (a London-based guild), I took a three-week trip to the Amazon basin in Brazil. The next year, I financed my own eight-week trip through peninsular Malaysia, Australia, Papua New Guinea (P.N.G.) and the Solomon Islands—all areas that support dense rain forests. My stay in these

countries was briefer than I would have liked, because I couldn't spend too much time away from my cabinet shop in Oxford, England. Therefore, my views are shaped more from observation than from thorough, academic-like research afforded by a long stay in an area.

I started my trip with many preconceived notions of ecological disaster. In the course of the two trips, my views on the subject were broadened, and I can see now that the issue is more com-

plex than I once thought. It's certain that forest products must be harvested to meet the economic and social needs of the developing nations in which they are located. The question remains whether the changes will be for the long-term benefit of these nations, and ourselves, or whether they will be to our collective detriment.

Timbering in the tropics: While on Bougainville, I saw loggers felling 150-ft.-tall trees, some of them with 100 ft. of trunk to the first branch. A man wielding a chainsaw with a 3-ft.-long bar stepped up to each tree and in five minutes, felled what took centuries to grow. Roaring bulldozers and log skidders crashed, smashed and ground through the jungle, tearing up undergrowth and spewing diesel fumes. It's easy to look on this destruction and say it should be banned. But the developing countries I visited cannot simply leave their forests alone; they need the income from their timber exports. Worldwide tropical hardwood timber exports are worth $8 billion a year in U.S. currency, and the tropical-timber trade accounts for about 60% of the world's hardwood trade.

Yet using rain forests as a resource need not destroy them. For instance, The Hyundai Group (a major international industrial corporation based in Seoul, South Korea) representatives in the nearby Solomon Islands proudly showed me how they observed logging regulations, keeping the required 164 ft. (50 meters) from streams, rivers and ponds and not logging on slopes with more than a 20% grade. Even small companies can carefully harvest small quantities of high-quality timber. I saw such a logging operation in the Ewingar Forest in the state of New South Wales, Australia. I was several miles into the logging area before I discovered a single felled tree. Short logging trails had been cut at an angle off the main road and trees were carefully dropped into these trails so they would do minimum damage as they fell.

Environmentalists often give the impression that tropical forests will be logged out tomorrow. After visiting Guadalcanal in the Solomon Islands, I learned that much of the forested terrain in tropical countries often is too steep or swampy to log economically. I heard from various sources that in another five years, Guadalcanal would be logged out. In fact, this applies only to the 15% of the island accessible for logging; the rest is too mountainous or swampy. P.N.G. consists of 46 million hectares, and of that, only 15 million are considered accessible for logging (1 hectare = 2.47 acres). In addition to natural barriers, all the countries I visited have legislation limiting the amount of timber that can be cut. Malay-

sia enacted a National Forest Policy in 1977 that declared 39% of the country's total area to be a permanent forest estate. Of this, 7.9 million hectares are loggable, while 3.7 million are protected forest. The policy was a reaction to massive timber cutting there—one third of the country's forest had been cleared in the last 20 years. Incidentally, this was not Malaysia's first step to protect its forests. In 1938, it set aside 4,343 square kilometers of rain forest for Taman Negara National Park.

I'm not naively saying that tropical deforestation is easily controlled with legislation. It's virtually impossible to police remote jungle logging, and corruption is a way of life in many developing nations. Timber money is said to run politics in Sarawak (a region north of Borneo belonging to Malaysia). And, a couple of thousand miles east, I arrived in P.N.G. only to find some key government people I needed to talk to had disappeared in the wake of a timber-price scandal. Allegedly, the quantity, grades and species of timber shipments had been purposefully misrecorded so less export tax would be due on them. A commission of inquiry had been established to investigate the scandal. I wonder if the commission would also learn of the activities of a timber company I visited there. I was bumping along a logging trail in a truck with the company's manager when he let it slip that two logging teams (I'd estimate 10 or 20 men) were felling illegally, in preserved forest, that day.

Tree plantations: I believe the rain forest's recuperative powers and its own inaccessibility will probably have more to do with saving it from destruction than high-minded conservation goals. I visited a forest in Guadalcanal that had been logged 20 years ago and found the dense undergrowth that had sprung up was hiding most traces of previous activity, at least to my uneducated eye. The only clue of logging was that the giant trees were gone. Still, the load on the jungle can and should be reduced by growing tree plantations for construction materials or paper pulp, neither of which require the high-quality forest trees being felled to provide them.

Plantations are still new and somewhat experimental. Those begun 30 years ago are only now starting to pay off, and the ones I visited in P.N.G. and peninsular Malaysia would still not be harvestable for another 10 or 15 years. Plantation trees are more easily harvestable and more uniform than their natural counterparts. Their uniformity makes them less ecologically diverse

This rain forest, near Manaus, Brazil, was cleared in typical fashion—the area was clear-cut, then burned, with much of the wood being wasted. Cleared rain forests are poor sites for farming. Their topsoil is too thin and too deficient in nutrients to grow crops, and they can hardly support grazing cattle.

Above, a worker bucks up a log at a sawmill on Bougainville, P.N.G., while the mill's waste and marginal logs burn in the background. Many sawmills in developing nations aren't equipped to process wood beyond basic sawing. This is changing, however, as developing nations look to boost their income by exporting finished and semi-finished wood products. Right, the author's guide walks atop a tree felled on Bougainville. Rain forest trees are often 150 ft. tall with 100 ft. of trunk to the first branch.

than the native rain forest trees, however, so plantations can be wiped out from insect attack and disease that the natural forest withstands.

The Stettin Bay Lumber Co., owned jointly 25% by the P.N.G. government and 75% by the Japanese, was involved in a large-scale plantation program growing kamarere, teak and erima for construction lumber and pulp. I visited their kamarere plantation on New Britain island and, much to my surprise, found it quite beautiful. The rows of kamarere trees were almost like a large-scale sculplture. Walking through it in the leaf-filtered sunlight, I thought that if it had been woods at home, it would have been the subject of a preservation order on account of its natural beauty. Plantation trees are generally harvested in 15- to 30-year cycles, but the kamarare can be harvested sooner. After six years, trees about 4 in. in diameter are cut for poles, and final harvesting is done 14 years later when the trees are 15 in. to 16 in. in diameter at breast height. Apparantly, plantations aren't enough to meet the company's needs. It's cutting trees on 200,000 hectares of natural forest and negotiating to log on another 100,000 hectares.

Peninsular Malaysia is "recycling" plantation-grown Para rubber trees for use as construction lumber. The trees need to be cut down and replanted every 25 years, but rather than burn the logs, as in the past, they are sawn for lumber. A bland wood, it glues and stains well and is well-suited for inexpensive furniture. I saw several attractive chairs made from it at The Malaysian Timber Promotion Board in Kuala Lumpur.

Ultimately, economic arguments carry more weight in developing nations than environmental ones. If timber was more valuable, that is if timber-producing nations were paid more for it, then they'd treat it more like a sustainable resource. They would be more inclined to enforce timber-cutting quotas, crack down on illegal cutting and replant for the future. Similarly, taxes on timber exports or timber income could pay for plantations, forest research and selective, small-scale felling.

I'd be willing to pay more for timber, because I've seen how expensive it is to extract from the jungle. Though many woodworkers would object at first to paying more for exotic timbers (they are expensive enough already), I suspect they'd be more willing if they knew the money was subsidizing timber research. □

Lucinda Leech builds custom furniture at her shop in Oxford, England.

Taking Stock in Forest and Shop

*Saving money and lumber through timber management
and resourceful woodworking*

by Richard Jagels

Innovative forestry practices are gaining wider attention as one way to help ensure a continuing source of wood. Motorists driving along the interstates in Maine and in Mississippi can occasionally glimpse innovative forestry in action on the median strips. Both states have, at times, logged the medians to save taxpayers money and more efficiently use our nation's wood resource. Successful forest management practices also shine in operations like the Indian reservation in Menominee, Wis. (see the photo above and *FWW* #100, p. 71). Those creative forestry techniques are just one facet of attempts to husband our precious wood resources more effectively. But wise and efficient wood use will also extend the supply of wood. I'll explore these topics and aim the discussion at some of the ways woodworkers can save both money and their resources.

Changing forests, changing forestry

Historically, forests have been seen as something to tame and to convert to agriculture. But as virgin timber sources disappear, a new environmental ethic seeks to preserve the few remaining tracts of "natural" forests. In farming, land tenure has helped to achieve at least a minimal level of stability and sustainability. But forests more often have been logged until near depletion, and then the harvesters have moved on to new territory. In the United States, destructive logging has followed a counterclockwise path from New England, to the Midwest, to the Northwest and then to the South. Then, in the middle part of this century, we found cheaper overseas sources of tropical hardwoods. As an unplanned consequence, we now have a large inventory of domestic hardwoods.

New Forestry—For the past few years, professional foresters have been talking about a New Forestry—one aimed at managing forests to provide a wider range of value, including protection of genetic stock (biodiversity), watersheds and wildlife, while continuing to supply wood and fiber. Two forestry professors at the University of Maine have proposed a triad approach to forest land allocation: A portion of the resource is set aside as ecological reserves, a portion is managed as a natural forest and a segment is intensively managed as high-yield plantations (refer to *New Forestry in Eastern Spruce-Fir Forests* by R.S. Seymour and M.L. Hunter Jr., 1992, Univ. of Maine). The greatest biological diversity would be maintained in the reserves, and the least diversity would be in the plantations. The natural forest would yield high-quality lumber and veneer, while plantations would produce fiber for paper and reconstituted building materials.

For New Forestry to take hold, certain sociological and economic changes have to occur. A good analogy of these changes can be seen in the field of recycling. It was easy in the beginning to propose that we recycle more products in this country (stage I). Now (stage II) people have to put more labor and thought into managing their waste. The next step (stage III) requires investment in recycling facilities. But for the entire process to work, all three stages must happen at once. The same logic applies to managing a forest, and a likely outcome will be a higher cost for wood and wood products. However, the outlook is not as gloomy as one might suppose. Today, logging volumes are close to the growing-stock inventory only in the Pacific Northwest. For areas east of the Mississippi River, we have considerable reserves, particularly in hardwoods, of which we remove less than half the growing stock. For more about hardwood abundance, see the box at right.

More efficient ways to use and work wood

Converting the world's forests to sustainable production will take time and political will. In the meantime, woodworkers can take several meaningful steps to more efficiently use present resources and encourage sustainable forest management.

Using composites and laminations—Glued-up members and composite sheet goods are important ways the wood-products industry conserves wood. Modern glues permit the construction of large structural members with small pieces of wood. For example, products such as Glu-Lam and Com-Ply ingeniously use wood shorts and particleboard.

Composites and laminations hold promise for woodworkers as well. A realistic look at old-growth forests reveals that there are few remaining large-dimension Douglas-fir and other softwood timbers like those that timber framers desire. But luckily, there are big-timber alternatives on the horizon. For example, wood technologists in Hokkaido, Japan, are experimenting with gluing thick-surface veneers onto low-grade, pre-kerfed stock and laminations to produce the look of large-dimension, solid timbers.

Using veneers and thinner stock—Using veneer in place of solid stock is particularly helpful in conserving valuable woods in short supply. For the woodworker who doesn't want to do ve-

Sizing up logs at the sawmill—Millworkers use lumber rules to estimate board footage (left). The timbers, which come from Wisconsin's Menominee Indian reservation, are sorted by species and graded by size and quality. This forestry operation is successful because it is carefully managed; both young and old trees are harvested and both hardwoods and softwoods are logged. The whole operation is coordinated with a detailed computer model.

Photos except where noted: Scott Landis

<small>Photo: John Clark</small>

***All cut from native trees—**The boards leaning against Clark's shop include Florida maple, black walnut, black cherry, longleaf pine, red bay and paint-protected walnut. He obtained the wood for little cost: sweat equity and some modest milling fees.*

Using overlooked hardwoods

by John T. Clark

As a forester in the Southeast United States for more than 35 years, I've found that many native hardwoods in my area are misused or overlooked. Even though there are fine hardwoods in parts of the Southeast, few loggers are knowledgeable of their value, and fewer still are mills that will accept hardwood.

Bountiful hardwoods: In the late 1950s, Southern mills shipped hardwoods to furniture manufacturers in the North. With the coming of particleboard, that changed. Today "trash" hardwood species with a stumpage value of $3 per ton are used for fuel, pulpwood, cross ties and pallets. Only small amounts of top-quality hardwoods are sawn into lumber for furnituremakers.

I've found an enormous mix of fine hardwoods (see the photo above) growing locally on slopes, creek bottoms and in my backyard. I've used some 40 species, including yellow poplar, Osage orange, chinaberry, sweet bay and camphorwood.

Impoverished tropical woods: Hardwood abundance is not the story in all parts of the South, however. Extreme South Florida is the only area in the continental United States where tropical woods grow. But this region has been cut over, developed and farmed to such an extent that from Orlando south, there are few merchantable trees and even fewer sawmills.

Occasionally, windfall events, like hurricane Andrew, provide a bonanza of tropical woods for woodworkers. For example, in November 1992, Fairchild Tropical Gardens in Coral Gables, Fla., sold 1,300 downed exotic trees. But the availability of U.S.-grown tropical timbers is generally as scarce as the species themselves.

Cultivate and harvest your own trees: Despite the shortages, never fear that the Southeast is running out of good trees. Because southern trees usually reproduce rapidly, little planting is needed. Landowners can profit by thinning trees, eliminating the culls early to encourage the more desirable species.

To harvest local trees, portable bandsaw sawmills, like the Wood-Mizer (8180 W. 10th St., Indianapolis, Ind. 46214), are ideal. If you don't want to cut the lumber yourself, small-sawmill operators can be hired for as little as $100 per 1,000 bd. ft. But the real benefit comes when quality woods are used by craftspeople rather than made into pallets, disposable diapers or paper. □

John Clark operates Chartered Foresters in Quincy, Fla. For more Florida hardwood information, contact C. Leon Irvin, Florida Division of Forestry, 125 Conner Blvd., Tallahassee, Fla. 32301.

neering, he or she can still resaw boards into ¼-in. or ⅜-in.-thick pieces, which are easily handled and glued up to make thicker components. And often, narrower boards and smaller structural members will do the job alone. Every board that you resaw doubles the surface area that you can cover with it. And if you already do a lot of resawing, consider cutting boards closer to final dimension and planing only one side if the opposite side will be hidden in the piece (such as drawer bottoms and cabinet backs). Our forebears did this to save work and manpower—we can do it to extend our wood supply.

Using thin-kerf blades—By shifting to thinner blades, the wood products industry has increased its profits. Thin-kerf sawblades are readily available for both circular saws and bandsaws. These blades not only reduce wood waste and dust, but they require less power and are easier on equipment.

Using recycled and scrap wood— More and more builders are recycling logs and timbers. Large, clear timbers (trusses, beams and columns) are often available from demolition sites, such as old factories, mills and barns or from dredging swamps, bogs and rivers. And for smaller-dimensioned stock, woodworkers can reuse hardwood from pallets. I recently picked up free pallets that contained 2x4s of lauan (Philippine mahogany) and other tropical hardwoods. In the shop, you can save scrapwood to be used again in small projects or to be re-glued for large ones. At the very least, scraps can be used to heat your shop rather than being hauled to an overburdened landfill.

Using premium woods wisely— High-quality woods have generally achieved their status for sound reasons. Often a particular wood has properties not found in other species. Teak for boat decking, rosewood for musical instruments, greenheart for marine piling are a few examples. To extend the supply of valuable woods, consider restricting exotics to appropriate high-value situations (e.g. use teak for decking—not interior boat trim). And more and more cabinetmakers are charging clients a surcharge when the piece they are building requires an exotic or premium wood.

Hardwood surpluses can ease softwood shortages

For decades in this country, we have framed houses with softwood lumber. As a consequence we have, or will soon face, regional shortages in softwood supply (Douglas-fir in the Northwest and spruce and fir in the Northeast). At the same time, we have an abundant supply of low-density hardwoods, such as tulip-poplar, gum, cottonwood and

aspen, which research has shown can be used satisfactorily for construction and other purposes.

Many higher density hardwoods are also in copious supply and could be substituted for exotic woods. Cherry, for instance, is a good substitute for mahogany in many cases. But we also have locally abundant sources of little-used hardwoods in the United States and in the tropics. The bottom photo on this page shows how alternative woods can be used resourcefully by furnituremakers. In addition, there are artificial substitutes for certain exotics. For example, in lieu of using ebony for the splines and pegs of a Greene and Greene reproduction chair, Thomas Stangeland of Seattle, Wash., used EBON-X, which is simply walnut impregnated with dye. He built the rest of the chair from certified "well-managed" mahogany from Belize.

By establishing relationships with local sawmills, woodworkers

Photo: Mark Van S.

Fiddleback western maple, *culled from Douglas-fir logging operations in Washington state, was used by cabinetmaker Judith Ames to build her* Cloud chair *for a 1992 theme exhibit, "Environmentally Friendly," at a Seattle furniture gallery.*

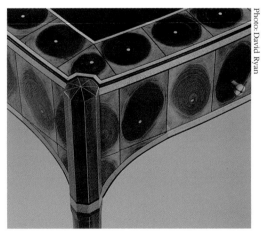

Photo: David Ryan

Writing desk from overlooked woods—*Silas Kopf made this desk using storm-damaged walnut limbs, oak salvaged from a bog, maple and EBON-X (an ebony substitute made from dyed walnut). Kopf fashioned the desk's tapered legs, paneled apron and marquetry bordered top. The curved core stock is plantation-grown poplar plywood; the flat core panels are medium-density fiberboard.*

can influence the kind and quality of wood they obtain. During the past decade, furnituremakers on the West Coast have begun to use the native hardwoods of the region (see the photo at left), like oak, bigleaf maple and Pacific madrone. Not only has this resulted in wider availability of hardwoods but also local landowners have been given new incentives for sustainable forest management. And the incentive to use wider tree diversity extends well beyond the borders of this country. Foresters in the tropics have long grappled with having forests with a multitude of species per hectare and only one or two of commercial value, which sets the stage for destructive logging. Luckily, more tropical foresters are considering using a wider array of species. For a further discussion of this issue, see "Managing a Rain Forest" on pp. 113-117.

Banding together conserves stock, saves dollars

Woodworkers can further influence the supply, quality and sustainability of their wood resource by forming or joining associations or cooperatives like the Institute for Sustainable Forestry (ISF). Groups can also save money by purchasing in larger quantities. One group of woodworkers from the United States and Canada, Woodworkers Alliance for Rainforest Protection (WARP), is seeking to find uses for a wider array of species by establishing a shop-testing program that will evaluate lesser-known species of tropical woods. By using their collective voices, groups can help influence industry practices and governmental policies. □

Dick Jagels is a professor of forest biology and an amateur woodworker. He is the author of Tropical Forests—Slowing the Destruction *(misc. publication 710, July 1990, Maine Agricultural Experiment Station, University of Maine, Orono).*

Index

If you enjoyed this book, you're going to love our magazine.

A year's subscription to *Fine Woodworking* brings you the kind of practical, hands-on information you found in this book and much more. In issue after issue, you'll find projects that teach new skills, demonstrations of tools and techniques, new design ideas, old-world traditions, shop tests, coverage of current woodworking events, and breathtaking examples of the woodworker's art for inspiration.

To try an issue, just fill out one of the attached subscription cards, or call us toll free at 1-800-888-8286. As always, we guarantee your satisfaction.

Subscribe Today!
6 issues for just $29

Taunton
M A G A Z I N E S
for fellow enthusiasts

Taunton Direct, Inc.
63 South Main Street
P.O. Box 5507
Newtown, CT 06470-5507